Using Literature to Help
Troubled Teenagers
Cope with End-of-Life Issues

Recent Titles in
The Greenwood Press "Using Literature to Help Troubled Teenagers" Series

Using Literature to Help Troubled Teenagers Cope with Family Issues
Joan F. Kaywell, editor

Using Literature to Help Troubled Teenagers Cope with Societal Issues
Pamela S. Carroll, editor

Using Literature to Help Troubled Teenagers Cope with Identity Issues
Jeffrey S. Kaplan, editor

Using Literature to Help Troubled Teenagers Cope with Health Issues
Cynthia Ann Bowman, editor

Using Literature to Help Troubled Teenagers Cope with End-of-Life Issues

Edited by
Janet Allen

The Greenwood Press "Using Literature
to Help Troubled Teenagers" Series
Joan Kaywell, Series Adviser

Greenwood Press
Westport, Connecticut • London

Library of Congress Cataloging-in-Publication Data

Using literature to help troubled teenagers cope with end-of-life issues / edited by Janet Allen.

p. cm.—(The Greenwood Press "Using literature to help troubled teenagers" series)
Includes bibliographical references and index.
ISBN 0–313–30781–4 (alk. paper)
1. Grief in adolescence. 2. Bereavement in adolescence. 3. Loss (Psychology) in adolescence. 4. Teenagers and death. 5. Bibliotherapy for teenagers. 6. Young adult literature—Study and teaching (Secondary) I. Title. II. Series.
BF724.3.G73A55 2002
155.9'37'0835—dc21 2001023852

British Library Cataloguing in Publication Data is available.

Library of Congress Catalog Card Number: 2001023852
ISBN: 0–313–30781–4

First published in 2002

Greenwood Press, 88 Post Road West, Westport, CT 06881
An imprint of Greenwood Publishing Group, Inc.
www.greenwood.com

Printed in the United States of America

The paper used in this book complies with the
Permanent Paper Standard issued by the National
Information Standards Organization (Z39.48–1984).

10 9 8 7 6 5 4 3 2 1

Dedicated to the memory of Robert Cormier
(1925–2000)

Our hero in literature and life

Contents

Series Foreword

The idea for this six-volume series—addressing family issues, identity issues, social issues, abuse issues, health issues, and death and dying issues—came while I, myself, was going to a therapist to help me deal with the loss of a loved one. My therapy revealed that I was a "severe trauma survivor" and I had to process the emotions of a bad period of time during my childhood. I was amazed that a trauma of my youth could be triggered by an emotional upset in my adult life. After an amazing breakthrough that occurred after extensive reading, writing, and talking, I looked at my therapist and said, "My God! I'm like the gifted child with the best teacher. What about all of those children who survive situations worse than mine and do not choose education as their escape of choice?" I began to wonder about the huge number of troubled teenagers who were not getting the professional treatment they needed. I pondered about those adolescents who were fortunate enough to get psychological treatment but were illiterate. Finally, I began to question if there were ways to help them while also improving their literacy development.

My thinking generated two theories on which this series is based: (1) Being literate increases a person's chances of emotional health, and (2) Twenty-five percent of today's students are "unteachable." The first theory was generated by my pondering these two statistics: 80% of our prisoners are illiterate (Hodgkinson, 1991), and 80% of our prisoners have been sexually abused (Child Abuse Council, 1993). If a correlation actually exists between these two statistics, then it suggests a strong need for literacy skills in order for a person to be able to address emotional turmoil in healthy or constructive ways. The second theory came out of work I did for my book, *Adolescents at Risk: A Guide to Fiction and Nonfiction for Young Adults, Parents and Professionals* (Greenwood Press, 1993), and my involvement in working with teachers and students in middle and secondary schools. Some of the emotional baggage our youth bring to school is way too heavy for them to handle without help. These students simply cannot handle additional academic responsibilities when they are "not right" emotionally.

THEORY ONE: BEING LITERATE INCREASES A PERSON'S CHANCES OF EMOTIONAL HEALTH

Well-educated adults who experience intense emotional pain, whether it is from the loss of a loved one or from a traumatic event, have several options available for dealing with their feelings. Most will find comfort in talking with friends or family members, and some will resort to reading books to find the help they need. For example, reading Dr. Elisabeth Kübler-Ross's five stages for coping with death—denial, anger, bargaining, depression, and acceptance or growth—might help a person understand the various stages he or she is going through after the death of a friend or relative. Sometimes, however, additional help is needed when an individual is experiencing extreme emotions and is unable to handle them.

Consider a mother whose improper left-hand turn causes the death of her seven-year-old daughter and the injury of her four-year-old daughter. It is quite probable that the mother will need to seek additional help from a therapist who will help her deal with such a trauma. A psychologist or psychiatrist will, more than likely, get her to talk openly about her feelings, read some books written by others who have survived such a tragedy, and do regular journal writing. A psychiatrist may also prescribe some medication during this emotionally challenging time. This parent's literacy skills of talking, reading, and writing are essential to her getting through this difficult period of her life.

Now, consider her four-year-old daughter who is also experiencing extreme grief over the loss of her beloved older sister. If this child is taken to counseling, the therapist will probably get her to talk, role-play, and draw out her feelings. These are the literacy skills appropriate to the developmental level of a four-year-old child. Such a child, if not taken to a counselor when needed, will manifest her emotions in one of two ways—either by acting out or by withdrawing.

Lev Vygotsky, a well-respected learning theorist, suggests that without words there could be no thoughts and the more words a person has at his or her disposal, the bigger that person's world. If what Vygotsky suggests is true, then a person with a limited or no vocabulary is only capable of operating at an emotional level. *The Story of My Life* by Helen Keller adds credibility to that view. In the introduction to the biography, written by Robert Russell, he describes Helen Keller's frustration at not being able to communicate:

> Perhaps the main cause for her early tantrums was plain frustration at not being able to communicate. . . . Not being able to hear, Helen had nothing to imitate, so she had no language. This meant more than simply not being able to talk. It meant having nothing clear to talk about because for her things had no names. Without names, things have no distinctness or individuality. Without language, we could not describe the difference between an elephant and an egg. Without the words we would have no clear conception of either elephant or egg. The name of a thing confers identity upon it and makes it possible for us to think about it. Without names for love or sorrow, we do not know we are experiencing them. Without words, we could not say, "I love you," and human beings need to say this and much more. Helen had the need, too, but she had not the means. As she grew older and the need increased, no wonder her fits of anger and misery grew. (pp. 7–9)

Helen, herself, writes,

> [T]he desire to express myself grew. The few signs I used became less and less adequate, and my failures to make myself understood were invariably followed by outbursts of passion. I felt as if invisible hands were holding me, and I made frantic efforts to free myself. I struggled—not that struggling helped matters, but the spirit of resistance was strong within me; I generally broke down in tears and physical exhaustion. If my mother happened to be near I crept into her arms, too miserable even to remember the cause of the tempest. After awhile the need of some means of communication became so urgent that these outbursts occurred daily, sometimes hourly. (p. 28)

If Vygotsky's theory reflected by the illuminating words of a deaf, blind, and mute child is true, then it is no wonder that 80% of our prisoners are illiterate victims of abuse.

THEORY TWO: 25% OF TODAY'S TEENAGERS ARE "UNTEACHABLE" BY TODAY'S STANDARDS

Teachers are finding it increasingly difficult to teach their students, and I believe that 25% of teenagers are "unteachable" by today's standards. A small percentage of these troubled youth do choose academics as their escape of choice, and they are the overachievers to the "nth" degree. That is not to say that all overachievers are emotionally disturbed teenagers, but some of them are learning, not because of their teachers, but because their very survival depends upon it. I know. I was one of them. The other adolescents going through inordinately difficult times (beyond the difficulty inherent in adolescence itself) might not find the curriculum very relevant to their lives. Their escapes of choice include rampant sex, drug use, gang membership, and other self-destructive behaviors. Perhaps the violence permeating our schools is a direct result of the utter frustration of some of our youth.

Consider these data describing the modern teenage family. At any given time, 25% of American children live with one parent, usually a divorced or never-married mother (Edwards & Young, 1992). Fifty percent of America's youth will spend some school years being raised by a single parent, and almost four million school-age children are being reared by neither parent (Hodgkinson, 1991). In 1990, 20% of American children grew up in poverty, and it is probable that 25% will be raised in poverty by the year 2000 (Howe, 1991). Children in homeless families often experience developmental delays, severe depression, anxiety, and learning disorders (Bassuk & Rubin, 1987).

Between one-fourth and one-third of school-aged children are living in a family with one or more alcoholics (Gress, 1988). Fourteen percent of children between the ages of 3 and 17 experience some form of family violence (Craig, 1992). Approximately 27% of girls and 16% of boys are sexually abused before the age of 18 (Krueger, 1993), and experts believe that it is reasonable to say that 25% of children will be sexually abused before adulthood (Child Abuse Council, 1993). Remember to note that eight out of ten criminals in prison were abused when they were children (Child Abuse Council, 1993).

Consider these data describing the modern teenager. Approximately two out of ten school-aged youth are affected by anorexia nervosa and bulimia (Phelps & Bajorek, 1991) and between 14% to 23% have vomited to lose weight (National Centers for Disease Control, 1991). By the time students become high school seniors, 90% have experimented with alcohol use and nearly two-thirds have used drugs (National Institute on

Drug Abuse, 1992). In 1987, 40% of seniors admitted they had used dangerous drugs and 60% had used marijuana (National Adolescent Student Health Survey). In 1974, the average age American high school students tried marijuana was 16; in 1984, the average age was twelve (Nowinski, 1990).

By the age of 15, a fourth of the girls and a third of the boys are sexually active (Gibbs, 1993), and three out of four teenagers have had sexual intercourse by their senior year (Males, 1993). Seventy-five percent of the mothers who gave birth between the ages of 15 and 17 are on welfare (Simkins, 1984). In 1989, AIDS was the sixth leading cause of death for 15- to 24-year-olds (Tonks, 1992–1993), and many AIDS experts see adolescents as the third wave of individuals affected by HIV (Kaywell, 1993). Thirty-nine percent of sexually active teenagers said they preferred not to use any method of contraception (Harris Planned Parenthood Poll, 1986).

Ten percent of our students are gay (Williams, 1993), and the suicide rate for gay and lesbian teenagers is two to six times higher than that of heterosexual teens (Krueger, 1993). Suicide is the second leading cause of teenage deaths; "accidents" rated first (National Centers for Disease Control, 1987). An adolescent commits suicide every one hour and 47 minutes (National Center for Health Statistics, 1987), and nine children die from gunshot wounds every day in America (Edelman, 1989). For those children growing up in poor, high crime neighborhoods, one in three has seen a homicide by the time they reach adolescence (Beck, 1992).

Consider these data describing the dropout problem. In 1988, the dropout rate among high school students was 28.9% (Monroe, Borzi, & Burrell, 1992). More than 80% of America's one million prisoners are high school dropouts (Hodgkinson, 1991). We spend more than $20,000 per year per prisoner (Hodgkinson, 1991) but spend less than $4,000 per year per student. Forty-five percent of special education students drop out of high school (Wagner, 1989).

Numbers and statistics such as these are often incomprehensible, but consider the data in light of a 12th grade classroom of 30 students. Eight to 15 are being raised by a single parent, six are in poverty, eight to ten are being raised in families with alcoholics, four have experienced some form of family violence, and eight of the female and five of the male students have been sexually violated. Six are anorectic or bulimic, 27 have used alcohol, 18 have used marijuana, and 12 have used dangerous drugs. Twenty-two have had sexual intercourse and 12 of them used no protection. Three students are gay. Eight will drop out of school, and six of those eight will become criminals. Everyday in our country, two adolescents commit suicide by lunchtime.

These are the students that our teachers must teach every day, and these are the students who need help beyond what schools are currently able to provide. Think about the young adults who are both illiterate and in pain! Is there anything that can be done to help these young people with their problems while increasing their literacy skills? Since most of our nation's prisoners are illiterate—the acting out side—and most homeless people are not exactly Rhodes scholars—the withdrawal side—it seems logical to try to help these adolescents while they are still within the educational system.

Perhaps this series, which actually pairs literacy experts with therapists, can help the caretakers of our nation's distraught youth—teachers, counselors, parents, clergy, and librarians—acquire understanding and knowledge on how to better help these troubled teenagers. The series provides a unique approach to guide these caretakers working with troubled teenagers. Experts discuss young adult literature, while therapists provide analysis and advice for protagonists in these novels. Annotated bibliographies provide the reader with similar sources that can be used to help teenagers discuss these issues while increasing their literacy skills.

Joan F. Kaywell

REFERENCES

Bassuk, E. L., & Rubin, L. (1987). Homeless children: A neglected population. *American Journal of Orthopsychiatry, 57* (2), p. 279 ff.

Beck, J. (1992, May 19). Inner-city kids beat the odds to survive. *The Tampa Tribune.*

Craig, S. E. (1992, September). The educational needs of children living with violence. *Phi Delta Kappan, 74* (1), p. 67 ff.

Edelman, M. W. (1989, May). Defending America's children. *Educational Leadership, 46* (8), p. 77 ff.

Edwards, P. A., & Young, L. S. J. (1992, September). Beyond parents: Family, community, and school involvement. *Phi Delta Kappan, 74* (1), p. 72 ff.

Gibbs, N. (1993, May 24). How should we teach our children about sex? *Time, 140* (21), p. 60 ff.

Gress, J. R. (1988, March). Alcoholism's hidden curriculum. *Educational Leadership, 45* (6), p. 18 ff.

Hodgkinson, H. (1991, September). Reform versus reality. *Phi Delta Kappan, 73* (1), p. 9 ff.

Howe II, H. (1991, November). America 2000: A bumpy ride on four trains. *Phi Delta Kappan, 73* (3), p. 192 ff.

Kaywell, J. F. (1993). *Adolescents at risk. A guide to fiction and nonfiction for young adults, parents and professionals.* Westport, CT: Greenwood Press.

Keller, H. (1967). *The story of my life.* New York: Scholastic.

Krueger, M. M. (1993, March). Everyone is an exception: Assumptions to avoid in the sex education classroom. *Phi Delta Kappan, 74* (7), p. 569 ff.

Males, M. (1993, March). Schools, society, and "teen" pregnancy. *Phi Delta Kappan, 74* (7), p. 566 ff.

Monroe, C., Borzi, M. G., & Burrell, R. D. (1992, January). Communication apprehension among high school dropouts. *The School Counselor, 39* (4), p. 273 ff.

Nowinski, J. (1990). *Substance abuse in adolescents and young adults.* New York: Norton.

Phelps, L. & Bajorek, E. (1991). Eating disorders of the adolescent: Current issues in etiology, assessment, and treatment. *School Psychology Review, 20* (1), p. 9 ff.

Simkins, L. (1984, spring). Consequences of teenage pregnancy and motherhood. *Adolescence, 19* (73), p. 39 ff.

Tonks, D. (1992–1993, December–January). Can you save your students' lives? Educating to prevent AIDS. *Educational Leadership, 50* (4), p. 48 ff.

Wagner, M. (1989). *Youth with disabilities during transition: An overview of descriptive findings from the national longitudinal transition study.* Stanford, CA: SRI International.

Williams, R. F. (1993, spring). Gay and lesbian teenagers: A reading ladder for students, media specialists, and parents. *The ALAN Review, 20* (3), p. 12 ff.

A Letter from Robert Cormier

Dear Reader,

Everybody dies but nobody should ever die. Especially somebody young and vibrant, on the threshold of life. In fact we never expect young people to die. Nobody ever goes to school in the morning expecting to find out that a classmate died last night. Or yesterday afternoon. In a car crash. Or from a sudden violent illness.

Yet it happens.

How do you cope?

As a writer I have faced that question in my novels. A novel isn't real life but it is often inspired by actual events and actual people, some of whom have died. When somebody like Kate Forrester in *After the First Death* or Barney Snow in *The Bumblebee Flies Anyway* face death, I must somehow cope as a writer, but the coping must be real, both to me and to the reader.

I've always believed that a writer's job is simply to bring up questions—because nobody has the answers to life-and-death mysteries—but I think it's important to provide hints to the answers.

Barney Snow ventures outside the hospital and sees flowers beginning to fade but observes a nearby tree beginning to display new life, new flowers. "One life ending and another beginning . . . the continuity of life, nature at work in the world. . . . maybe there was a kind of continuity in people, too. Nature at work in people. Or was it God?"

The hint of an answer—that's all we really have. We can draw comfort from the hints, the comfort of knowing we are a part of the whole, part of all humanity, linked to one another. In this link with other people, this sharing of our futures, we can somehow find a bit of solace, a sweet slant of light in all the darkness. That light for many, myself included, is God. For others, it may be something else. But for all of us, it's being human, sharing that common destiny, and somehow deriving strength from knowing we are not alone.

I wish I could tell you more than that—but I can't.

Sincerely,
Robert Cormier

Acknowledgments

Janet Allen wishes to gratefully acknowledge those people who have made this book a reality.

For the authors of young adult literature who shared their writing, letters of encouragement, and insights on behalf of the students whose teachers and counselors may read this book, I want to thank them for the power of their words in our children's lives.

For the students who willingly shared their writing to bring the reality of these issues to our minds and hearts, I thank you for helping us hear what we need to hear.

For the dedicated educators and mental health professionals who worked together to bring their combined expertise to all of us, I thank them for their professionalism and inspiration.

For Anne Cobb, who diligently worked at getting permissions and the logistics of the chapter breaks written by young adult authors, I'm thankful for her continued professionalism and passion for the work.

For Denise Beasley, whose tireless efforts went into making this book a reality, I am thankful that we have been able to do together the work that matters to us both. Dee's help to many of the chapter authors with related readings, format, editing, and creativity have made each of the chapters stronger and richer. Her energy for the task and her diligence in seeing it through the completed manuscript stage has been a source of comfort and professionalism for me.

Introduction: Shared Grieving and Celebration

Janet Allen

What I am trying to convey to you is that if we grownups would be more honest, and instead of making such an incredible nightmare out of dying, we could convey to children where we are at and what we feel; if we would not be embarrassed to shed tears or to express our anger and rage (if we have any), and if we would not try to shield our children from the windstorms of life but instead share with them, then the children of the next generation will not have such a horrible problem with death and dying.

Elisabeth Kübler-Ross, *The Tunnel and the Light* (1999, 19)

While I was still teaching in my high school classroom, I was teaching children's literature as an adjunct at the local university. All the students in the class were elementary teachers and we laughed and cried our way through hundreds of children's books during that semester. One novel that brought us all to our knees was Katherine Paterson's *Bridge to Terabithia*. No one in the class had read it, and they were all stunned at the raw courage of the characters in the face of such loss. We talked about how we might have tried to help Jess Aarons through his time of grief had he been a student in one of our classrooms. We reread Mrs. Myers's tearful comment to Jess, "This morning when I came in, someone had already taken out her desk" (125), and discussed the importance of the desk staying there as a reminder that part of Leslie would always be with them. We adults talked about the ways we remember those who had died and about the spontaneous moments of grief we had each experienced years after the death.

A year later I received a letter from one of the teachers who had been a student in that children's literature class. She relayed to me her renewed sense of gratitude for having read *Bridge to Terabithia* to her students when one of those students was killed in a house fire that year. She remembered our discussion of the missing desk and asked that this child's desk be left in the room. Students made gifts and wrote letters to the child and left them on her desk. And she didn't rush their grief. She told me that throughout the remainder of that year, students would think of something funny, or something traumatic or something that made them angry, write about it, and leave the writing in the child's desk. At the end of the year, students made a class memory book and left one on the child's desk.

These children were given the gift of time and a safe place for honest grieving and celebration for their friend. This teacher understood that grief would not be over in a matter of days. The book you are holding is about using literature and informed mentoring to provide that same support for all children who are experiencing loss. The first chapter is written from the perspective of a chaplain for a Florida high school and its football team and the community's police chaplain. In his role as football chaplain, Steve Puckett is called in for Critical Incidence Stress Debriefings. His chapter guides us through the stages of grieving, the role of literature in that grieving, and the importance of providing teenagers a place and time to tell their stories.

All other chapters in this book share the format of the other books in The Greenwood Press "Using Literature to Help Troubled Teenagers" Series. Each chapter is a collaboration between a literacy educator and someone in the counseling field. The literacy educator chose one or more core novels as the focus for the chapter. The therapist read the book and analyzed the characters' end-of-life issues from the perspective of ways to offer intervention and support. The literacy educator looked at how she might teach the novels and the ways she would deal with those end-of-life issues while reading the novels with her students. In each of these chapters I have asked the literacy educators to make their writing practical. I want teachers and students to benefit from this combined expertise by being able to implement some of the strategies and activities into their teaching when it is appropriate. We hope that you will find the suggestions useful when adapted to your individual teaching situations.

A unique aspect in our book is the inclusion of the voices of writers of young adult literature in the form of letters they have written, which can be shared with students who are suffering personal or collective loss. These writers' words can be found between chapters and can be used in conjunction with one or more of the chapters or by themselves as models for facing end-of-life issues. All the authors have shared with us a letter and one or more pieces of writing in order to show students how they come face-to-face with grief in their personal and writing lives. It is my hope that students discover in these authors' words some models for finding a way through, rather than a way around, grief.

End-of-life issues can be difficult for us as adults, and so the thought of dealing with these issues with our students is often overwhelming. Each new encounter with literature that focuses on issues of death and dying brings all our individual losses back to us. Safe classrooms are required when dealing with these issues in literature that matters to students. I have yet to see a student sob at the characters' deaths in any of Shakespeare's plays. Conversely, it is almost impossible for students and teachers to get through the end of Irene Hunt's *Lottery Rose* or Beatrice Sparks's *It Happened to Nancy* without heightened emotions and tears.

We have purposely chosen texts for these chapters that will affect our students and their thinking. We want these works of literature to help break the silence around death. In Theresa Nelson's novel, *Earthshine*, a support group leader starts a support meeting but breaks down in tears. She automatically apologizes and then rethinks that apology. "Oh, for heaven's sake, what am I apologizing for? My friend died today, my friend Tommy who was funny and smart and kind and a lot braver than I am, and I'm standing here apologizing? Well, I won't do it anymore, that's all. I'm mad and I'm not going to pretend I'm not" (47).

It is certainly a time when the children in our care need us to help them stop pretending that death is not a natural part of life—as natural as the grief we share at its arrival.

REFERENCES

Hunt, Irene. (1970). *The lottery rose*. New York: Tempo Books.

Kübler-Ross, Elisabeth. (1999). *The tunnel and the light: Essential insights on living and dying with a letter to a child with cancer*. New York: Marlowe.

Nelson, Theresa. (1994). *Earthshine*. New York: Orchard Books.

Paterson, Katherine. (1977). *Bridge to Terabithia*. New York: HarperCollins Publishers.

Sparks, Beatrice, ed. (1994). *It happened to Nancy*. New York: Avon Books.

"Grey"
Angela Shelf Medearis

All the color has left the world,
everything is black and white,
I can't tell night from day,
or decipher day from night.
Nothing is funny anymore,
life is just a routine.
I don't want to bathe or change my clothes,
I like not being clean.

I don't know how long I've been this way,
or how things were before.
I feel like I'm chained inside myself
in a room without windows or doors.

I'm in the deepest pit of despair,
and the walls are too smooth to climb out.
I'm begging for help
in my own way
in a whisper that sounds like a shout.

CHAPTER 1

Helping Teens Cope through Sharing Their Stories about Death

Steve Puckett

> If you sit with a child and care for him, and if you are not afraid of his answers, then he will tell you practically everything about himself.
>
> Elisabeth Kübler-Ross, *The Tunnel and the Light* (1999, 17)

Dylan was an All-American athlete at a local high school. He had already committed to playing football for a major college and was due to receive a full scholarship. His mother proudly wore his number at every game. Her son was going to get what she'd always wanted for him, a college education. But Dylan lost his life in a tragic accident at the beach when he was pulled under by a rip current and drowned.

Joey was an introverted kid who seemed to do well in school, but since his mother died he had struggled with deep bouts of depression. He went out of his way to get along with others and even though he was shy was liked by his classmates. His father noticed he spent a lot of time alone in his room watching TV and playing video games, but he thought this behavior normal for a fourteen-year-old. One day Joey took a .357 magnum handgun from his dad's closet and went off to school. A few hours later he went into the boys' bathroom and killed himself.

Megan and Melissa were identical twins who were the youngest of five children. Their parents loved them deeply. They were very outgoing as sophomores in high school: Megan was a thespian and Melissa was a reporter for the school TV station. One bright, sunny day a state trooper drove up to Megan and Melissa's school to deliver the news that their parents had been killed in an automobile accident.

If you are an administrator, teacher, or parent, you probably can relate to these stories. These stories, with the names changed and a few details altered, are true stories that repeat themselves hundreds of times in schools all across our nation every day.

My first real experience with death came in 1962 when I was 6 years old. My next-door neighbor had an aneurysm that burst in her brain while she gave birth to a baby girl. Her baby daughter lived. She didn't.

Death had not been completely sterilized in 1962. In those days, bodies were often laid out in their homes. Community members brought food to the family at their home, visited awhile, and paid their respects. Children were a part of this process. Death was understood as a part of life. No family member died alone, and settling the death accounts was a family matter.

I walked into the front hall of the house with my parents, and there she was, in a dark, muscadine-colored casket. Her lipstick was bright, cherry red, her hair had been styled, and she wore a navy blue frock.

Even though it might sound strange in today's context of death, being in that house with a new baby and new casket seemed right. The whole community, along with the family, shared the sadness of that event. Her husband and her family told their stories of what happened in her death and things they remembered about her life. There was a context for the story-that-begged-to-be-told to be shared. A foundation was laid for a husband, two young boys, and a new baby girl to start over.

About forty years later, I know that what I learned from that first experience with death still needs to be heard. Death needs a context, a context where its story can be told, and a place where death's connection with life can be understood.

In 1987 I served on a Critical Incidence Stress Debriefing team (CISD) for Brevard County, Florida. Our team helped emergency services personnel deal with traumatic experiences that went beyond their routine duties.

One such experience occurred on April 23, 1987, when William Cruse went on a shooting spree in Palm Bay, Florida, and killed six people, including two police officers, and wounded fourteen others. In order to help the emergency service personnel such as police officers, EMTs, etc., cope with this kind of tragedy, our CISD team brought together, in small groups of eight or ten, those employees directly involved for a debriefing. During these debriefings, we encouraged each person to tell his or her story. "What happened?" "What was your role?" "What did you do?" Finally, "How did you feel?"

This kind of group dynamic has power and the power is in the telling of the story. Death has a context, a setting, and tragic as it may be, death is a part of life. Sharing your experience with death is important, whatever your age.

As teachers, administrators, and parents we will see death close up and far away many times during our lives. So will our children. "An estimated 3.5 million grieving children are struggling to make sense of the frightening new world created by the loss of a parent" (Emswiler and Emswiler, 2000, 5). This statistic grows larger when we take into account the deaths of siblings, grandparents, close relatives, and friends. We can help children survive when we provide a place for their stories of death to be told. Donna Schuurman, director of the Dougy Center for Grieving Children, concurs, "The one thing that is the most helpful to children who are grieving is to be listened to. They are needing to tell the story" (*The Tomorrow Children Face When a Parent Dies*, 1997).

In her book, *Part of Me Died, Too* (1995), Virginia Lynn Fry shares the creative ways that kids tell their survival stories after the death of a significant person in their lives. She is the director of the Hospice Council of Vermont and is a bereavement counselor with the hospice in Montpelier. Fry calls these stories about death "stories of creative survival." In her book she tells the story of eleven young people who experienced the death of a family member or friend. These kids, guided by a counselor, use creative activities like drawing and writing to tell their experiences with death and to explore their feelings.

The goal, of course, is healing the wounds that death has created. The healing process goes through several stages as the person shares her story. Elisabeth Kübler-Ross's landmark book, *On Death and Dying* (1969), outlines the stages that a dying person goes through: denial, anger, bargaining, depression, and acceptance. She explains further how the immediate family experiences some of the same emotional reactions including denial and anger, resentment and guilt. "When anger, resentment, and guilt can be worked through, the family will then go through a preparatory grief, just as the dying person does. The more this grief can be expressed before death, the less unbearable it becomes afterward" (176).

In her classic work *The Grieving Child*, Helen Fitzgerald says, "The most common feelings experienced by children reacting to death are denial, anger, guilt, depression, and fear" (105). The feelings that kids experience are similar to adults' feelings about death with one significant difference. Emswiler and Emswiler believe children feel even less in control of their world than adults do (2000, 13).

Their attempts to cope with death and grief are expressed in different ways, the differences depending on their age and life experiences. Drops in academic performance, complaints of being sick or not feeling well, fighting, and disruptive behaviors in the classroom are grief indicators in kids. Children need adults who can understand these attempts to cope with loss and grief. Their coping can be examined using Kübler-Ross's five stages. Although I will describe them as stages, *processes* might be a better word because the stages don't necessarily occur in sequence and they can recur at different moments in the person's life.

DENIAL

Kids learn denial at a very early age. Your first child is now 3 years old. One day you enter your kitchen and discover the cabinet door under your sink open and dog food spilled all over the floor. Your child is standing there with one piece of dog food in his mouth and one in each hand. You ask him what happened and he responds, "I didn't do it." That's a real-life explanation of denial. Your child wants to escape the consequences of his choice, and so he denies it happened.

Shock from a sudden death or the revelation that a loved one is near death can lead to a denial that permits temporary postponement of the consequences of the event. So when death comes to a loved one, shock often leads the survivor to say, "This can't be true. I can't accept that this has happened to me. It must be a dream." Denial can go on for a lengthy period without a healthy environment that allows the person in grief to honestly face the reality of death.

An excerpt from Agee's *A Death in the Family* provides us with a moment in the life of a child which illustrates how adults can, unknowingly and with the desire to protect a child, foster denial for a longer period of time than normal. In this scene, 6-year-old Rufus Follet asks his mother about the accident that killed his father.

> When you want to know more about it (and her eyes become still more vibrant) just ask me and I'll tell you because you ought to know. "How did he get hurt," Rufus wanted to ask, but he knew by her eyes that she did not mean at all what she said, not now, anyway, not this minute, he need not ask; and now he did not want to ask because he too was afraid; he nodded to let her know he understood her. (33)

Denial, when understood properly, is a normal part of the young person's grieving process. Children also use denial as a coping mechanism. The child may even casually respond when asked about a loved one's death,

"Oh, yeah, he died," and then go on to play video games or watch TV. The impact of death has not yet penetrated his heart and mind. Children may not grieve initially while they are still in shock, but their grieving process is often longer than that of adults. A temporary putting aside of the pain of death is a part of the preparation for the next stage.

ANGER

> When the first stage of denial cannot be maintained any longer, it is replaced by feelings of anger, rage, envy, and resentment. . . . this stage of anger is very difficult to cope with from the view of family and staff. The reason for this is the fact that this anger is displaced in all directions and projected onto the environment at times almost at random.
>
> Kübler-Ross, 1969, 64–65

In Paterson's *Bridge to Terabithia*, 11-year-old Jess Aarons's best friend and kindred spirit, Leslie, dies in a tragic fall swinging from a rope they used to cross a stream. Jess visits Leslie's family to pay his respects and discovers that her family is having her cremated and that he will never see her again. As he returns home, his anger is evident in this scene with his younger sister, May Belle.

> He remembered running up the hill toward his own house with angry tears streaming down his face. He banged through the door. May Belle was standing there, her brown eyes wide open. "Did you see her?" she asks excitedly. "Did you see her laid out?"

> He hit her. In the face. As hard as he had ever hit anything in his life. She stumbled backward from him with a little yelp. He went into the bedroom and felt under the mattress until he retrieved all his papers and the paints that Leslie had given him at Christmastime. . . .

> He ran out the kitchen door and down the field all the way to the stream without looking back. . . . Above from the crab apple tree the frayed end of the rope swung gently. . . .
> He screamed something without words and flung the papers and paints into the dirty brown water. . . . There was nowhere to go. Nowhere. Ever again. He put his head down on his knee. (114–15)

Jess did not plan to lash out at his sister, but she was a handy target when he returned home from his visit to Leslie's house. His father sees Jess throw away the gifts Leslie gave him. He comments, "That was a damn fool thing to do" (115). But grief is not guided by logic. As Emerson once said, "Sorrow makes us all children again."

Kids can have a hard time admitting their anger. Their anger may come out in yelling, criticism, teasing, or fighting. Others may use sports, art, or writing to release their anger. Destructively, some kids will use drugs or alcohol. As with denial, some kids will disguise their anger with cheerfulness or in some other way pretend it isn't there.

Dr. William Worden, Dr. Steven Nickman, and Dr. Phyllis Silverman conducted a study in the Boston area among seventy families with children ages six to seventeen who experienced the death of a parent. They tracked these grieving children and compared their behaviors and attitudes to those of nongrieving children. Dr. Worden says that when kids express their anger more aggressively, they do so because of their sense of powerlessness and their unspoken and unresolved fears. He concludes, "It may be that such behavior was a means of getting a strong reaction from the surviving parent as well as giving the child a greater sense of empowerment" (1996, 63).

A popular feature in many children's grief programs is a room for getting out aggressive anger in a healthy way. These "hurricane" rooms provide a safe environment for expressing anger. They often include things like telephone books or magazines to rip apart, bubble wrap to stomp on, foam bats to hit the walls with, a punching bag with gloves, a tape recorder to yell into, and pillows or duffel bags filled with clean rags to wrestle with (Emswiler and Emswiler, 2000, 94).

GUILT

In Eda LeShan's book *Learning to Say Good-by When a Parent Dies*, she tells Tony's story. Because of his guilt, Tony had never been able to grieve for his mother's death in a natural way. On the night she died, Tony begged her to play checkers with him even though she said she didn't feel very well. While they were playing, his mother got a terrible pain in her chest and died because of a heart condition that she had had since she was a young girl. Naturally, Tony's conclusion was that he had killed his mother because he insisted that she play with him even though she didn't feel well (65–69).

LeShan also writes about sixteen-year-old Helen Colon's guilt, which surfaced when she thought about the times she watched television and her mother asked her to make her coffee. She had put her mother off by saying she would do it later. She felt guilty after her mother's death when this memory surfaced (47).

Almost every person who goes through the death of a loved one, feels some form of guilt, whether deep or shallow. "If only I had . . . , then maybe he would still be alive." In *Bereaved Children and Teens*, Grollman says,

Guilt takes many forms. It can be manifested outwardly through aggression and hostility: "Why didn't you call the ambulance faster?" By projecting guilt on someone else, children absolve themselves of blame. Or, in an attempt to fight off unhappy thoughts, they may idealize the person, becoming obsessed with only the good qualities of the one who died. They may try to compensate for the loss of a loved one by assuming her characteristics and mannerisms. Guilt may also be turned inward and cause depression. They are no longer able to focus on schoolwork. They are too preoccupied to join others in play. Some cannot sleep, and when they do, they have recurrent nightmares. Unresolved grief takes the form of withdrawal, delinquency, excessive excitability, self-pity, and defiance. (10–11)

In Judith Guest's *Ordinary People*, Conrad Jarrett has deep feelings of guilt about his brother's drowning on a lake while they were sailing together. He spends eight months in a hospital after attempting suicide. The novel chronicles his gut-wrenching attempt to find normalcy in the midst of his overwhelming guilt from his feeling of responsibility for his brother's death. This is the classic guilt response of "If only I had. . . ." At the climax of the book, he finally is able to take ownership of his feelings in an early-morning session with his therapist.

"Ah, God, I don't know. I don't know, it just keeps coming. I can't make it stop!"

"Don't then."

"I can't! I can't get through this! It's all hanging over my head!"

"What's hanging over your head?"

"I don't know!" He looks up, dazed, drawing a deep breath. "I need something. I want something—I want to get off the hook!"

"For what?"

He begins to cry again. "For killing him, don't you know that? For letting him drown!" (222–23)

Owning the guilt and expressing it to another person helps to lessen its power. This is yet another grieving process that leads the survivor to a point where he can grieve in a healthy way.

DEPRESSION

Fitzgerald says, "A period of depression almost always follows a major loss" (1992, 126). Withdrawal, difficulty concentrating, personality changes, poor eating and sleeping habits, and less interest in others are some of the symptoms of depression. One way to recognize depression in a child is to take note of any changes in the items such as toys, dolls, or books that are important to her.

Fitzgerald suggests that a child experiencing normal depression (depression that lingers for about a month) after a death can be helped by evoking memories of the loved one using drawings, keepsakes, photographs, scrapbooks, videos or home movies, games, or plays (129–31).

For instance, in Couloumbis's *Getting Near to Baby*, Willa Jo's baby sibling, referred to as Baby throughout the book, dies and her mom paints pictures of Baby with the angels. Finally, as her mother becomes more depressed, she begins focusing on the paintings and almost ignores her two living children.

> "Why do you keep painting Baby with the angels, Mom?" . . . "Why don't you paint Baby the way we remember her?" . . . she finally said, "Maybe it's because I already know how Baby was here with us. I'm painting the part I don't know," she said. "I'm painting so I'll understand" (159).

In Peggy Mann's *There Are Two Kinds of Terrible*, Robbie and his dad experience similar feelings when left alone after his mom dies of cancer. Through the support of his friend, Jud, Robbie manages pretty well, but his father is in deep depression much of the time and he can't understand why. One day he discovers a special picture album under his dad's pillow. It was his mom's "old-fashioned" album. The album contained pictures of her as a baby, as a little girl, and a few pictures of her in school. But the pictures in the album that help Robbie the most are the pictures of his dad and mom in the early years of their marriage, from the honeymoon to his baby years.

> I kept turning slowly through the album; pages headed OUR FIRST APART-MENT . . . LAKE PLACID SUMMER . . . VISIT TO MUNCIE, INDIANA . . . ENG-LISH SUMMER . . . and then . . . ROBBIE ARRIVES. Me in a baby carriage . . .

my mom holding me as I slept and her looking down at me with this sweet smile. . . . Suddenly I realized that this was the book Dad had on his lap that night when I found him asleep by the TV. And the fact that he had it under his pillow . . . maybe he looked at this book every night before he went to sleep. . . . Then I had what might be the most important shot of understanding in my life. (123–24)

Understanding, in whatever form it comes, helps the child and the adult move from depression and apathy toward acceptance.

ACCEPTANCE

Health is not equivalent to happiness, surfeit, or success. It is foremost a matter of being wholly one with whatever circumstances we find ourselves in. Even our death is a healthy event if we fully embrace the fact of our dying. . . . The issue is awareness of living in the present. Whatever our present existence consists of, if we are at one with it, we are healthy.

Latner, 1973, 64

Does anyone ever accept the death of someone who is deeply loved? The answer to that question is "yes." For some people, acceptance may come in a few months, for others acceptance may take years. For a few, because of unresolved grief issues like anger, resentment, or depression, acceptance may never come. The goal for parents, administrators, and teachers is to facilitate the grieving process so that all the grief issues can be dealt with in healthy ways and in healthy environments so children can move to acceptance.

One novel that demonstrates acceptance is Mavis Jukes's *Blackberries in the Dark*. Readers feel Austin's pain during a visit to his grandmother after his grandfather has died. He is very sad that he will not be able to fly-fish with his grandpa. One day while he is down by the stream his grandma comes bursting clumsily out of the woods with all the fly-fishing gear. Their efforts to put together the fishing reel and to try to catch a trout bring them to this moment of acceptance:

"Grandpa would like us doing this—wouldn't he," said Austin. "He would be happy we're learning to fly-fish at Two Rock Creek."

"Yes," said Austin's grandmother. "And tomorrow we'll learn to drive the tractor." (39)

CONCLUSION

Raising the level of awareness among parents, teachers, and administrators allows more than one person to make note of changes in the behavior or performance of the child given to their care. Having parents communicate with school personnel about a death in the family or of a close friend is vital to helping the child work through grief. If there is a change in the child's behavior or performance, parents and school officials can work on a strategy to help the child process grief and seek outside intervention if necessary.

I note here that children need not only the opportunity to tell their stories and express their feelings, but a place, a *safe* place to tell that story. Those safe places can be professional centers like the Dougy Center in Portland, Oregon; the Center for Grieving Children in Portland, Maine; the Cove in Guilford, Connecticut; or the kitchen table or den in a home. Kübler-Ross says the important ingredients are caring and openness with a desire to hear with your heart (1999, 19).

Since you have taken the time to read this chapter, I am convinced that the mental well-being of children may begin with you. You care and you want to make a difference in a child's life.

I leave you with this thought. You can help a teenager tell his story by formulating your own story. Bring to mind your first experience with death. What happened? Did your family include you in the process? How did you feel? What were you told? What smells and sounds do you associate with that experience? Your reflections, when combined with the resources in this book, can help you support the life of a grieving child. If you only have time to read one book on the list at the end of this chapter, please get a copy of *The Tunnel and the Light* by Elisabeth Kübler-Ross. Her letter to Dougy, a nine-year-old cancer patient, will show you how just one individual with a commitment to children can change lives.

RECOMMENDED READINGS

Fiction

Agee, James. (1998). *A death in the family*. New York: Random House. ISBN: 0–375–70123–0 (12+). PB, 310 pp.

Jay Follet leaves his house in Knoxville, Tennessee, to tend to his father, whom he believes is dying. The summons turns out to be a false alarm, but on his way back to his family, Jay has a car accident and is killed instantly. The book moves from the viewpoints of his wife, brother, and young son Rufus as they struggle with his death.

Blume, Judy. (1982). *Tiger eyes*. New York: Bantam Doubleday Dell. ISBN: 0–440–98469–6 (9–12). PB, 224 pp.

When Davey's father is killed during a robbery of a 7–11 store, she undergoes anger, depression, and grief.

Coman, Carolyn. (1998). *Tell me everything*. New York: Penguin Putnam Books. ISBN: 0–140–38791–9 (6–12). PB, 160 pp.

Roz runs away to find answers about her mother's death.

Couloumbis, Audrey. (1999). *Getting near to baby*. New York: Penguin Putnam Books. ISBN: 0–399–23389–X (6–12). HC, 224 pp.

This Newbery honor book tells the story of twelve-year-old Willa Jo and her little sister. Their baby sister has died and when their mother slips into a depression they go to live with their Aunt Patty. Willa Jo is searching for answers and trying to comfort little sister, who hasn't spoken since the baby's death.

Deaver, Julie. (1989). *Say goodnight, Gracie*. New York: HarperCollins. ISBN: 0–064–47007–5 (6–12). PB, 224 pp.

Even though they have opposite personalities, Morgan and Jimmy become friends. When Jimmy is killed, Morgan must come to terms with his death.

Draper, Sharon M. (1996). *Tears of a tiger*. New York: Simon & Schuster. ISBN: 0–689–80698–1 (9–12). PB, 180 pp.

After a night of drinking, Andy gets behind the wheel and ends up killing his best friend, a passenger in the car. Ridden with guilt, he can't contemplate a future for himself.

Guest, Judith. (1982). *Ordinary people*. New York: Penguin Books. ISBN: 0–140–06517–2 (9–12+). PB, 263 pp.

This is a story of a typical American family, living a typical American life. Then the unthinkable happens. The death of Buck, the family's elder son, brings Conrad to depression, which eventually leads him to attempt to take his own life. The book follows Conrad and his parents as they recover from the painful tragedies they have recently suffered.

Hesse, Karen. (1995). *Phoenix rising*. New York: Puffin Books. ISBN: 0–140–37628–3 (6–8). PB, 182 pp.

Nyle and her grandmother survive a nuclear power plant accident and take in a mother and son who have been injured. In the midst of destruction and death, Nyle tries to find hope.

Holt, Kimberly Willis. (1999). *When Zachary Beaver came to town*. New York: Henry Holt. ISBN: 0–805–06116–9 (6–8). HC, 227 pp.

Willis explores southern-flavored small-town life. Toby's quirky, yet ultimately rewarding, coming-of-age story will serve as a gentle reminder to teens that sometimes the best way to work through your problems is by helping others with theirs.

L'Engle, Madeleine. (1981). *A ring of endless light*. New York: Bantam Doubleday Dell. ISBN: 0–440–97232–9 (6–8). PB, 332 pp.

When her grandfather is dying of leukemia, a fifteen-year-old girl finds solace with dolphins.

McDaniel, Lurlene. (1996). *Angels watching over me*. New York: Bantam Books. ISBN: 0–553–56724–1 (6–12). PB, 176 pp.

When Leah enters the hospital for tests, she discovers she has a life-threatening illness and has a romantic encounter with Ethan, the brother of her Amish roommate. The two sequels after this book show Leah's continued struggle with cancer and concern over whether she and Ethan can love each other despite their different religious and cultural backgrounds.

McDaniel, Lurlene. (1990). *Somewhere between life and death*. New York: Bantam Books. ISBN: 0–553–28349–9 (6–12). PB, 148 pp.

As in most of the McDaniel books, the main character, a family member, or a friend experiences the shock and grief of a death.

Park, Barbara. (1996). *Mick Harte was here*. New York: Random House. ISBN: 0–679–88203–0 (4–8). PB, 89 pp.

A 13-year-old girl recalls her brother's death from a bicycle accident. This touching story includes poignant touches of humor and heartache.

Paterson, Katherine. (1987). *Bridge to Terabithia*. New York: HarperCollins. ISBN: 0–064–40184–7 (4–8). PB, 144 pp.

A young boy and girl form a close, special friendship, but joy turns to grief when the girl dies unexpectedly.

Paulsen, Gary. (1995). *Tracker*. New York: Simon & Schuster. ISBN: 0–689–80412–1 (6–8). PB, 90 pp.

Somehow 13-year-old John equates tracking and killing a deer with forestalling his grandfather's cancer, but the encounter with the deer changes his perspective.

Peck, Richard. (1986). *Remembering the good times*. New York: Bantam Doubleday Dell. ISBN: 0–440–97339–2 (9–12). PB, 192 pp.

The frustrations of a group of gifted high school students in an apathetic but affluent community lead to tragedy.

Rodowsky, Colby. (1988). *Remembering Mog*. New York: Farrar, Straus, and Giroux. ISBN: 03–380–72922–9 (11–12+). PB, 136 pp.

Annie tries to deal with her own life while she and her parents cope with the murder of her sister Mog.

Rylant, Cynthia. (1993). *Missing May*. New York: Bantam Doubleday Dell. ISBN: 0–440–40865–2 (4–8). PB, 96 pp.

After her aunt dies, twelve-year-old Summer and her uncle leave their home to search for answers about living.

White, Ruth. (1998). *Belle Prater's boy*. New York: Bantam Doubleday Dell. ISBN: 0–440–41372–9 (6–8). PB, 196 pp.

Cousins Woodrow and Gypsy find comfort in each other as Woodrow tries to accept his mother's disappearance and Gypsy her father's death.

Zindel, Paul. (1981). *The Pigman*. New York: Bantam Doubleday Dell. ISBN: 0–553–26321–8 (6–12). PB, 158 pp.

A teen boy and girl trade off writing chapters as they describe their adventures with Mr. Pignatti, whom they nickname the Pigman. Humorous and adventurous incidents result.

Nonfiction

Buckman, Robert. (1992). *I don't know what to say: How to help and support someone who is dying*. New York: Vintage Books. ISBN: 0–679–73202–0. PB, 272 pp.

Dr. Buckman, himself once diagnosed as having a fatal illness, addresses the patient's need for information as well as the needs of his or her family and friends, the way to support a dying parent or child, and the complications of caring for those afflicted with AIDS or cancer.

Emswiler, Mary Ann, and James P. Emswiler. (2000). *Guiding your child through grief.* New York: Bantam Books. ISBN: 0–553–38025–7. PB, 304 pp.

Sharing their years of personal insights and anecdotes in dealing with grieving youth, the Emswilers explain how grief affects the family, how to communicate with grieving children, how to create and use "holding communities," and rituals that might help. They deal with issues such as complicated mourning, caring for caregivers, stepparenting a grieving child, and tips for teachers and health professionals. There is a question-and-answer section and a bibliography.

Fitzgerald, Helen. (1992). *The grieving child: A parent's guide.* New York: Simon & Schuster. ISBN: 0–671–76762–3. PB, 207 pp.

Fitzgerald provides much-needed guidance on grief. She addresses areas like visiting the seriously ill or dying, especially difficult situations, including suicide and murder, attending a funeral, and the role religion can play.

Fry, Virginia L. (1995). *Part of me died, too: Stories of creative survival among bereaved children and teenagers.* New York: Dutton Children's Books. HC, 218 pp. ISBN: 0–525–45068–8. HC, 218 pp.

Fry, a bereavement counselor, shares how she leads young people to use their creative talents to ease their emotional turmoil. Each of the eleven real-life stories she includes is followed by a selection of reasonable self-help activities—make a trouble doll, stitch a memory quilt, etc. The narratives, from young people ranging in age from toddler to teen, encompass a wide variety of situations.

Grollman, Earl A. (1993). *Straight talk about death for teenagers: How to cope with losing someone you love.* Boston: Beacon Press. ISBN: 0–807–02501–1. PB, 146 pp.

Grollman addresses issues of death particularly affecting teenagers, such as normal reactions to the shock of death, how grief can alter relationships, and how to work through grief.

Grollman, Earl A. (1991). *Talking about death: A dialogue between parent and child.* Boston: Beacon Press. ISBN: 0–807–02363–9. PB, 118 pp.

Whether through war, a natural disaster, or the serious illness of a loved one or pet, many children must face the reality of death much sooner than their parents would like. This book is designed to help parents and children talk about this difficult time.

Grollman, Earl A., ed (1996). *Bereaved children and teens*. Boston: Beacon Press. ISBN: 0–807–02307–8. PB, 238 pp.

A guide to helping children and adolescents cope with the emotional, religious, social, and physical aspects of a loved one's death. Topics include how adolescents grieve differently from adults and concrete ways to help children cope.

Hipp, Earl. (1995). *Help for the hard times: Getting through loss*. Center City, MN: Hazeldon Information Services. ISBN: 1–568–38085–2. PB, 122 pp.

Hipp presents a guide that helps teens understand how they experience grief and loss, how our culture in general doesn't often acknowledge their losses or give them tools to grieve, and how they can keep their loss from overflowing. The book is filled with illustrations.

Johnson, Joy. (1999). *Keys to helping children deal with death and grief*. New York: Baron's Education Series. ISBN: 0–764–10963–4. PB, 208 pp.

An experienced bereavement specialist tells parents how to explain the concept of death in ways that will be understandable to children. She helps parents anticipate children's responses and needs, shows how to cope with funeral rites in meaningful ways, and points out the importance of incorporating the loss into a positive sense of personal memories.

Krementz, Jill. (1993). *How it feels when a parent dies*. New York: Alfred A. Knopf. ISBN: 0–844–66675–0. PB, 110 pp.

Eighteen children from age 7 to 17 speak openly of their experiences and feelings. As they speak we see them in photos with their surviving parent and with other family members, showing how they have survived the loss of the family member and have continued on with their lives.

Kübler-Ross, Elisabeth. (1997). *Death: The final stage of growth*. New York: Simon & Schuster. ISBN: 0–684–83941–5. PB, 181 pp.

Why do we treat death as a taboo? What are the sources of our fears? How do we express our grief, and how do we accept the death of a person close to us? How can we prepare for our own death? Drawing on our own and other cultures' views of death and dying, Kübler-Ross provides some illuminating answers to these and other questions. She offers a spectrum of viewpoints, including those of ministers, rabbis, doctors, nurses, and sociologists and the personal accounts of those near death and of their survivors.

Kübler-Ross, Elisabeth. (1997). *Living with death and dying*. New York: Simon & Schuster. ISBN: 0–684–83936–9. PB, 192 pp.

Kübler-Ross, the world's foremost expert on death and dying, shares her tools for understanding how the dying convey their innermost knowledge and needs. Expanding on the workshops that have made her famous and loved around the world, she shows us the importance of meaningful dialogue in helping patients to die with peace and dignity.

Kübler-Ross, Elisabeth. (1997). *On children and death*. New York: Simon & Schuster. ISBN: 0–684–83939–3. PB, 288 pp.

This book is based on a decade of working with dying children. The book offers the families of dead and dying children the help and hope they need to survive. Kübler-Ross speaks directly to the fears, doubts, anger, confusion, and anguish of parents confronting the terminal illness or sudden death of a child.

Kübler-Ross, Elisabeth. (1997). *On death and dying*. New York: Simon & Schuster. ISBN: 0–684–83938–5. PB, 272 pp.

This is the classic study of death and dying. This book grew out of Kübler-Ross's famous interdisciplinary seminar on death, life, and transition. In this remarkable book, Dr. Kübler-Ross explores the now-famous five stages of death: denial and isolation, anger, bargaining, depression, and acceptance. Through sample interviews and conversations, she gives the reader a better understanding of how imminent death affects the patient, the professionals who serve that patient, and the patient's family, bringing hope to all who are involved.

Kübler-Ross, Elisabeth. (1997). *Questions and answers on death and dying*. New York: Simon & Schuster. ISBN: 0–684–83937–7. PB, 177 pp.

This companion volume to *On Death and Dying* consists of the questions that are most frequently asked of Kübler-Ross and her answers to them. She discusses accepting the end of life, suicide, terminal illness, euthanasia, how to tell a patient he or she is critically ill, and how to deal with all the special difficulties surrounding death.

Kübler-Ross, Elisabeth. (2000). *To live until we say good-bye*. New York: Simon & Schuster. ISBN: 0–684–83948–2. PB, 160 pp.

This is a visual record of Kübler-Ross's work. Through the photographs of Mal Warshaw, the book gives an intimate view of Kübler-Ross's counseling work with terminally ill patients as she brings them to an acceptance of death.

Kübler-Ross, Elisabeth. (1999). *The tunnel and the light: Essential insights on living and dying with a letter to a child with cancer.* New York: Marlowe. ISBN: 1–569–24690–4. PB, 192 pp.

This book is an introduction to the beliefs, work, and life of psychiatrist Elisabeth Kübler-Ross and is based on her more than 30 years of experience with the dying. The appendix of the book contains her moving letter to a 9-year-old boy who has cancer, "the Dougy letter."

Staudacher, Carol. (1994). *A time to grieve: Meditations for healing after the death of a loved one.* San Francisco: HarperCollins. ISBN: 0–062–50845–8. PB, 256 pp.

This book is a collection of down-to-earth thoughts and meditations, including the authentic voices of survivors, for anyone grieving the loss of a loved one.

Worden, J. William. (1996). *Children and grief: When a parent dies.* New York: Guilford Press. ISBN: 1–572–30148–1. HC, 225 pp.

This book, based on three doctors's study of children who experienced the death of a parent, integrates theory, research, and practical suggestions. The book also contains helpful information that will be as useful to the general public as to professionals.

Picture Books

Heegaard, Marge. (1992). *When something terrible happens.* Minneapolis: Woodland. ISBN: 0–962–05023–7. PB, 32 pp.

Heegard's book helps children explore feelings in a nonthreatening manner that focuses on strengths. The book is general enough for kids to personalize it with whatever issue is troubling them. The pages are large and allow the child to draw illustrations, and the directed art therapy format makes it simple to use.

Jukes, Mavis. (1994). *Blackberries in the dark.* New York: Alfred A. Knopf. ISBN: 0–679–86570–5. PB, 60 pp.

The story of a 9-year-old boy's first extended visit to his grandparent's house after the death of his grandfather, where he explores his grief and finds acceptance of his loss.

Munsch, Robert. (1989). *Love you forever.* Willowdale, ON, Canada: Firefly Books. ISBN: 0–920–66836–4. HC, 32 pp.

The mother sings to her sleeping baby: "I'll love you forever / I'll love you for always / As long as I'm living / My baby you'll be." She still sings the same song when her baby has turned into a fractious two-year-old, a slovenly nine-year-old, and then a raucous teen. So far so ordinary, but this is one persistent lady. When her son grows up and leaves home, she takes to driving across town with a ladder on the car roof, climbing through her grown son's window, and rocking the sleeping man in the same way. Then, inevitably, the day comes when she's too old and sick to hold him, and the roles are at last reversed.

Viorst, Judith. 1975. *The tenth good thing about Barney.* New York: Simon & Schuster. ISBN: 0–689–71203–0. PB, 25 pp.

The death of a cat teaches a child a lasting lesson about death.

Winsch, Jane Loretta. 1995. *After the funeral.* Mahwah, NJ: Paulist Press. ISBN: 0–809–16625–9. PB, 32 pp.

This is a good book to read to children before and after the funeral. The book deals directly with death and what comes after death. The book helps children move toward acceptance, understanding, and hope.

REFERENCES

Agee, James. (1957). *A death in the family.* Thorndike, ME: Center Point.

Couloumbis, Audrey. (1999). *Getting near to baby.* New York: G. P. Putnam's Sons.

Emswiler, Mary Ann, & James P. Emswiler. (2000). *Guiding your child through grief.* New York: Bantam Books.

Fitzgerald, Helen. (1992). *The grieving child: A parent's guide.* New York: Simon & Schuster.

Fry, Virginia Lynn. (1995). *Part of me died, too: Stories of creative survival among bereaved children and teenagers.* New York: Dutton Children's Books.

Grollman, Earl A. (1995). *Bereaved children and teens.* Boston: Beacon Press.

Guest, Judith. (1976). *Ordinary people.* New York: Penguin Books.

Jukes, Mavis. (1985). *Blackberries in the dark.* New York: Alfred A. Knopf.

Kübler-Ross, Elisabeth. (1969). *On death and dying.* New York: Collier Books.

Kübler-Ross, Elisabeth. (1999). *The tunnel and the light: Essential insights on living and dying with a letter to a child with cancer.* New York: Marlowe.

Latner, Joel. (1973). *The Gestalt therapy book.* New York: Julian Press.

LeShan, Eda. (1976). *Learning to say good-by when a parent dies.* New York: Macmillan.

Mann, Peggy. (1977). *There are two kinds of terrible.* New York: Avon Camelot Books.

Paterson, Katherine. (1978). *Bridge to Terabithia*. New York: Avon Camelot Books.

Schuurman, Donna, dir. (1997). *The tomorrow children face when a parent dies*. Videocassette. Sparrowhawke Productions.

Worden, J. William. (1996). *Children and grief: When a parent dies*. New York: Guilford Press.

A Letter from Angela Shelf Medearis

Dear Friend,

I know how depressing life can be sometimes when you're a teenager. It's hard to imagine that things will ever get any better, but they do. Most teens who are considering suicide are too afraid to ask for help or discuss their problems because they feel that no one really understands them. It's hard to believe that anyone else could understand the pain you're in or possibly help you. Death seems to be the only way out. If I could talk to anyone who has ever felt this way, I'd tell them that there is a way out but you have to live your life in order to find it. Sometimes, when life is at its darkest point, you need to take the focus off of yourself and place it on someone else who needs your help. And by all means, find someone to talk to. Talking helps. If you can't stand to talk to someone face to face, call a help line for depression or suicide. You can find the numbers in the phone book. Hang in there.

Love,
Angela Shelf Medearis

"Immune"
Angela Shelf Medearis

I am young.
Therefore,
I am immune
to
AIDS
WAR
CANCER
AND OTHER DEADLY
ILLNESSES
and those WEIRD THINGS that happen to
other people
on TV.
I am young, and
strong, and alive.
Nothing can happen to me.
The only thing I haven't figured out is . . .
why do they make
coffins
in different sizes?

CHAPTER 2

Discovering Life in Death: Confronting AIDS-Related End-of-Life Issues in *It Happened to Nancy*

Janet Allen and Myrna Lewin

An illness in stages, a very long flight of steps that led assuredly to death, but whose every step represented a unique apprenticeship. It was a disease that gave death time to live and its victims time to die, time to discover time, and in the end to discover life.

Herve Guibert (1955–1991)

Children are confronted with end-of-life issues every day as they see friends, family members, victims of tragedy, and public figures leave life as we know it. Children expect death. They expect pets to die and they expect people to die with advanced age or diseases. They see random and violent deaths in the news and at the movies. Unfortunately, they have even come to expect a certain number of those kinds of deaths. Most adolescents, however, still do not see themselves as potential victims of AIDS-related deaths. Nancy's diary entry after hearing her diagnosis reflects that disbelief.

I have . . . *The HIV virus.* . . . I can't feel; I can't think. I may be dumb and young and naïve, but I'm not stupid. Someone's made the most horrible of horrible mistakes. How could *I* have AIDS . . . I've never had a blood transfusion . . . used a dirty needle. I've never had . . . (Sparks, 1994, 75)

The National Vital Statistics Reports (Hoyert et al., 1999) showed a total of 2,314,245 deaths registered in the United States in 1997. Of that number, deaths related to HIV infections were the eighth leading cause of death in 1996 and dropped to the fourteenth leading cause in 1997. While this decrease in percentages is promising, the statistics indicate a continuing toll among young people thirteen to twenty-four years old.

While all death is significant, those adolescents with AIDS or who are supporting someone with AIDS often confront special challenges. In *Straight Talk about Death for Teenagers: How to Cope with Losing Someone You Love*, Grollman characterizes AIDS as a "stigmatic death" (1993, 66). That stigma may make many adolescents shy away from coming to a significant understanding of the disease. Mark Samos, a sixteen-year-old high school student, displays and explains these emotions in a poem he recently wrote regarding his mother's battle as a drug user with AIDS.

> The last time I saw my mother was in the warm summer, 2000.
> Waving goodbye to me from her small second floor hotel window.
> Tears pouring from her eyes
> A knot in my throat
> is this the last time
> alive?
> A small hotel room
> a mere window of her poor hard life
> insecurity
> imprisonment
> freedom from disease
> her skin silky white
> the track marks on her fragile arms
> pale grey
> the color of death
> in her eyes
> sends cold chills to my spine
> loneliness in my heart
> I love and miss her dearly
> I don't know why
> I say it is because she is my
> mother
> It's my duty as a son
> She has lived a long hard life
> She stripped herself of dignity,
> Sold her body to feed me
> drug-user
> but with a mother's love
> I will always love her in return
> She's a fighter

not a quitter
a leader
not a follower
She will grasp onto life
like the string of a kite
fleeting, dancing in the
winds of turmoil
my mother
my lesson
she taught through actions
I learned the lessons well
My daily mantra,
Will she make it through the day?
I love you mom
I forgive you
I don't want to be selfish God,
but, please, don't take her yet
mom, you'll always be in my heart

Buckman (1992) gives us several reasons why this difficult time needs to be treated with logical *and* humane thinking and actions. "AIDS is a disease that puts its victims into a special category—one that some people think should prevent them from getting the kind of humane treatment any other sick person claims as a right. As a result, AIDS patients are not only facing the social taboos associated with death and dying, but must also confront the other taboos of homosexuality and immorality, adding to the already heavy burden of facing death at a young age" (217). For those adolescents who are victims of this disease and for those who support their friends and family members who have the disease, like Mark, Dr. Beatrice Sparks's work, *It Happened to Nancy*, can serve as the springboard for research, discussion, new understanding of AIDS, and support.

IT HAPPENED TO NANCY

This nonfiction work is based on the diary of a junior high school girl who is infected with the AIDS virus as the result of a date rape. Our look at Nancy's diary begins with her entry after she meets a handsome stranger, Collin, who came to her rescue at a concert. Her diary is filled with all the predictable drama of first love, as a fourteen-year-old would report the experience. She is a normal teenager whose diary entries reflect what Nightingale and Wolverton (1993) term "rolelessness." Finding a place to belong and making that transition safely is a difficult stage for most adolescents, and Nancy is no exception. "Adolescents have no prepared place in society that is appreciated or approved; nonetheless they must tackle two major tasks, usually on their own: identity formation and development of self-worth and self-efficacy. The transition from elementary to middle or junior high school or the easy access to potentially life-threatening substances and activities can make adolescence a particularly difficult time" (472–73). Unfortunately for Nancy, the place and the person she chooses for belonging is not safe.

The diary entries reflect her increased obsession with Collin as well as her decreased time and honesty with those who have been important to her—her mother and her childhood friends, who are collectively called "the gaggle." Nancy isn't at all suspicious of Collin's interest in her in spite of the fact that she is in junior high and he is supposedly in college. She revels in his comments, his attention, and his expressed need for her. Her interest in Collin and her meetings with him are kept a secret from her parents and her friends, and this secrecy eventually leads to disaster. When Nancy's mother is away on business, Nancy chooses to stay home alone so she can see Collin. He gives Nancy liquor and then proceeds to rape her.

After Collin leaves, Nancy is left wondering what she has done that might have made her responsible for this "unpredictable" behavior on Collin's part. She still tries to defend him in her mind and in her diary but is devastated from both the event and the disillusionment. This pain makes it almost impossible for her to break her silence about the event. In *Straight Talk about Date Rape*, Mufson and Kranz (1993) cite a reason for this reticence: "The prospect that there may be medical aftereffects of an already traumatic experience adds further emotional pain to an already upsetting experience" (102). When she finally admits to herself and her mother what has really happened, it is already too late. Collin has infected Nancy with the HIV virus and she is left to deal with the consequences of this single sexual encounter.

Nancy's reality changes by the day as she has one difficult decision after another to make. Initially, only Nancy, her parents, and the health-care professionals know that she is HIV-positive. As her condition deteriorates rapidly, she misses more school and begins lying to her friends about trips to Arizona to visit her father so she can mask the extended absences. While HIV can typically take five to ten years to turn into AIDS, Nancy's already weakened immune system affords her only a few months. When that happens, Nancy has to confide in her friends and begins finding there the comfort she has always experienced with them.

The diary entries reflect Nancy's recursive process through the stages of grieving: denial/isolation, anger, bargaining, depression, acceptance (Kübler-Ross, 1993). She has to move from denial quickly, since her symptoms escalate so rapidly. That denial, however, returns each time Nancy's symptoms abate and during those times she looks to the future. She makes plans for college and career, marriage and children. During her intense periods of sickness with pneumonia, rectal ulcers, and weight loss, Nancy has to let go of those dreams and the letting go of those dreams fills her with anger.

> I DO NOT WANT TO DIE! I'M JUST FIFTEEN YEARS OLD! THIS IS SUPPOSED TO BE THE BEST PART OF MY LIFE. WHEN I TURN FROM A GIRL INTO A WOMAN! (Sparks, 1994, 111)

Nancy doesn't bargain much. In fact, she accepts early and quickly that her future is limited. "I've got to face it. . . . I AM GOING TO DIE. . . . I'm not going to have a career . . . husband . . . family" (76). Her acceptance leads her to hope for small things: being well enough to attend her sixteenth birthday party; having enough strength to keep up with the gaggle; and hiding the physical aspects of her disease. As she becomes closer to Lew and his family and closer to both her parents, she realizes that she has the most important things in her life. That realization, however, can't keep her from severe depression when her symptoms quickly overtake her life. "I'm beginning to see the really black side of AIDS that everyone tries to hide. Guess I'll just pretend that everything is okay with me. Then I'll die" (77).

This depression keeps Nancy in bed some days and she begins not eating. There are long spaces between diary entries and days where she writes but doesn't know the date. Her depression finally leads her mother to send Nancy for a vacation with her father who lives in Arizona. Leaving the scene of her rape (her home with her mother) and the school/community, who know about her disease, helps Nancy once again discover living. While in Arizona, she begins doing office work for her father's friend and meets Adam there. Nancy develops an interest in music and begins playing in a small band with Adam's family. Depression is behind her and her life seems good again until she develops rectal ulcers and her health once again deteriorates.

Nancy's weight is down to 81 pounds and she gets increasingly weak. She doesn't want to return to her mother and friends in this condition, and she believes the strain of her disease is too much on her father. The maid has quit in fear of her own health and her father is beginning to show the strain of holding home and business together. Nancy has nearly given up. "Everyone, including me, will be so much better off when I finally die" (181).

Nancy's mother flies to Arizona and together they decide to ask Nancy's Aunt Thelma, an artist in Idaho, if Nancy can come to stay with her. After a night of indecision, Thelma decides to welcome Nancy to her home. Nancy's acceptance of her disease and the safe environment she finds with Thelma allow Nancy the opportunity to cherish the time she has. "I must live only for the *here*—the *now!* It's the only way I can handle my life at this point" (210). In addition to Thelma and Melvin, the ranch caretaker, she finds comfort in Cougar, a tomcat, and a wolf/dog named Red Alert. Together they explore the woods and fields and Nancy begins to find peace. "My heart is leaping within me. Life is good" (211).

The peaceful place and Thelma's invitation to Dr. B. (who put together one of her favorite books, *Go Ask Alice*) to come and visit with Nancy bring Nancy to a place where she can begin to think about her legacy. Nancy had decided to give up. "I want to lock myself in my room and never, NEVER, NEVER COME OUT!" But, the idea of Nancy leaving her diary to help others renews her spirit and gives her a will to live. "Dr. B. and I have to finish my book to help other kids! *That* will be my legacy. I will never have children to live after me . . . to make a difference in the world" (217). She died in her sleep two days after her final diary entry and just two short years after her rape. Nancy had been given the gift of a safe place to tell her story and that story has helped many students who are struggling to find value in their experiences with death.

FROM THE THERAPIST'S POINT OF VIEW

If Nancy had been my client, I don't think I could or would have been able to help her better, or more, than the help she received. In her unfortunate circumstance, she was surely fortunate with her network of family, friends, physicians, and the variety of peaceful places she had available to her. But her best ally was her astonishingly well-developed SELF. In doing an assessment, I look for strengths of self and of a support system. Nancy had both of these. Sadly, in spite of these strengths, her innocence and vulnerability, both from divorce and illness, were characteristics that made her an easy target for Collin. Highlighting those supports that were helpful to Nancy can help us examine how Nancy and her significant others survived this tragedy.

Especially important for Nancy was a safe environment and knowledge of people to help her shed the shame that she would inevitably feel. The nonjudgmental social worker, police, and physician allowed her room to process and keep her humanness when she saw herself as a bad person for not obeying her mother's teachings. The relationship with her mother and her parents' seeming ability to give her unconditional love, even when the marriage failed, were immeasurably significant for Nancy. She spent surprisingly little time in self-pity and appeared to have been very thoughtful of her mother's and her friends' well-being. This is an attribute that a therapist would have looked to foster, but Nancy's own ego supplied it. This proved very useful to her in the eighteen months of her illness.

Journaling as Nancy did is a tool many therapists use to teach their clients to express feelings and to allow those feelings to be separated from the self. Nancy's writing allowed her to rid herself of anxieties and fears as they formed. This helped her avoid getting stuck in a depression from not being able to distinguish one feeling from another. Sadness, desperation, and anger need not be constant companions if expressed and faced, and Nancy's writing helped her discover that. She did an excellent job of doing something about her pain once she recognized it in her written words. For example, as she saw herself writing angry wishes, she often chastised herself, then forgave herself the thought and was able to do the "right things." This method seemed to be a mainstay for her in dealing with anger, loneliness, and embarrassment with friends as well as the emotional pain of having AIDS. This self-acceptance is a skill some adults never achieve and something I strive to teach, foster, and infuse in each of my clients with each connection. Nancy's journal helped her reestablish that sense of self when it faltered.

Nancy's peer friendships in her gaggle—EL, Dorie, Margie, and Lew (and later with Adam)—were essential for her to sustain the energy and sense of belonging in which she could die feeling loved. Her parents' homes, her trip to the beach with her parents, the weekends with her mother were love manifested. I would have sought those for her had she not had them. The peer groups and support of teachers and counselors at schools often provide this network for children who don't have those supports in home and family.

Significant in Nancy's support group was the acceptance and celebration of Nancy's choices. She was not made to feel suffocated and at a loss for control by those who loved and cared for her. This is demonstrated most poignantly in Nancy's choice and the invitation to her last home and final resting place. Melvin and Aunt Thelma, Cougar and Red

Alert were spiritual teachers. She had little time to sort out beliefs on life, let alone death, in her short time on earth. The beautiful land and her last connection to it as well as the demonstrations of love and connectedness she received in that place were simple and serene lessons of the supreme awareness that life equals relationships plus responsibility. Nancy learned that death is part of that life even when it moves more quickly than we could have imagined.

In death, people who are given or seize the opportunity usually attempt to find value in what they have done or what they leave behind. The work of many therapists at this stage is in helping people discover that legacy. Nancy's writings have certainly left a legacy for her generation. She left her life with a powerful message for her known and unmet friends: know your sexual partners; choose well; and beware of who your enemies could be. These are hard lessons for anyone—Nancy's legacy is in making the importance of those lessons both understandable and realistic.

IN THE CLASSROOM

Seneca (d. AD 65) said, "It takes the whole of life to learn how to live, and—even more surprising—it takes the whole of life to learn how to die." Nancy chose as her legacy the writing of a book to help others understand what she learned about learning how to live and how to die. That legacy provides educators the opportunity to share Nancy's story with adolescents so they can benefit from Nancy's developing understandings of risk, family, friends, and plans. Nancy's diary entries bring readers into her thought processes in ways that few informational texts could. Students are not reading statistics that seem to relate to unknown others; they experience the AIDS-related information connected to a character they come to know, care for, and respect. This format and students' connections to Nancy provide rich opportunities for discussion and deeper understandings of end-of-life issues as well as AIDS-related issues.

Building Background Knowledge

When Kyle Gonzalez read *It Happened to Nancy* to her middle school students, she was immediately struck by the amount of vague "information" her students possessed about the topic of HIV and AIDS (Allen & Gonzalez, 1998). After reading the beginning of Nancy's diary, students had some background knowledge for how Nancy contracted the

HIV virus but still seemed sketchy at the general information level. When students were asked to generate what they knew about HIV and AIDS, they generated the following list:

- Sex
- Using/sharing needles
- Fighting/someone scratches you and has AIDS
- It kills you
- If someone has AIDS and bites your skin and breaks it
- Does not hurt you
- You can't get it by having contact with someone
- It's a virus
- Started by a monkey
- You might get it from sex

This lack of knowledge led Kyle and me to a university science educator who came to Kyle's class and did an experiment with the students. This experiment was modeled after an article written by Richard C. Jones, "The Plague Generation: An Exercise in AIDS Awareness" (1993). When the science educator, Dr. Judy Johnson, came to class, students had lots of questions. After giving each student a plastic cup of liquid, she asked them to move around the room and exchange the liquid in their cups with three people they trusted. She asked students to think of questions they would ask before they exchanged the liquids. After several minutes, all the cups began to turn various shades of pink, and students were ready to discuss the transmission of communicable diseases.

As background knowledge increases, students read Nancy's diary with a heightened awareness of the responsibility each person has for personal choices. They also began to see the role of education in making informed choices. Using a class graphic organizer such as the B-K-W-L-Q (see Figure 2.1) to document students' knowledge and questions can then lead them to research in other texts, on the Internet, and in art. Each new piece of background leads students into other works of fiction and non-fiction to gain multiple perspectives on end-of-life issues (see Related Reading suggestions). The information gathered from related readings can be used to create bulletin boards presenting answered questions and knowledge quests related to the topic.

Figure 2.1
B-K-W-L-Q

Build Background	What do I know?	What do I want to know?	What did I learn?	What new questions do I have?
It Happened to Nancy	* Sex * Using/sharing needles * Fighting/someone scratches you and they have AIDS * It kills you * If someone has AIDS and bites your skin and breaks it * Does not hurt you * You can't get it by having contact with someone * It's a virus * Started by a monkey * You might get it from sex	1. When are those stupid scientists that we're paying our tax money to going to find a cure? 2. How do they say the monkey started it? 3. Can you get AIDS from mosquitoes? 4. Can you get it from kissing? 5. How did it start? 6. Why? 7. Nothing 8. Are they going to find a cure?		

Source: Yellow Brick Roads: Shared and Guided Paths to Independent Reading by Janet Allen (Portland, ME: Stenhouse Publishers).

Focused Discussions

I have found that discussing AIDS-related end-of-life issues can be one of the most difficult discussions for adolescents. In *Part of Me Died, Too* Fry (1995) supports that difficulty. "AIDS and suicide are the hardest deaths for society to accept. People often feel that those who die from AIDS or suicide have done something wrong" (152). In many of the related novels and nonfiction I read, the end-of-life issues related to HIV and AIDS were made more difficult because of embarrassment, perceived needs for secrecy, feelings of isolation and guilt, and notions of the disease as punishment for bad or risky behavior. In Reese's (1997) book, *A Young Man's Journey with AIDS: The Story of Nick Trevor*, the author describes her son's feelings around these issues and how detrimental and consuming those feelings were to living his life. "Guilt is a heavy burden to carry. It can tire one out; it was exhausting Nick. There is a big difference between acquiring the results of having lived an at-risk lifestyle and deserving a terrible disease" (68).

Because this issue has these added emotional dimensions, I believe that discussions have to be safe for adolescents as participants and listeners. One of the ways these discussions can be focused and effective is for students to come to discussion prepared to participate because they have given thought to how they might contribute. We have all experienced the devastating effects of one student saying something that occurs to him in the heat of discussion that quickly has tempers flaring. While we can't entirely take away that possibility, asking students to give advance thought and make a commitment to some of the things they would like to consider during discussion can help.

Looking at Nancy's vulnerability at the beginning of this book is critical for adolescent readers. It would be easy for some readers to cite Nancy's "stupidity," but most adolescents would agree they have experienced many of the same feelings of loss of connection with parents, low self-esteem, poor body image, and a sense of being unloved and unwanted that made Nancy vulnerable to Collin's attention. That vulnerability blinded Nancy to what might otherwise have been warning signals: Collin's unwillingness to give details about his life; his mysterious appearances/disappearances; and his need for a fourteen-year-old girl. Using the graphic organizer Looking at Our Options (see Figure 2.2) can focus the class discussion on less risky ways Nancy might have begun to resolve those feelings of inadequacy. In this discussion, students could choose Collin as one of Nancy's options but might also explore other options for Nancy while they are just beginning the reading of

Figure 2.2
Looking at Our Options

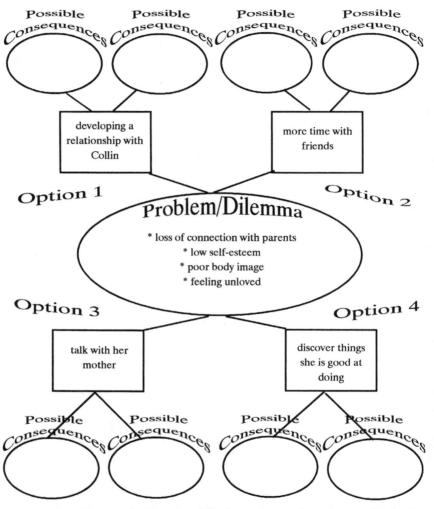

Source: *Yellow Brick Roads: Shared and Guided Paths to Independent Reading* by Janet Allen (Portland, ME: Stenhouse Publishers).

Nancy's diary: more time with friends, finding things she is good at doing, makeup and beauty makeovers, and talking with her mother.

One graphic organizer that can help students with focused discussions during their reading is the Choice and Consequences Log (see Figure 2.3). During the reading, students can discover or teachers can highlight moments of critical opportunity when the main character has a choice to

Figure 2.3
Choice and Consequences Log

Critical Moment of Opportunity	Your Choice for Character	Character's Choice	Consequences
* (10) "I'll leave a note for Mom saying I'm going to the mall to pick up something for one of my classes...Umm, I'll tell her I might be a little late." * (22) Nancy chose to spend the night at her house alone with Collin. "I told her I had real bad cramps, and I wanted to sleep in my own bed. * (25) After the rape: "I've cleaned up the house, gotten rid of every single thing that remains of...him. I even took the trash to the canister outside the building. I don't want it anywhere near me."			

make. Readers can examine the critical moment; write about the choice they would make for the character; compare their choices against what the character chose to do; and examine the consequences of those choices. As with most young adult literature, this work of nonfiction has many critical moments for choices. Some are listed here as possible places to model the thinking, writing, and discussion that can follow this activity.

I discovered a variation of this activity in Young's (1993) novel, *Losing David*. In their AIDS support group, Andrea talked about "junk thoughts" (80). She gave each member of the group the assignment of keeping a journal of all their junk thoughts and then finding a way to turn each of those junk thoughts into something positive. Students could use the opportunity to record Nancy's junk thoughts as a class activity and explore the roles of optimism and pessimism in the healing process.

A final possible support for focused discussions is giving students the opportunity to bring to the discussion table notes and quotes they found interesting in their reading. They can use these notes and quotes to make personal connections and develop questions they have for Nancy, their peers, and the knowledgeable others who might be part of the discussion (texts, web sites, teachers, counselors). Students can track their notes in a triple-entry journal (see Figure 2.4) so their thoughts are more organized when it is time for discussion.

These ideas for assisting in focused discussion do not limit students' abilities to have epiphanies of understanding nor do they necessarily create stilted, fill-in-the blanks discussions. If used in supportive but not restrictive ways, these organizers can be a place to begin. They can give the shiest member of the class entry into a discussion they might otherwise consider too embarrassing or uncomfortable. They can also give the discussion facilitator a point of return when the discussion gets into broad generalizations and heightened emotions.

Dreams and Legacies

Acknowledging and celebrating the end of life is a difficult place for most adolescents. In Hoffman's (1998) *At Risk*, when Charlie is told that his young sister has AIDS, he is stunned as he attempts to absorb this future loss: "He always thought he was smart, and now, quite suddenly, he sees that science has made him stupid. He really believed that, given enough time, science could answer any question, but it cannot answer what is most important: What if there's no time left?" (77). Many of the texts I read supported the importance of providing children with the

Figure 2.4
Triple-Entry Journal

Noting & Worth Remembering	Making Connections	Questioning

opportunity to explore the legacy of the lived life in order to help them find acceptance for what seems so gut-wrenching and unacceptable. This step is critical for the person who is the victim of the disease and it is important for the families, friends, and caregivers who are grieving over the loss. Legacies can be public or private, but acceptance of death is often attached to a celebration of the life. Many have chosen to make their lives public as a way of helping others understand AIDS and the life issues surrounding the disease. In Nick Trevor's story, he left a public presentation a few months before his death saying, "That felt real good." Nick's mother said Nick had been filled with self-pity, but "giving his talk made him feel something he hadn't felt in a long time: worthwhile" (Reese, 1997, 95). Since the core book is a legacy, reading the book lends itself to students finding ways to celebrate the lives of those they have lost.

The AIDS Memorial Quilt is one of the most visible projects of this kind. The project was begun in 1985 to keep the lives of individuals in our hearts and minds rather than just the statistics of AIDS-related deaths. Panels are six feet by three feet of cloth where family members and friends cut words and symbols representing the loved one from other materials and attach those representations onto the cloth background. These panels are sent to an AIDS headquarters and added to other panels from other parts of the country. Parts of the quilt then travel to different places so people can see the quilt. After reading *It Happened to Nancy*, Kyle Gonzalez's students had the opportunity to visit the AIDS Memorial Quilt exhibit, and the quilt had a significant impact on the students' thinking. "As students began to write about the experience, I realized anew the importance of including adolescents in the conversations we have about important life issues" (Allen & Gonzalez, 1998, 126).

This project can serve as a model for remembering those we have lost. Each class member can create a quilt panel that represents someone they have lost. The symbolic choices they make for their panels can help students hold onto the things the loved one has left behind. If some students feel uncomfortable sharing personal losses as quilt panels, they can do panels for characters in novels they have read. In this way, all students get the opportunity to experience the critical role of creating a legacy.

One of the most touching and authentic examples I have seen of continuing Nancy's legacy occurred in Nancy Roberts's middle school class in Sarasota, Florida. After her students completed their reading of *It Happened to Nancy*, they wrote letters to Nancy telling her of the impact of her legacy on their lives. The letters were poignant reminders of the ways that literature can help teenagers find their way. One young woman wrote, "By publishing this book you have led me to a better understanding of this disease. Yes, I have heard about HIV in the news and seen it on T.V., but I figured, 'Hey, it won't happened to kids like me!' "

For students who are fortunate enough to read this book and have the support of counselors, teachers, parents, and mentors to help them make honest connections between Nancy's life and their own choices, they will leave this reading experience wiser and more able to deal with living and dying issues. In April 2000 reports from the Centers for Disease Control and Prevention, UNAIDS, and the World Health Organization provide us with statistics give renewed fervor for making adolescents more aware:

- 1,800 children are infected with HIV each day worldwide.
- More than 33.6 million are infected with HIV worldwide and 1.2 million of them are children.
- Every day, 7,000 people ten to twenty-four years of age worldwide acquire the virus. This translates into five young people every minute or 2.6 million infections a year.
- Worldwide, more than half of all new HIV infections acquired after infancy occur among young people ten to twenty-four years old.

"It can't happen to me." But, it can and it does. Nancy Roberts's students left their reading of this book knowing it can happen to them, or to someone close to them. Students wrote that this book helped them realize they needed to be thankful for the lives they had. They wrote about understanding the responsibilities that come with making adult choices. They wrote about learning that death is a part of life. And they wrote to thank Nancy for the legacy she left them. "Thank you for saving my life and the lives of many others. You made us think twice. I know I'll take this book with me in my decisions for the rest of my life."

Irvin (1996) points to the critical role of the adult in helping students discover alternatives to risky behaviors. "Given that many 'at risk' behaviors, such as drug and alcohol abuse and early sexual experiences, begin during early adolescence, it seems logical that success in developmental tasks and positive interactions with adults may reduce the need that some adolescents feel to engage in those behaviors" (222). Education is our best hope for changing the statistics, and literature can play a significant role in that education. *It Happened to Nancy* can and does provide the springboard for honest talk that may well save some adolescents' lives. It can also help each of us as we discover the life in the midst of death.

RECOMMENDED READINGS

Fiction

Arrick, Fran. (1992). *What you don't know can kill you.* New York: Bantam Doubleday Dell Books for Young Readers. ISBN: 0–440–21894–2 (6–12). PB, 154 pp.

Debra Geddes, and almost everyone in the community, thinks Ellen Geddes has a perfect life. During the screening for the donated blood, Ellen tests HIV-positive. The novel takes readers through Ellen and her family's unwilling acceptance and transition into living with this disease. When Jack, the boyfriend, decides to commit suicide, he asks Ellen to join him so they will die with everyone believing they were still perfect. Ellen opts for life. Jack's death then makes Ellen's HIV public knowledge and the family has to learn how to live with this open discussion.

Baer, Judy. (1993). *The discovery.* Minneapolis: Bethany House. ISBN: 1–55661–330–X (6–12). PB, 127 pp.

Nancy Kelvin is a well-loved pediatric nurse and an active part of her church and community. When she becomes engaged to Mike, the wedding plans quickly begin. All plans are shattered, however, when they discover that her weight loss is not stress from the wedding but AIDS-related. The novel is told through the perspective of Mike's brother, Todd, and his girlfriend as they try to understand how something like this could happen. Written from a religious perspective, this novel addresses religion as well as AIDS issues.

Cleage, Pearl. (1997). *What looks like crazy on an ordinary day . . .* New York: Avon Books. ISBN: 0–380–79487–X (12+). PB, 244 pp.

Ava Johnson has lived her life for more than a decade finding pleasure in freedom and life in Atlanta. When Ava finds her way back to her childhood home of Idlewild, she discovers that many of her criticisms of small-town living have changed. Diagnosed with HIV and determining when and whom she should tell become the focus of Ava's new life. Her involvement in the lives of those in the community and living with AIDS—as well as discovering the love of her life—lead to Ava's legacy. Mature readers will appreciate the honest portrayals of life's tough decisions.

Cunningham, Michael. (1990). *A home at the end of the world*. New York: Picador USA/Farrar, Straus, and Giroux. ISBN: 0–312–20231–8 (12+). PB, 343 pp.

The story of two boyhood friends, Jonathan—well cared for, close to his mom, alone—and Bobby—wild, troubled, and covetous of Jonathan's home. Jonathan and Bobby have a brief homosexual relationship during their adolescence and then separate after high school. Several years later, after Jonathan's family becomes Bobby's family, Jonathan's parents move to Arizona and Bobby moves to New York, where he lives with Clare and Jonathan. Eventually, Clare and Bobby develop a sexual relationship and Clare becomes pregnant (always a dream of Clare's and Jonathan's in spite of Jonathan's homosexuality). Finally, all three, plus the baby, move away from the city and into the country where they find a home together. A former partner of Jonathan's arrives having been diagnosed with AIDS, and Clare's anxiety that she will be left out causes her to run away and leave Bobby and Jonathan. The tough family and social decisions brought about by the disease brings the reader to a deep understanding of home and safety.

Durant, Penny Raife. (1992). *When heroes die*. New York: Atheneum/Macmillan. ISBN: 0–689–31764–6 (4–8). HC, 136 pp.

Gary's Uncle Rob has been his hero forever—the kind of hero you would like to have as a real father. Uncle Rob drives a Corvette, plays basketball, and gives advice to Gary about girls. When Uncle Rob becomes increasingly sick, Rob and Gary's mother finally tell Gary that Rob has AIDS. The disease progresses rapidly when Rob gets pneumonia until Rob dies. During this time of loss, Gary struggles not only with the loss of a father figure, a hero, and a confidant, but also with his the dilemma of his own sexuality.

Fox, Paula. (1995). *The eagle kite*. New York: Bantam Doubleday Dell. ISBN: 0–440–21972–8 (6–12). PB, 127 pp.

When thirteen-year-old Liam has to confront his father's diagnosis of AIDS, he does not believe his mother's explanation that his father has contracted the disease from a blood transfusion. He remembers seeing his father on the beach with a man during a family vacation and that memory haunts him. Liam sets out to confront his father about the lies and secrets and to build an honest relationship while there is time.

Hoffman, Alice. (1998). *At risk*. New York: Berkley. ISBN: 0–425–16529–9 (6–12). PB, 259 pp.

At Risk is a sad yet inspirational story about an eleven-year-old girl named Amanda, who becomes infected with the AIDS virus after getting a blood transfusion a few years before. We see her attempt to live her life in a normal way: family, school, and gymnastics. We also have the opportunity to glimpse how the family and the community view her disease. This book was first published in 1988; we do not today often see much of the hysteria that was connected with AIDS more than a decade ago. This book, however, brings readers back to the importance of community and support especially when ignorance and hysteria would otherwise prevail. Readers today would still learn from the courage of this family.

Humphreys, Martha. (1991). *Until whatever*. New York: Scholastic. ISBN: 0–590–46616–X (6–12). PB, 150 pp.

When school begins in September, the entire school community knows that Connie Tibbs has AIDS. The office nurse at a local doctor's office has told her daughter and she tells the other students. This causes an outcry of fear and rage, resulting in Connie's being shunned by the students and adults at that high school. When Karen, a former childhood friend, chooses to befriend Connie, the other students begin abandoning and eventually attacking Karen. As Connie and Karen go through some of the awareness stages of the reality of AIDS, both learn the value of real friendship and support.

Kerr, M. E. (1986). *Night kites*. New York: HarperCollins. ISBN: 0–06–447035–0 (9–12). PB, 216 pp.

Seventeen-year-old Erick believes he has a normal life at Seaville High until he becomes attracted to Nicki Marr. Nicki is everything Erick's friends would have criticized in the past. She is an outsider who doesn't care to be inside. Erick's journey with Nicki begins to parallel the journey he has to take with his older brother, Pete. When Erick has to confront Pete's otherness because of AIDS, he really begins to understand what it is to find your own way. One of the earliest young adult novels related to AIDS, this book remains one of the finest.

Levy, Marilyn. (1990). *Rumors and whispers*. New York: Ballantine. ISBN: 0–449–70327–4 (9–12). PB, 153 pp.

Sarah Alexander has lived her life in a small town in Ohio until her father's job requires him to move to southern California in her senior year of high school. The change in lifestyle is significant, which makes Sarah miss Ohio even more. Her brother, however, seems to adjust quickly to his new life. Several factors pull Sarah's family apart: Her brother comes out of the closet; her art teacher is forced to face public scrutiny and dismissal when students and parents discover he has AIDS; and Sarah's relationship with David Light and his family foster Sarah's independence. A satisfying response by the school board in spite of public outcry teaches Sarah about some of the social aspects of AIDS. Her relationship with David's father, an AIDS researcher, teaches her the medical implications.

McDaniel, Lurlene. (1993). *Baby Alicia is dying*. New York: Bantam Books. ISBN: 0–553–29605–1 (6–12). PB, 185 pp.

When ninth grader Desi Mitchell's aunt suggests that she begin working at Atlanta's ChildCare House, it seems to be just another school project. Desi quickly becomes attached to an infant who is living at ChildCare—living and dying with AIDS. Desi's involvement increases each day as she spends more and more time with Alicia. In part, Desi is compensating for the love she doesn't feel from her parents. As Desi's connection to Alicia becomes more and more involved, readers are led to understand the trauma of loving someone who is dying.

McDaniel, Lurlene. (1992). *One last wish: Sixteen and dying*. New York: Bantam Books. ISBN: 0–553–29932–8 (6–12). PB, 139 pp.

When Anne Wingate and her father discover that Anne is HIV-positive, neither of them can accept Anne's future. Anne has received a blood transfusion that was tainted and this eventually leads to a downward spiral in her life. An anonymous benefactor promises to grant a wish to Anne and she decides she wants to spend a summer on a ranch in the west. Her father isn't convinced this is best, but Anne insists on spending her days as she would want. She develops a relationship while there with Morgan, and that relationship ends up sustaining her dad after her death.

Nelson, Theresa. (1994). *Earthshine*. New York: Orchard Books. ISBN: 0–440–21989–2 (6–12). PB, 182 pp.

This book has no pretenses—Slim (and the readers) know from the beginning that Slim's dad, Mack, is living and dying with AIDS. We encounter Slim as she is part of a support group for kids living with PWAs (Persons With AIDS). Slim, her dad Mack's friend Larry, and Slim's friend Isaiah (whose mother has AIDS) form a unique and supportive family unit. As Slim tries desperately to hold to her belief that her dad will live in spite of the disease, Isaiah frantically looks for miracles. A book rich in hope and rich in love that sustains, this book leaves readers believing in miracles in spite of Mack's ultimate death.

Peck, Richard. (1998). *Strays like us*. New York: Dial Books. ISBN: 0–8037–2291–5 (6–12). HC, 155 pp.

Twelve-year-old Molly is left with her great-aunt Fay when her drug-addict mother can no longer take care of her. Willis McKinney, the next-door neighbor who lives with his grandparents and is Molly's age, believes he and Molly should stick together, since they are both strays and won't be welcome in the town. Molly's entrance into the social stratum of junior high is rocky until Willis makes her acceptable for the other students. In the end, Willis hasn't been a stray like Molly. Willis father is dying of AIDS and is being kept alive and comfortable by Willis's grandmother and Aunt Fay. When Willis's dad dies, he suffers from the ignorance of the community about AIDS. Molly has to confront the knowledge that her mother is never going to return for her. Aunt Fay introduces Molly to her real grandmother as a way to keep social services from taking her away. Through all this Willis and Molly forge a friendship out of their mutual recognition that they are survivors.

Uyemoto, Holly. (1989). *Rebel without a clue*. New York: Crown. ISBN: 0–517–57170–6 (12+). HC, 194 pp.

This is the story of a male model who comes home to California from New York and tells his best friend he has AIDS. The book does not show the progression from HIV to AIDS; rather, it highlights the emotion around telling his friends and "family" who are in California. The 1980s slang and the lack of character development would make this a difficult read for many students. The book is out of print and there are many other young adult novels that cover this topic in more realistic ways, but, I believe, this book does give us a glimpse of a time, a place, and a series of events that make us think from alternative perspectives.

Young, Alida E. (1993). *Losing David*. New York: Trumpet Club. ISBN: 0–440–82446–X (6–12). PB, 151 pp.

Kim Roberts (fourteen) has been infected by the AIDS virus from a blood transfusion which occurred when she was seven. Her parents have recently moved to a new community after Kim was ostracized at school and social gatherings because of the lack of AIDS education and subsequent hysteria. Her parents have moved to the new community to get away from such hysteria and to move to a place with a medical support system and Hope House. While Kim's initial response to the diagnosis and disease was to retreat, her eventual involvement as a patient and a volunteer at Hope House helps her learn to live her life, not plan her death.

Nonfiction

Basso, Michael J. (1997). *The underground guide to teenage sexuality*. Minneapolis: Fairview Press. ISBN: 1–57749–034–7. PB, 230 pp.

When I read this book, I could not help but think how this book would have helped Nancy (Sparks, 1994) as she began and ended her adolescence. The book is informative and well written with diagrams and statistics to support the text. Chapters include everything from anatomy and birth control to "how to say no" to sex. I would characterize this book as a must-have book for secondary classrooms where students are asking about AIDS and other sexually transmitted diseases.

Blake, Jeanne. (1990). *Risky times: How to be AIDS-smart and stay healthy*. New York: Workman. ISBN: 0–89480–656–4. PB, 158 pp.

The multi-genre format of this informational text would be very appealing to most student readers. The columns of text cover everything from definitions and decision making to getting help if infected. The sidebars of most pages have pictures and quotes from people who have AIDS or who are going through some of the issues related to sexuality and diseases.

Bode, Janet. (1990). *The voices of rape: Healing the hurt*. New York: Dell. ISBN: 0–440–21301–0. PB, 134 pp.

This informational text is another book I would highly recommend for its authentic voices (adolescents who have been raped) and its wealth of important information related to rape and the consequences of that violence. Chapters examine aspects of rape (survival, police action, getting help) as well the hope that comes with finding the right support.

CityKids Speak on Relationships. (1994). New York: Random House and Jim Henson Productions. ISBN: 0–679–86553–5. PB, 46 pp.

The CityKids Publishing Committee has compiled a book written by kids in New York City. While not specifically focused on AIDS, the discussions of sexuality and relationships lead to some painfully honest narratives. The narrative by a young woman who finds out her friend has AIDS highlights the stages of denial, aversion, and education that many go through as they live with those who have AIDS.

Ford, Michael Thomas. (1993). *100 questions and answers about AIDS: What you need to know now*. New York: New Discovery Books. ISBN: 9–780688–126971. PB, 202 pp.

A rich resource for young adults, this book provides factual information for readers asking about health and AIDS-related issues. Sections include general information, fact and fiction, keeping safe, and testing and beyond. Each chapter is punctuated with interviews that bring the factual information to life. The appendices provide annotated safe places and resources of information.

Ford, Michael Thomas. (1995). *The voices of AIDS: Twelve unforget-table people talk about how AIDS has changed their lives.* New York: William Morrow. ISBN: 0–688–05323–8. PB, 225 pp.

The chapters in this book highlight real people whose lives AIDS has affected. These are not the athletes and stars whose voices are often associated with the disease. These are the people who live next door to each of us. They are the people who are trying to make a difference in what we know and what we do about the AIDS epidemic. There are fast facts related to AIDS throughout the book, but the book's merit for your students is they will recognize the voices in the book as their own or those of others like them.

Giblin, James Cross. (1995). *When plague strikes: The black death, smallpox, AIDS.* New York: HarperCollins. ISBN: 0–06–025854–3. HC, 212 pp.

Giblin examines the historical, social, psychological, and political impact of three plagues: the Black Death, smallpox, and AIDS. Extremely well written and interesting chronology of each of the diseases in separate topic-related sections. AIDS, as the most recent, is then compared to the other two. The author provides reference citations, scientific research, and the immediacy of known victims in this informative narration of AIDS, both worldwide and in the United States. An excellent resource in the middle and high school classroom or library.

Gonzales, Doreen. (1996). *AIDS: Ten stories of courage.* Springfield, NJ: Enslow. ISBN: 0–89490–766–2. HC, 112 pp.

This volume of Enslow's Collective Biographies series focuses on ten individuals who chose to share their AIDS stories with the world. Their stories add to our collective knowledge of the disease, the heartache and the triumph. This book is less clinical in its approach; rather, it gives honest, poignant accounts of living and dying with AIDS from people such as Magic Johnson, Arthur Ashe, and Ryan White.

Hyde, Margaret O., & Elizabeth H. Forsyth, M.D. (1992). *AIDS: What does it mean to you?* New York: Walker. ISBN: 0–8027–8202–7. HC, 117 pp.

In its fourth edition, this informational text discusses the causes, symptoms, and treatments of AIDS. The book examines treatments for the disease and the opportunistic infections related to the disease. Clear explanations and visuals would make this a good research source for students, although students should be cautioned that any information may be very dated since much has changed since 1992.

Jukes, Mavis. (1996). *It's a girl thing: How to stay healthy, safe, and in charge*. New York: Alfred A. Knopf. ISBN: 0–679–88771–7. PB, 207 pp.

This book is a candid look at the ways girls' bodies change and develop and the impact of those changes on their lives. Readable text covers topics such as menstruation, puberty, general health, drugs, sex, sexually transmitted diseases including AIDS, pregnancy, and staying safe. Significant statistics and facts are highlighted for easy reference.

Madaras, Lynda. (1988). *Lynda Madaras talks to teens about AIDS: An essential guide for parents, teachers, and young people*. New York: Newmarket Press. ISBN: 1–55704–010–9. HC, 101 pp.

An early informative text about the AIDS epidemic, how the disease is contracted, and ways adolescents can protect themselves and their friends. Short and easy to read with some diagrams and visuals, this book would be beneficial for student research.

Monette, Paul. (1988). *Borrowed time*. Orlando, FL: Harcourt, Brace. ISBN: 0–15–600581–6. PB, 342 pp.

This biography takes us deeply into the life of Paul Monette as he helped his friend of twelve years fight AIDS. This book is both a love story and an incredible look at the ravages of the disease. The information on AIDS in a decade when AIDS was not well known is still valuable and accurate over a decade later. More important, this is a book about making commitments to people and finding ways to honor the spirit and life of a person whose body has been stolen by disease—any disease.

Mufson, Susan, & Rachel Kranz. (1993). *Straight talk about date rape*. New York: Facts on File. ISBN: 0–8160–3752–3. PB, 123 pp.

Factual information related to the psychology behind rape, the aftermath, and recommendations for survival is related in a way that will give adolescents solid support in a dangerous situation. This book makes clear the connection between date rapists and increased risks for all sexually transmitted diseases.

Price, Mark de Solla. (1995). *Living positively in a world with HIV/AIDS*. New York: Avon Books. ISBN: 0–380–77623–5. PB, 272 pp.

This book is fairly unique in the nonfiction texts I collected because a person who has lived with HIV/AIDS wrote it. He takes us through his decision making, his moves toward acceptance and finding realistic solutions, and his hopes that center on taking care and making healthy choices.

Reese, Luellen. (1997). *A young man's journey with AIDS: The story of Nick Trevor.* New York: Franklin Watts. ISBN: 0–531–11366–3. HC, 160 pp.

This biographical account of Nick Trevor's (a.k.a. Jonathan Reese) life is told through letters, AIDS-informative chapter breaks, Nick's writing, Kim's writing, Nick's speeches, and his mother's perceptions. The account is told in the third person, Nick Trevor's point of view, after his death. Readers are allowed into the private thoughts and daily struggles from a point prior to Nick discovering he had AIDS, when he was living a teenage life of rebellion, until just after his death. This informative text is a legacy to what it takes to live and die with AIDS. Medications, treatments, and procedures are made understandable because of the human face attached to the medical language.

Roberts, Tara, ed. (1997). *Am I the last virgin?* New York: Aladdin Paperbacks. ISBN: 0–689–81254–X. PB, 145 pp.

The collection of essays discusses the sexual coming-of-age experiences of ten African-American women. Each essay is honest and informative. Students will fight for the opportunity to look inside the lives of others and compare their own problems and experiences to those reflected in this book. "Quilt of Comfort" is written from the perspective of a young woman who believed that AIDS happened to other people.

Zylstra, Mignon M., & David Biebel. (1996). *When AIDS comes home: Answers to the most commonly asked questions: what to say, what to do, and how to live with AIDS.* Nashville, TN: Thomas Nelson. ISBN: 0–7852–7714–5. PB, 193 pp.

This book deals with AIDS questions and information from a medical and religious perspective. There are fast facts sections with bullets of information for PWAs and their caregivers. These sections are connected to each chapter and offer concrete support for acceptance and moving forward. Older readers who are searching to understand the disease in terms of medicine and spirituality will find this text especially helpful.

Picture Books

Devore, Cynthia DiLaura. (1993). *A week past forever.* Minneapolis: Abdo & Daughters. ISBN: 1–56239–246–8. HC, 32 pp.

Paolos and his niece, Nita, have shared a wonderful relationship, and so Paolos decides to honestly share the magnitude of his illness with her when he has AIDS. Nita's parents leave her at the beach so Paolos can talk with Nita in their

"Enchanted Beach" setting. He talks about the disease in terms of knowing how to make good choices. He explains to her that in her life she needs to take careful steps when taking risks. Nita assures her uncle that she will love him "one week past forever."

Girard, Linda Walvoord. (1991). *Alex, the kid with AIDS*. Morton Grove, IL: Albert Whitman. ISBN: 0–8075–0245–6. HC, 32 pp.

Michael's fourth grade year in school is changed when he becomes friends with Alex. Alex has acquired AIDS from a blood transfusion and the school and community have decided to give the students information so they can understand the disease. Alex and Michael's teacher has to learn how to treat Alex just like all the other students in spite of his disease and Alex has to learn that being special can have both positive and negative aspects. Simple, direct text relating some of the challenges for children in understanding AIDS.

Jordan, MaryKate. (1989). *Losing Uncle Tim*. Morton Grove, IL: Albert Whitman. ISBN: 0–8075–4758–1. PB, 32 pp.

Daniel has a significant relationship with his interesting Uncle Tim who travels around the globe finding antiques and treasures to sell in their store. As Uncle Tim gets weaker and less able to do his work, his mother tells Daniel that Tim has AIDS. Daniel goes through the awareness stages of what the disease means and what it means to him in relation to his Uncle Tim. He finds a way to remember his Uncle through his words.

Newman, Leslea. (1995). *Too far away to touch*. New York: Clarion Books. ISBN: 0–395–90018–2. PB, 32 pp.

Zoe's relationship with her Uncle Leonard is filled with exciting adventures. When Uncle Leonard takes Zoe to the planetarium, she finds the stars mysterious and exciting. On their return home, Uncle Leonard covers her ceiling with glow-in-the-dark stars and they decide the stars are "too far away to touch, but close enough to see." As Uncle Leonard's disease progresses, Zoe has to believe that soon Uncle Leonard will be part of that same starry sky.

Wiener, Lori S., Aprille Best, Philip A. Pizzo, compilers. (1994). *Be a friend: Children who live with HIV speak*. Morton Grove, IL: Albert Whitman. ISBN: 0–8075–0590–0. HC, 40 pp.

Be a Friend is an incredible collection of art and writing by children with AIDS. The voices of these children are represented in three categories: I Often Wonder; Living with HIV; and Family, Friends, and AIDS. In "I Often Wonder," children explore life and death, the cause of their disease, and the impact of that disease on those they love. "Living with AIDS" gives readers insight into the struggles and triumphs these children live each day: telling friends, sickness, weight loss, self-conscious acts, making new friends who also have AIDS, and living with the knowledge that death may be around the next corner. "Family, Friends, and AIDS" helps us understand the child/adolescent perspective of concern for those they see grieving. This collection has art, letters to God, letters to family, essays, thoughts, and poetry. Perhaps Robert Coles expresses the value of this book best in his foreword: "to meet these wonderfully alert, sensitive, thoughtful fellow pilgrims, who have so very much to tell about how to live this life, how to try to understand it, no matter the trials that have come their way" (13).

Poetry

Klein, Michael, ed. (1989). *Poets for life: Seventy-six poets respond to AIDS*. New York: Persea Books. ISBN: 0–89255–170–4. PB, 244 pp.

Poets for Life is an incredible anthology of poetry that speaks to the spirit of the disease. Other books in the related readings highlight statistics and medical research. This anthology offers promise and hope, redemption and memories for those who have helped us see the human side of AIDS.

AIDS-RELATED RESOURCES

Places to Find Help

Advocates for Youth
1025 Vermont Ave. NW, Suite 200
Washington, DC 20005
(202) 347–5700
http://www.advocatesforyouth.org/
Advocates for Youth attempts to increase the opportunities for youth to make healthy decisions about sexuality. They supply information, training, and advocacy to organizations and teachers serving youth.

AIDS Alliance for Children, Youth and Families
AIDS Alliance for Children, Youth and Families
1600 K St. NW, Suite 300
Washington, DC 20006
(202) 785–3564
www.aidspolicycenter.org/
Formerly known as the AIDS Policy Center for Children, Youth and Families, the alliance offers policy research, education, and advocacy on HIV/AIDS prevention, care, and research issues.

AIDS Education Global Information Service (AEGIS)
www.aegis.com/
The largest international HIV and AIDS website, updated hourly. Provides comprehensive information on all aspects of HIV and AIDS.

American Institute for Teen AIDS Prevention
P.O. Box 136116
Fort Worth, TX 76136
(817) 237–0230
Provides educational publications and videotapes relating to prevention of HIV and AIDS.

CDC National Prevention Information Network
www.cdcnpin.org/
(800) 458–5231
Formerly known as the National AIDS Clearinghouse, they provide information for patients, health-care workers, and the general public related to HIV and AIDS, tuberculosis, and sexually transmitted diseases. Provides publications, newsletters, listservs, as well as research information.

Health Initiatives for Youth (HIFY)
1242 Market Street, 3d floor
San Francisco, CA 94102
(415) 487–5777
www.hify.com/index2.htm
Their mission is to improve the health and well-being of young people through education and initiative. They provide educational resources to youth and counselors and teachers to help adolescents take charge of their own well-being.

HIV/AIDS & Adolescents: A Guide to Selected Resources
http://www.hivpositive.com/f-Resources/f-17-NewslettersInfo/f-teenagers/R-adol.html
Created by the Centers for Disease Control, offers young people and teachers links to resources, journals, newsletters, and materials concerning adolescents and HIV and AIDS.

HIV InSite
University of California, San Francisco
http://hivinsite.ucsf.edu/
A comprehensive website that offers information on HIV and AIDS: medical advice, prevention and education information, policy and social issues, and pertinent international news on HIV and AIDS issues.

Mother's Voices
165 West 46th Street, Suite 701

New York, NY 10036
1–888-MVOICES (686–4237)
www.mvoices.org
Assists, educates, and encourages mothers to unite in HIV and AIDS prevention efforts by providing advocacy, education, and awareness programs.

National AIDS Hotline
(800) 342-AIDS (1–800–342–2437) (toll-free)
(800) 344–7432 (toll-free—Spanish)
(800) 243–7889 (toll-free—TTY)
www.ashastd.org/nah/nah.html
Operated by the Centers for Disease Control, they answer HIV and AIDS and STD questions about prevention, risk, testing, treatment, and related concerns. They also provide referrals and send publications.

National Association of People with AIDS (NAPWA)
1413 K St. NW, 7th floor
Washington, DC 20005
(202) 898–0414
www.napwa.org/
Offers information on AIDS education as well as medical and counseling referrals.

Sexuality Information and Education Council of the U.S. (SIECUS)
130 W. 42d St. Suite 350
New York, NY 10036–7802
(212) 819–9770
www.siecus.org/
SIECUS develops, collects, and disseminates information regarding comprehensive sexual education and HIV and AIDS education and promotes the right of individuals to make responsible sexual choices.

Teen AIDS Hotline
(800) 440–8336
Staffed by teens for teens.

Publications, Pamphlets, and Kits

Advocacy Kit
1025 Vermont Ave. NW, Suite 200
Washington, DC 20005
(202) 347–5700
http://www.advocatesforyouth.org/publications/pubsdp.htm#Advocacy%20Kit
Provides an excellent array of resources to begin an advocacy group for young adults ($30.00/kit).

Be a Force for Change: Talking with Young People about HIV
www.cdoupin.org/cgi-bin/webic.exe
Provides tips and information for talking about HIV prevention with young people (free of charge).

Bridges
www.hify.com/bridges.htm
Discusses trends, policies, and stories as they relate to youth, HIV, and health providers ($20.00/4 quarterly issues).

Guidelines for Effective School Health Education to Prevent the Spread of AIDS (January 29, 1998, vol. 37, No. S-2)
www.cdcnpin.org/cgi-bin/webic.exe
Provides statistics, tips, and background information to educators in order to prepare proper HIV educational training to adolescents (free of charge).

What Are Young Gay Men's HIV Prevention Needs?
www.cdcnpin.org/cgi-bin/webic.exe
A fact sheet offering prevention and transmission information specifically targeted toward young gay men (free of charge).

Young People at Risk: HIV/AIDS among America's Youth
www.cdcnpin.org/cgi-bin/webic.exe
Fact sheet published by the CDC that provides youth with specific prevention strategies (free of charge).

Videos

I Have AIDS—A Teenager's Story
www.cdcnpin.org/cgi-bin/webic.exe
Tells the story of Ryan White and gives information about prevention and transmission of HIV (free of charge).

REFERENCES

Allen, Janet, & Kyle Gonzalez. (1998). *There's room for me here: Literacy workshop in the middle school.* Portland, ME: Stenhouse.

Buckman, Robert. (1992). *"I don't know what to say . . ." How to help and support someone who is dying.* New York: Vintage Books.

Centers for Disease Control. (2000). Reports from UNAIDS and the World Health Organization. Atlanta: U.S. Department of Health and Human Services.

Fry, Virginia Lynn. (1995). *Part of me died, too: Stories of creative survival among bereaved children and teenagers.* New York: Dutton Children's Books.

Grollman, Earl A. (1993). *Straight talk about death for teenagers: How to cope with losing someone you love.* Boston: Beacon Press.

Hoffman, Alice. (1998). *At risk.* New York: Berkley.

Hoyert, Donna L, Kenneth D. Kochanek, & Sherry L. Murphy. Deaths: Final data for (1997). *National Vital Statistics Reports* 47, no. 19 (June 30, 1999).

Irvin, Judith. (1996). "Developmental tasks of early adolescence: How adult awareness can reduce at-risk behavior." *Clearing House* 69, no. 4:222–25.

Jones, Richard C. (1993). "The plague generation: An exercise in AIDS awareness." *Science Teacher* 60, no. 8:34–41.

Kübler-Ross, Elisabeth. (1993). *AIDS: The ultimate challenge.* New York: Collier Books.

Mufson, Susan, & Rachel Kranz. (1993). *Straight talk about date rape.* New York: Facts on File.

Nightingale, Elena O., & Lisa Wolverton. (1993). "Adolescent rolelessness in modern society." *Teachers College Record* 94, no. 3:472–85.

Reese, Luellen. (1997). *A young man's journey with AIDS: The story of Nick Trevor.* New York: Franklin Watts.

Sparks, Beatrice, ed. (1994). *It happened to Nancy: A true story from her diary.* New York: Avon Books.

Young, Alida E. (1993). *Losing David.* New York: Trumpet Club.

A Letter from Paul B. Janeczko

"So Many Days" grew from my interest in Buddhism. I wanted Nick to show the Buddhist sense of the current moment, the Now that is such an important part of their belief system. I wanted Nick to contrast with the narrator of the poem, who is so concerned with his father's death, something he cannot control. So, Nick tells his son, "Worry doesn't make life smoother." Or, to use the words of Chogyam Trungpa, a Tibetan Buddhist master, "Hope and Fear cannot alter the seasons."

This is not to say that we should not have hopes and fears, or that we shouldn't plan. Or, that we shouldn't grieve the loss of a love. Rather, we should take the time to enjoy all the blessings that are part of our life. Our parents, our friends, algebra, music, work. Be mindful of all these things. Be mindful even in the mundane, like washing the dishes or mowing the lawn. We need to pay attention. To notice. By being mindful we will see and feel so much more of what our life has to offer.

Yes, life will end for all living things. That is part of the deal. There is no way around it. Nick knows it. That's why he tells his son, "We get so many days. Period." But by living mindfully, concentrating on what is before us, we will get the full measure of living from those days that are our gift on earth.

Peace,
Paul B. Janeczko

"So Many Days"
Paul B. Janeczko

I never thought about it
until Todd Lambert's father—
younger than Nick,
thinner, tan—dropped
dead
while mowing the lawn.

No warning, Todd said.
Never sick.
Just fell to his knees
then over on his side
as if sleeping
with broken glasses.

Which made me shadow Nick,
looking for strain and exertion,
and do chores with new enthusiasm:
hauling trash, raking leaves, and,
most important, mowing the lawn.
Until Nick grew suspicious
and cornered me over a glass of lemonade.
"It's not Father's Day," he began,
making a face
as if he had a real puzzle on his hands,
"and my birthday's not for months."

After my explanation
he said, "We get so many days. Period.
Not one more, not one less
than we're entitled to."

Nick squeezed my shoulder.
"I appreciate your help,"
he said, "I do,
but worry doesn't make life
smoother."

He drained his glass,
looked at it with regret,
and set it on the table
before walking outside,
ready to tempt fate
with the pull of the lawn-mower cord.

CHAPTER 3

Giving Words to the Grief: Using *Two Moons in August, Saying It Out Loud,* and *Tiger Eyes* to Explore the Death of a Parent

Denise P. Beasley and Carin M. Beasley

My mom dying was like the worst
thing that could happen to me.
It felt like my world came
crashing down.
I used to feel angry at her for
leaving me.
But she was very sick, and she
finally stopped suffering.
I had a bad attitude and was
bitter towards almost everyone.
But later on I figured it
was not worth it.
For a long time, and sometimes even
now I was sad and angry.
I had very low self-esteem.
My dad wanted me to come live with him, so I had to leave
my brother, sisters, aunt, cousins,
and childhood friends all behind.
But now I know that God does
everything for a reason.

Myrlande Desulme, 17

After a parent dies, an adolescent's life changes forever, because her
parents play such an important role in defining what type of person she

is and will be. Parents' attitudes, beliefs, and actions help her gauge what her place is in the world, and their values help her evaluate the moral actions of those around her. Wilby (1995) believes that when adolescents lose a parent they are "already going through a kind of bereavement, losing parts of themselves and the people around them as bodies, personalities and through changes in relationships. A parent's death at the same time is a double blow; an additional loss and shock at a time of considerable change" (234).

Tyson-Rawson's (1996) research found that after the death of a parent, "it is not uncommon for adolescents to report that they have difficulty remembering daily events—such as school—for months . . . and that periods of sadness recur at unexpected times even after the acute phase of bereavement" (156). She also discovered that after the death of a parent, "the risk of depressive symptoms for bereaved adolescents 12 to 15 years of age was found to be twice that of children from 8 to 11 years, with girls at twice the risk of boys" (156). Doette Drummond, an eighteen-year-old girl whose father died when she was nine, recalls

> I did not believe that my dad would be taken away from me at such a young age. This was not any ordinary death, he was out fishing and never returned so they just said "he's dead," after all the search party and yet nothing. . . . I finally accepted the fact that he was dead. . . . Sometimes I still think it's my fault. I feel that maybe if I was not born then all this would not have happened. Now I realize it's not my fault, because my dad loved me more than I could imagine. I do miss him and hope one day he will return to me.

It is believed that adolescents who must face the death of a parent are forced to grow up and mature more quickly than their peers who have not suffered such a loss. Grollman (1993) reminds us that these young adults may be forced to accept new household responsibilities such as "shopping, cooking, cleaning, taking care of a younger sibling, getting an after-school job. Life was hectic enough with homework, music, sports, drama practice—and now this" (45). Therefore, it is important to show teens how to recognize their pain, how to find time for themselves, and how to discuss their feelings with others.

Grief is a universal experience that all individuals endure as a normal and natural response to loss. It is important to clarify that there is no "right" way to experience grief and that adolescents grieve differently from adults. Their limited life experiences and their stages of development and maturation affect how they view and cope with death. Citing

Van Eerdewegh, Clayton, et al. (1985), Valente, Saunders, and Street (1988) believe "adolescents may be more prone to negative consequences of bereavement because, unlike children, they are no longer protected psychologically by immature cognitive skills and concrete thinking that could buffer them from the full impact of bereavement" (13).

UNDERSTANDING THE STAGES OF GRIEF

Symptoms of grief include, but are not limited to, anger, rage, fear, depression, numbness, tiredness, frustration, helplessness, hopelessness, and guilt. Grief can also affect thinking patterns, including memory impairment, confusion, disorientation, and denial. It is important to familiarize adolescents with the steps of the grieving process and answer any questions they have about this process. Before planning any treatment for a young adult in the midst of bereavement, it is vital to determine where the teen is on the continuum of the grieving process.

During the process of bereavement, the relationship between an adolescent and her family is in a state of transition as the adolescent attempts to become more independent from the family. As she strives for autonomy, she experiences inevitable mood swings that may inhibit family members from providing the emotional support needed during this difficult time. Instead, the adolescent may seek alternative forms of release such as attention-seeking behavior, social withdrawal, refusal to attend school, sleeping difficulties, changes in eating patterns, and physiological symptoms such as aches and pains of unknown origin. During this time, teens may also turn to drugs and alcohol as a means of avoiding the grieving process. This, in turn, creates increasing problems for the grieving youth, which further isolate her from the rest of the world. Some reactions to a death that signify the need for outside intervention include

- Pretending absolutely nothing has happened
- Constant anger toward anyone and everyone
- Pervasive depression and isolation from friends and family
- Physical assaults on others
- Cruelty to animals
- Excessive misbehavior, fighting, or other serious socially delinquent acts
- Involvement with drugs or alcohol
- Frequent panic or anxiety attacks
- Truancy or a phobic fear of school

- Threat of suicide
- Persistent physical illness (Aldrich, 1993; McIntier, 1993).

HOW TO HELP FAMILIES COPE WITH THE DEATH
OF A PARENT

All families interact in a complicated network of communication patterns such as unspoken rules, family traditions, expectations, and role obligations. Using the systems approach of family dynamics is the most effective way to promote change within the family unit. From this perspective, meaning is derived from the relationship *between* individuals, rather than focusing on the individuals themselves (Minuchin, 1984). In this model, behavior is approached as a recursive phenomenon (a behavior is both cause and effect), and communication patterns are investigated. In a systems approach, the family must work as an interactive meaning-making system. The grieving process for a family is focused on regaining stability and meaning, with the individual members grieving within the arena of the family system.

It is equally important to examine which life cycle stage the family is presently in. When dealing with grieving teenagers, the family must recognize the emotional issues connected to an adolescent's developmental stage and allow for the flexibility of family boundaries to foster the adolescent's independence. This requires the parents to shift the balance in the parent–child relationship. All family members can be "trained" in specific ways to provide comfort, consolation, love, companionship, and support to each other during this difficult time.

A significant component in assisting with adolescent bereavement is to support the surviving parent in maintaining open communication with the adolescent. Bowlby (1980) suggests that the therapist provide a supportive relationship for the parent by facilitating the expression of the feelings necessary for mourning to take a healthy course. The therapist should then advise the parent to encourage his/her children to also express their sorrow and distress. Grosshandler-Smith (1995) adds that adolescents must realize that "dealing with a grieving parent will take a great amount of patience and support" (80). It is also important for "children to see their surviving parent function outside of the roles that have been traditional in their families. Seeing a parent take on new nurturing or instrumental tasks can offer adolescents a new understanding of the potential for flexibility in adult roles" (Tyson-Rawson, 1996, 166).

Maria Luciano, a ninth grader, recalls her father's acknowledgment of her grief before her mother died in the following way, "My family tried to make me talk to her, but my father told them to let her talk to her when she's ready. When I went to talk to her I know that she didn't want to go until she had heard from me." No matter what the situation, it is crucial to remember that every person handles grief in his/her own way, and that family members must respect those differences. Grosshandler-Smith (1995) advises "be sensitive to how other people deal with their grief. Try different approaches to lessening the pain" (83).

NOVELS FOR DISCUSSION/TEACHING

Each novel chosen for analysis focuses on a unique aspect of the death of a parent. For instance, in two, the mothers die as a result of long-term illness, but one novel focuses on a mother's illness, which ultimately leads to her death; while the other explores death's effects on a family a year after the mother dies. The third novel investigates the unexpected and violent death of a father.

Saying It Out Loud by Joan Abelove

In this complex and insightful novel, Joan Abelove introduces the reader to sixteen-year-old Mindy, who must learn to cope, virtually on her own, with her mother's illness and eventual death from a brain tumor. Mindy's father refuses to discuss the severity of her mother's illness, and Mindy is forced to try to understand her mother's predicament, as well as prepare to leave for college on her own. During this difficult time Mindy realizes what a forceful presence her mother has been in her life, such as their similar interests in books, art, and music, which all flood Mindy's memories as she thinks back to times she has shared with her mother. Her father's distance forces Mindy to come to terms with her mother's illness and death in her own way, as she learns to deal with her conflicting emotions of anger, regret, guilt, and sadness.

Two Moons in August by Martha Brooks

As the main character, Sidonie, apprehensively awaits her sixteenth birthday, she must also prepare for the first anniversary of her mother's death. Martha Brooks describes how the family has become determined to go on with their lives by avoiding the emotional impacts the mother's death has had on each member of the family. Sidonie's father, a doctor, buries himself in his work, while Bobbie, her sister, tries to take on her mother's role in the family. Sidonie befriends Kieran, the boy across the street, who is emotionally detached from his father. As Sidonie tries to understand their father/son relationship, she begins to realize her ties to her family are steadily falling apart as well. She takes it upon herself to force her family members to realize their pain before they grow too emotionally detached from one another, and she is determined to do it before her birthday. When Sidonie's attempts turn into a near-tragedy, her family comes to terms with the loss they have avoided.

Tiger Eyes by Judy Blume

Judy Blume's ALA Best Book for Young Adults, *Tiger Eyes*, tells the story of fifteen-year-old Davey Wexler's family after the brutal murder of her father during a holdup. After the murder, Davey's mother moves the entire family across the country to New Mexico to live with an aunt and uncle they barely know. While living in New Mexico, Davey's mother shuts down, and Davey is forced to deal with her pain, confusion, and anger in her own way. She finds a friend, Wolf, who helps her comes to terms with her emotions and teaches Davey how she can help her mother and the rest of the family make the most of a difficult situation.

Help for the Main Characters

Each novel highlights a different family dynamic in reaction to the loss of a parent. Those clinically significant differences are discussed in terms of treatment planning. Remember that there is no "right" way or timetable for experiencing grief. Each of the characters must be made aware that their individual reactions are normal. This normalization process is crucial for establishing both comfort and a sense of direction for the grieving youth.

Mindy is faced with an emotionally distant father in the novel *Saying It Out Loud*. Her dad finds it difficult to speak openly about Mindy's mother's brain tumor. Therefore, in conversations between the father and daughter, the looming death is implied but never directly addressed. Clinically, this needs to be addressed in a family therapy session. Truthful and accurate information must be provided for Mindy to act from. Her father's misguided efforts to provide disinformation, in the guise of protecting her, seems to only complicate matters. Because, as Bowlby (1980) believes, only when the adolescent is given the truth can she face the situation with realism. It would be helpful to facilitate communication between Mindy and her father to help them express their painful feelings and find support from one another.

In the book *Tiger Eyes*, Davey, her seven-year-old brother, and her mother move across the country after her father's murder. The impact of moving, changing to a new school, and adjusting to a new social environment is very stressful and adds additional strain on Davey and her family. After moving into her aunt and uncle's strict home, Davey expresses her grief in her interactions with the family. Davey's mother becomes clinically depressed and withdraws from family and social activities and sleeps and cries excessively. The aunt and uncle do not talk openly about the mother's reactions, which further reinforces the unspoken rule that "uncomfortable issues are not to be addressed in this family." Clinically, these are significant issues that need to be identified and addressed. Family therapy with all members of this household would greatly improve their interactions and help them create a safe grieving environment. It is also of clinical significance for this "suddenly blended family" to openly identify roles and expectations of each other.

Sidonie's father is emotionally distant and seemingly unavailable in the book *Two Moons in August*. Her older sister, Bobbie, assumes the parental role in the family, while Sidonie develops a close friendship with Kieran, who also has difficulties with his father. It would be beneficial to bring Sidonie and Bobbie together in a therapeutic session to help them identify their source of conflict with each other. This would assist them in creating a unified relationship, which may encourage their father to address his grief. Sidonie must also address the effect that the unexpected death of her friend, Peter, creates for Sidonie. As a result of this experience, Sidonie withdraws from social relationships and demonstrates a reluctance to involve herself in other friendships. A therapist should highlight this reaction as a form of grieving and might use this as a means for Sidonie to connect to her feelings.

It is interesting to observe that although these three main characters have different family dynamics, they experience common phenomena in their reaction to their parents' deaths. Each girl must answer the question: to whom can I turn to discuss my grief? In each novel, every individual family member is in the midst of his/her own grieving, which leaves no one emotionally available to the main character. Therefore, each girl must either risk developing new relationships or begin strengthening existing friendships. Although each young adult seems vulnerable while seeking out support, each character discovers the cathartic effect of communicating her feelings of pain, guilt, anger, sorrow, and fear. This illustrates the important therapeutic role the peer group serves. The adolescent peer group normally provides a sense of belonging, uncritical acceptance of separation from family, submergence into a group, and identification with the power of the group (Van der Kolk, 1985).

The three characters experience different levels of frustration and difficulty in relating to their existing parent. Each parent engages in avoidance, social isolation, nondirective communication, and storytelling, which maintains the inability to discuss the grieving process openly. This lack of communication alienates the adolescent–parent relationship further and forces the young adult to build walls to protect herself from further emotional pain. Valente, Saunders, and Street (1988) believe the freedom to discuss death is a coping mechanism, but if the parent is afraid to express his/her feelings, the adolescent is not likely to believe that communication is an option in their relationship.

In forming treatment plans for the characters in the books, it is first necessary to establish long-term goals and short-term objectives, tailored to release the suppression of feelings of grief or denial of the loss. This is a critical goal in therapy, since suppression lends itself to prolonged grieving, which ultimately makes it more difficult for the individual to move toward resolution. Some appropriate long-term goals for Davey, Sidonie, and Mindy include

- Begin a healthy grieving process around the loss
- Complete the process of letting go of the lost parent
- Work through the grieving and letting-go process and reach the point of emotionally reinvesting in life with joy
- Create a supportive emotional environment in which to successfully grieve the loss
- Resolve the loss and begin reinvesting in relationships with others. (Jongsma and Peterson, 1995, 69)

In addition, some short-term objectives that each of the three girls might decide to achieve include

- Identify losses in life
- Increase understanding of the steps in the grief process
- Identify where she is on the continuum of the grieving process
- Begin verbalizing feelings associated with the loss
- State how the use of substances has helped to avoid feelings associated with the loss
- Tell the story of the loss

- Increase awareness of how avoiding dealing with the loss has negatively affected her life
- Identify the positive things about the deceased loved one or relationship and how things may be remembered
- Acknowledge dependency on the lost loved one and begin to refocus life on independent actions to meet emotional needs
- Verbalize and resolve feelings of guilt focused on herself or the deceased loved one that blocks the grief process. (Jongsma and Peterson, 1995, 69)

To meet these goals, the girls must first develop a trusting relationship with the therapist, which can be evidenced by the open communication of feelings and thoughts. Once the therapeutic relationship has been established, a series of interventions should be utilized to facilitate the storytelling of the adolescent's grief. Such behavioral and cognitive activities include play therapy, picture drawing, and guided imagery. These methods assist the adolescent in identifying feelings connected to the loss of a parent. The therapist might also ask the youth to write a list of positive things about her loved one and how she plans to remember each of these attributes. She might be asked to keep a daily grief journal where she records thoughts and feelings associated with the loss and how these emotions are triggered. These should be shared with the therapist. The creation of a memory box is a creative project that can be worked on in the therapy session and out.

Religion can be a powerful source of healing for those who find it comforting. Religion can help the youth develop rituals that aid in celebrating the life and memories of the deceased. The adolescents might also visit the grave and process their feelings through therapy. The therapist should work with clients to teach them behavioral techniques to help release their feelings of anger.

It is important to note that bereaved teenagers report that the most helpful activity after bereavement is simply talking about it. The therapist should facilitate this process. The importance of honest confrontation of the situation, and being able to talk it through, cannot be understated. There is general agreement that children and adolescents manage grief better when they have a supportive person to talk to about the bereavement experience (Valente, Saunders, & Street, 1988).

Unresolved grief is almost always about undelivered communication of an emotional nature. Myriads of feelings may be attached to things left unsaid. Some of the feelings a grieving adolescent might experience are happiness, sadness, guilt, love, fear, anger, relief, and compassion. It is vital that the therapist teaches the main character how to communicate these unspoken words, and then the therapist should remind her it is okay to say goodbye to the relationship that has ended. Frankie Rosario, a sixteen-year-old high school student, used poetry writing to help him come to terms with the guilt he felt over his father's death.

"Game Over"

The last time I saw my father
He had a volcano inside of him
ready to explode.
His heart full of grace,
yet so weak.
He played the family game as if it was his last
He socialized with the whole world.
Never hated anybody except the Devil himself.
Praised his beliefs to everyone
Expected much of his family
Especially me
He got mad at me once or twice
but that didn't stop him from being a good father.
Our family had many problems in our lives
he was always there to fix them,
overcoming many challenges in his life
except for one
October 3, 1997
his last challenge
a difficult one.
He assumed he was o.k.
Something bothering him
there were no signs pointing us in the right direction
until it was too late.
On that day
I got my father very upset
bent out of shape.
He yelled and screamed
I announced my surrender
He wouldn't quit fighting
He punched, jabbed, uppercutted like the heavyweight he was
I was knocked out for the count
by the end,
I was bruised from the head down.
My mother came home that afternoon from work
when she opened the door I approached her

with a black eye
badly beaten.
My father now wanted to box again verbally
with the first love of my life
they boxed back and forth cursing and swearing at each other
I wished that I was in paradise
but I was in hell.
Later that night
everybody sleeping
still aching from the bruises
my eyes wide open
a nocturnal owl
a loud sound from my parent's room
a scream of terror.
I rushed to my parent's room
the unthinkable thing happened
I saw them and that who raised me
lying on the floor
lifeless
call 911
cold to the touch
shrieking with turmoil
shocked with sadness
wishing I was dead
then it was all over
Game over.

This cathartic poem shows that Frankie is finally beginning to release the pain he has felt regarding his father's death for three years. Sometimes grief takes that long, especially with adolescents. The therapist must reiterate that grief does not have a timetable (Ragouzeos, 1987), and that bereavement takes as long as it takes.

IN THE CLASSROOM

The strategies that follow have been designed with the intention of using literature circles, where each group in the class reads a different one of the three core novels: *Two Moons in August, Tiger Eyes*, or *Saying It Out Loud*. This allows for a wide variety of discussion, for student choice, and for an excellent lesson in how each person approaches grief in his/her own way. But it is important to realize that the strategies are applicable to any novel that focuses on the death of a parent, and that each lesson can be adapted and will work effectively even if only one novel is used for the entire class.

Before Reading

Before reading the novels, students must understand the five stages of grief established by Elisabeth Kübler-Ross. Individually, or in groups, students should research and present information about each stage of grief. This information can be found on Internet sites such as those listed at the end of this chapter or in books, such as Corr and Balk (1996), *Handbook of Adolescent Death and Bereavement*, Fitzgerald (1992), *The Grieving Child*, and Grosshandler-Smith (1995), *Coping When a Parent Dies*. In their presentations, students should (1) discuss the emotions associated with that stage of grief, (2) role-play scenarios of someone immersed in that stage of grief, (3) discuss what mourners usually say when they are in that stage of the grieving process.

To model how these emotions connect to a person in the grieving process, the teacher may read aloud a picture book that illustrates a child experiencing the death of a parent. Some choices include Lucille Clifton (1983), *Everett Anderson's Goodbye*, Cindy Klein Cohen (1997), *Daddy's Promise*, and Cornelia Spelman (1996), *After Charlotte's Mom Died*. After the presentation of the book, students should discuss the steps of the grieving process the main character experiences. The teacher should once again stress that these steps do not always follow a distinct sequence.

During Reading

Stages of Grief

Just as with the picture book modeled above, students should record in reading logs the specific lines from their chosen novels that exemplify how the main character reacts during each stage of grief. Once again, it is imperative to remind them that the stages do not always occur in order. Each time the group meets, have individuals discuss their findings with the small group to see if the members agree or disagree with the results. Someone should keep a master list of the group's discoveries.

After the stages have been determined, students might create a comic strip or some sort of representation (collage, drawing, poem, song, etc.) that illustrates the character's actions during each stage. Students should share and discuss these creations with those students reading the other novels, which allows them to compare and contrast how the main characters cope with their grief both physically and emotionally.

Using Other Genres to Examine Grief

Have students examine poetry, short stories, and plays that illustrate the emotions that the main characters are feeling. Some suggestions include Nye's (1999) poetry collection *What Have You Lost*, Pastan's (1978) poems, *The Five Stages of Grief*, Casadagli, Gobey, and Griffin's (1992) short plays and poetry in *Grief: The Play, Writing and Workshops*, Dines' (1997) short story "Listening to My Father's Silence," and Hesse's (1997) individual poems from the novel *Out of the Dust*.

Dialogue Journals

Two books that use the voices of real children and teenagers who have dealt with the death of a loved one are Krementz (1994), *How It Feels When a Parent Dies*, and Fry (1995), *Part of Me Died, Too*. The vignettes contained in these books detail the events surrounding the tragedy young people have suffered and describe the strategies they utilize to accept the death of their loved one. These stories are told by children as young as three and as old as eighteen.

Teachers may have their students create dialogue journals between their main characters and a person from one of the vignettes. (If the additional readings are not available, students can exchange dialogue journals with the groups reading the other novels, since all the main characters are suffering a similar tragedy.) In order for dialogue journals to work, students should pretend that the two characters meet on the street. Have the students create a dialogue between the two characters as they describe their situations, their feelings, and their reactions to each other. Some questions students may consider are How can the characters help each other? What should they say? What happens when someone comes along who knows what it is like to lose a parent?

It is important to stress that the characters in each of the novels frequently say that they feel very alone and misunderstood. Grollman (1993), believes that "there are friends who will truly listen and say: 'I care about you.' 'You're not alone. I'm with you.' 'I remember when . . .' 'What can I do for you now?' 'You talk . . . I'll listen' " (103). By visualizing the characters in connection with someone in a similar situation, the students can imagine what might be said in their conversation. The teacher may also need to provide some additional ideas about what characters might *not* want to say in such situations. In *Straight Talk about Death for Teenagers* (1993), Grollman provides excellent scenarios that give insight into what should not be said during such conversations, which may serve as helpful examples.

Webb (1993) believes that children fear being different from their peers in having a deceased parent. "Unlike adults, who may obtain solace and comfort from the condolences of their friends, children *dread* this process, and frequently their peers feel equally uncomfortable at the prospect of having to speak to a bereaved friend" (13). By practicing these conversations with characters from novels, the students will be better equipped to know what to say to others who are grieving as they come in contact with them in "real life."

Effective versus Ineffective Coping Strategies

Lagorio (1993) suggests that students discuss a list of ineffective and effective coping behaviors that the main character exhibits. For example, does the main character blame others for her problems or situation, or does she talk with someone about her feelings? Have students list the coping behaviors the main characters utilize in the novels and then rate them as ineffective or effective. For the ineffective traits, have the students give advice about how the character could change her behavior to create a positive situation.

In order to demonstrate how the main characters cope in ways that are both similar and different, have each group share the positives and negatives they find. To extend this activity further, students could roleplay the ineffective behaviors as they happened in the book. The audience members may then discuss how the situation could have been handled more effectively. The actors may then reveal how the author chose to resolve the issue.

Guilt Resolution

Students create a list of things that the main character feels guilty about in reference to her deceased parent. After a discussion, students should list each of the guilts on individual slips of paper and the class should discuss ways to dispose of them. Some suggestions might be storing them in a locked box, recycling them, or using them to create a symbolic class sculpture made of papier-mâché. Participating in this process allows the students to see that they can "let their unfulfilled wishes dissolve and be transformed" (Lagorio, 1993, 82). The activity teaches students the importance of forgiving themselves and learning from past experiences.

"In Honor Of" Necklace

Students may apply such processes to their own lives by creating an "In Honor Of" necklace or bracelet. This necklace can be made by stringing beads on yarn, filament, or thread. Each bead on the "In Honor Of" necklace symbolizes a special wish, thought, or trait the child is grateful for. Students might even string a bead for each commitment he/she makes to a new behavior (Lagorio, 1993). This process shows the students how to create something positive from a negative situation. Have students connect this newfound knowledge to their main characters by examining specific events in the novels when the main character turns a negative into a positive. A picture book that describes the importance of this process is Eve Bunting's (2000) *Memory String*. When you read this book to the students, they will understand the special significance of each bead in the child's life.

For Further Discussion

The main characters in these novels must not only deal with the death of a parent, they must also face new roles and responsibilities. In addition, it is necessary for them to learn how to communicate with the parent who has not died. Have students discuss how the following quotes can be related to the situations their main characters have been placed in:

1. There may be other family members who pull away from you. They may be so engrossed in their own grief that they can't pay attention to you . . . maybe it's the wrong moment. Try again. Later they may be more receptive. Tell them what you need. If they can't listen, write them a letter. Very often family members want to share feelings but, mistakenly, try to protect you with silence. Tell them it's okay to talk about sad thoughts. All of you must come to grips with the change in your lives. All of you need to recover . . . dare to talk openly, even cry together. When words fail, hold each other . . . you need each other more now than ever before. (Grollman, 1993, 48)

2. If you are the older brother or sister in your family, your younger family members may look to you to help them deal with their questions, confusion, and pain. If your parent is ill and dying, talk to each other about what you can share with your parent at this time. It can be really helpful to be able to tell your mother how much you love her and that you'll all try to be there for each other when times are tough. (Grosshandler-Smith, 1995, 15–16)

3. Bringing out into the open your worries and fears to your parent will help him or her tune in to what you are feeling and where you are in the grieving process. Try not to shut him out. Work with her in solving the day-to-day problems. You may find that your role in the family changes, probably a little, possibly a lot. Even when you are dealing with the toughest pain and anger that you've ever felt in your life, reach out to your family and talk. Your mother or father needs to recognize your needs. (Grosshandler-Smith, 1995, 86)

4. Although the death of a spouse may place increased financial and emotional burdens on the survivor, it also offers the opportunity for children to see their surviving parent function outside of the roles that have been traditional in their families. Seeing a parent take on new nurturing or instrumental tasks can offer adolescents a new understanding of the potential for flexibility in adult roles. (Tyson-Rawson, 1996, 166)

After Reading

Creating a Funeral

In each of the novels presented, the main characters were excluded from making funeral arrangements for the deceased parent. Lagorio (1993) believes that if children "don't create some kind of memorial, children may hesitate to move forward for fear of forgetting about or not properly honoring the deceased" (83). Grosshandler-Smith (1995) suggests that the grieving child may want to be involved in making the plans, including helping to pick out the casket, choosing the clothing the deceased parent is buried in, selecting the reading or music played at the service, or saying a few words about his/her parent at the service or wake. It is imperative that the adolescent be prepared for what to expect at the funeral, including what things will look like and smell like. Stephanie West Allen's (1998) workbook, *Creating Your Own Funeral or Memorial Service*, provides ideas for allowing children to participate in funeral arrangements in the following ways: music, readings, eulogies, flowers, programs, memory displays, photos, videos, and more.

Using ideas from Allen's book, students could have the main character create a funeral for the deceased parent according to what information is known about their relationship. For instance, in *Two Moons in August* and *Saying It Out Loud*, the mothers loved to read, and each daughter remembers specific pieces of literature she shared with her mother. Students could find those pieces of literature and read a short passage from them and discuss what it symbolizes in the relationship between the two characters. The same could be done using artwork, music, videos, etc.

By participating in this activity, vicariously through the main characters, the students can better understand how important it is to honor the deceased with memories of the past. This activity allows them to see that a funeral becomes an expression of the person's personality, values, and life.

Memory Book

Students may also create a memory book that symbolizes the relationship between the deceased parent and the main character. This memory book may include special memories the main character has of her parent including such items as lessons taught, sports taught, books and music shared, and gifts given and received. By creating this permanent memento, the students realize that even though the person has died, the memories and lessons taught by the parent can last forever.

For Further Discussion

The death of a parent can serve as a catalyst for growth, maturity, and a new sense of self-awareness for adolescents who experience such a tragedy. By comparing the following quotes to the main characters in the novels, students can determine for themselves how the main character has changed as a result of the death of her parent:

1. Life changes forever when a parent dies. Your parents made your life possible. In part, they are responsible for who you are. Their attitudes and behavior help shape your view of the world. . . . You may spend the rest of your life looking for your "lost" parent in your relationships with others. (Grollman, 1993, 43)

2. The death of your father or mother is so painful that in most cases it is *the* turning point in your life. It may not seem that way at first . . . but in retrospect, as you travel the path that you are now on; you will look at life differently. (Grosshandler-Smith, 1995, 111)

3. Adolescents use such tragedies as means for growth; that is, coping with bereavement prompted the adolescents in question to proceed a bit more quickly than their peers into adulthood. . . . most studies indicate that coping with bereavement during adolescence leads to greater maturity, not regression or psychological disturbance. Rather than producing insurmountable obstacles to development, the trauma of bereavement more often promotes growth. (Corr & Balk, 1996, 14)

4. The idea of increased independence or autonomy resulting in the ability to meet one's own needs in the world is central to increased maturity. The discovery of capabilities that characterize adult behavior may come

as a surprise to the bereaved adolescents who are forced by the death of a parent to take on new responsibilities for their own welfare and, often, that of other family members. The death of a parent, then, has the potential to create a greater awareness of one's own capabilities. With greater autonomy and a clearer delineation of the self may also come the ability to discern and empathize with the pain of others. (Tyson-Rawson, 1996, 159)

Even after discussion and time, adolescents may still be reeling from the death of a parent and may still not understand why their parent had to die. Kelli-Ann Knowles, a tenth grader, wrote this poem about comprehending and coming to grips with her father's death:

> WHY?
> Why, why did he have to go?
> I know we all must die,
> But I didn't even get a chance
> To say goodbye.
> He was my father,
> No one can take his place.
> But if he loved me so much,
> Then why am I still asking the question
> WHY?

By providing our children with the gifts of space, time, and support, adults and peers can help grieving adolescents by being aware of that pain. We don't all grieve in the same way or at the same time but the need for honest grief is universal.

RECOMMENDED READINGS

Fiction

Coman, Carolyn. (1993). *Tell me everything*. New York: Farrar, Strauss, and Giroux. ISBN: 0–140–38791–9 (6–12). PB, 160 pp.

Twelve-year-old Roz moves in with her uncle after her mother's accidental death. Roz must come to terms with her mother's accident by reliving past events she shared with her mother.

Conly, Jane Leslie. (1995). *Crazy lady*. New York: Harper Trophy. ISBN: 0–064–40571–0 (6–12). PB, 180 pp.

After his mother's death, Vernon meets the town outcast and her mentally challenged son. As he observes their loving relationship, he realizes what he is missing in his life and decides to help them instead of tease them.

Creech, Sharon. (1996). *Walk two moons*. New York: HarperCollins. ISBN: 0–064–40517–6 (6–8). PB, 280 pp.

This Newbery-winning story within a story traces thirteen-year-old Sal's journey across the Midwest with her grandparents. In order to keep her grandparents amused on the trip, Sal tells them the story of her friend Phoebe, which is really Sal's own story of her memories of her mother.

Declements, Barthe. (1998). *I never asked you to understand me: A novel*. New York: Puffin Books. ISBN: 0–141–30059–0 (9–12+). PB, 144 pp.

After her mother suddenly dies, Didi's world collapses. After her grades plunge, she winds up at Cooperation High, the school for dropouts and druggies. In this novel, Didi begins a search for "self" and realizes that the only person who can help her is herself.

Hesse, Karen. (1997). *Out of the dust*. New York: Scholastic. ISBN: 0–590–37125–8 (6–12). PB, 227 pp.

In poetry, fourteen-year-old Billie Jo Kelby describes her life in the Oklahoma Dust Bowl during the Great Depression and describes her family's healing after the sudden death of her mother and brother. Newbery Medal winner.

Lantz, Francis Lin. (1999). *Fade far away*. New York: Avon Books. ISBN: 0–380–79372–5 (9–12). PB, 168 pp.

Fifteen-year-old Sienna realizes her father, a sculptor, is dying of a brain tumor. Sienna recognizes her father's physical limitations and helps him to create his final masterpiece before he dies, which allows Sienna to realize how important their relationship is to her.

Maguire, Gregory. (1998). *Oasis*. New York: Hyperion Press. ISBN: 0–786–81293–1 (6–8). PB, 170 pp.

After his father's sudden death, Hand must learn to live with his mother, who abandoned his family three years previously. This book chronicles the courage and strength a thirteen-year-old must acquire after losing a parent.

McDonald, Joyce. (1999). *Swallowing stones*. New York: Laurel Leaf. ISBN: 0–440–22672–4 (9–12). PB, 245 pp.

After Jenna's father was murdered by a stray bullet, Jenna not only deals with the fact that her father is dead, she must also realize it's unlikely they will catch his killer. While Michael, the killer, copes with the guilt of knowing he was the one who shot the gun that killed Jenna's dad.

Quindlen, Anna. (1997). *One true thing*. New York: Bantam Doubleday Dell. ISBN: 0–385–31920–7 (12+). PB, 289 pp.

After graduating from Harvard University, Ellen receives a job as a journalist in New York City but must return home to care for her mother, who is dying of cancer. During this time Ellen learns just who her mother is, and the two establish a bond that Ellen could never imagine.

Schnur, Steven. (1996). *Beyond providence*. San Diego, CA: Harcourt, Brace. ISBN: 0–152–00981–7 (6–8). PB, 245 pp.

Twelve-year-old Nathan's family falls apart after his mother's death, which requires that Nathan learn to play the peacekeeping role between his father and brother. Through hard work and determination, Nathan brings the family back together, and he learns self-reliance.

Sebestyen, Ouida. (1997). *Words by heart*. New York: Yearling Books. ISBN: 0–440–41346–X (4–8). PB, 144 pp.

Lena, a young African-American girl, practices her scriptures in order to win a Bible-quoting contest hoping to make her father proud. Because her classmates are white, she must face violence and her father's death, and she must learn to forgive.

Wallace, Daniel. (1999). *Big fish: A novel of mythic proportions*. New York: Penguin Books. ISBN: 0–140–28277–7 (12+). PB, 192 pp.

As Edward Bloom comes home to die, his son, William, gets to know his father better. As he listens and records his father's stories and tall tales, William comes to realize just who his father is and how much his father means to him. Each chapter serves as an individual story, or the novel can be read in its entirety.

Woodson, Jacqueline. (2000). *Miracle's boys*. New York: G. P. Putnam's Sons. ISBN: 0–399–23113–7 (6–12). HC, 131 pp.

Twelve-year-old Lafayette tells the story about his mother's death and how it has affected him and his two older brothers. One brother, Charlie, returns from reform school and blames her death on Lafayette, which Lafayette begins to believe. Ty'ree, the eldest brother, struggles to make ends meet and tries to support his younger brothers, while the threat of custody continuously hangs over his head.

Nonfiction

Allen, Stephanie West. (1998). *Creating your own funeral or memorial service: A workbook*. Denver: Kite Shade. ISBN: 0–964–42072–4. PB, 166 pp.

This workbook helps those who are dying begin to prepare their memorial or funeral service. As a result, the funeral becomes a work of art and an expression of the deceased's personality, values, and life.

Bode, Janet. (1995). *Death is hard to live with: Teenagers talk about how they cope with loss*. New York: Laurel Leaf. ISBN: 0–440–21929–9. PB, 192 pp.

After interviewing teens who have experienced the death of a friend or relative, Bode gives teens advice on how to deal with the shock, guilt, and tragedy of death.

Edelman, Hope. (1995). *Motherless daughters: The legacy of loss*. New York: Dell. ISBN: 0–385–31438–8. PB, 342 pp.

The editor polled 246 women across the United States, ranging in age from seventeen to eighty-two, about the impact on their lives of their mothers' deaths. The essays describe how the daughters' relationships changed with their fathers and their siblings, as well as how their identities changed because their motherly role model had disappeared.

Fry, Virginia L. (1995). *Part of me died, too: Stories of creative survival among bereaved children and teenagers*. New York: Dutton Children's Books. ISBN: 0–525–45068–8. HC, 218 pp.

Fry tells the true stories of eleven young people whose family members or friends have died. In each chapter she includes activities to help children explore their grief through writing, drawing, and other creative projects.

Gellman, Marc, & Thomas Hartman. (1999). *Lost and found: A kid's book for living through loss*. New York: Morrow Junior. ISBN: 0–688–15752–1. HC, 144 pp.

Rabbi Gellman and Monsignor Hartman explain all types of loss by talking directly to the reader about the role faith plays in relationships. Their casual dialogue does not force the reader to share in the same religious perspective.

Krementz, Jill. (1993). *How it feels when a parent dies*. New York: Alfred A. Knopf. ISBN: 0–844–66675–0. PB, 110 pp.

Eighteen children (ages seven to sixteen) discuss their experiences and feelings about the death of their parent.

Lagorio, Jeanne. (1993). *Life cycle: Classroom activities for helping children live with daily change and loss*. Tucson, AZ: Zephyr Press. ISBN: 0–963–31950–7. PB, 122 pp.

Provides activities and strategies to use with children in grades K–6 to help them understand grief, mourning, and loss.

Picture Books

Brisson, Pat. (1999). *Sky memories*. New York: Delacorte Press. ISBN: 0–385–32606–8. HC, 80 pp.

Ten-year-old Emily discusses her mother's inevitable death from cancer and tells the story of how the two of them analyze the sky and create visual images of the clouds at certain intervals during their life together.

Bunting, Eve. (2000). *The memory string*. New York: Houghton Mifflin. ISBN: 0–395–86146–2. HC, 33 pp.

As Laura looks at each button on her memory string, she is reminded of her family's heritage and is connected to her mother who has died. When the twine of Laura's memory string breaks, and she loses a button that was her mother's favorite, Laura's stepmother helps her find the lost button. This event helps Laura realize that the memory string is important for creating new memories too, which helps her come to terms with her mother's death.

Clifton, Lucille. (1983). *Everett Anderson's goodbye*. New York: Holt, Rinehart. ISBN: 0–805–00800–4. PB, 28 pp.

Using the genre of poetry, young Everett Anderson discusses his feelings as he goes through each stage of grief and eventually comes to terms with the death of his father.

Cohen, Cindy Klein. 1997. *Daddy's promise*. Bloomfield Hills, MI: Promise. ISBN: 0–965–64980–6. PB, 32 pp.

After his father dies, young Jesse struggles to understand the difficult concept of death. This text provides answers to common questions children have about death and offers suggestions for teaching them how to cope.

Klein, Lee. (1995). *The best gift for mom.* New York: Paulist Press. ISBN: 0–809–16627–5. PB, 28 pp.

Jonathan presents his mother with a special gift as she learns how to parent on her own during the difficult holiday season. The story proves that a family's love continues even after suffering tragedy and loss.

Spelman, Cornelia. (1996). *After Charlotte's mom died.* Boston: Albert Whitman. ISBN: 0–807–50196–4. HC, 24 pp.

Six months after her mother's death, Charlotte and her father visit a therapist to discuss their unexpressed feelings.

Drama, Poetry and Short Stories

Casadagli, Penny, Francis Gobey, & Caroline Griffin. (1992). *Grief: The play, writing and workshops.* London: David Fulton. ISBN: 1–853–46212–8. PB, 185 pp.

Includes a play, poetry, and advice for dealing with grief. Includes chapters such as "The grief of a deaf child," and "The loss of a twin," which all discuss the need to acknowledge and talk about grief.

Cormier, Robert. (1984). "In the heat." In Donald R. Gallo, ed, *Sixteen: Short stories by outstanding writers for young adults.* (1984). New York: Bantam Doubleday Dell. ISBN: 0–440–97757–6. PB, 179 pp.

This short story is told from the father's point of view as he grieves for his wife and observes his son at her funeral. The father thinks back to his own father's death and compares his feelings to those his son must be experiencing.

Dines, Carol. 1997. "Listening to my father's silence." In Dines, *Talk to me: Stories and a novella.* New York: Bantam Doubleday Dell. ISBN: 0–440–22026–2. PB, 223 pp.

In this story, Brian learns to cope with his mother's death after a long battle with breast cancer and is forced to choose between living his life and spending time with his mother before she dies.

Mazer, Norma Fox. 1999. "Meeting the Mugger." In Judy Blume, ed., *Places I Never Meant to Be.* (1999). New York: Simon & Schuster. ISBN: 0–689–82034–8. HC, 198 pp.

Fourteen-year-old Sarabeth recounts arguments she has with her mother before she dies of cancer. Sarabeth discusses her mother's denial of her cancer, and the advice she continuously gives to Sarabeth without heeding it herself. When her mother finally dies, Sarabeth realizes that the advice helps her make it through the tough times in her life as she continues on without her mother.

Nye, Naomi Shihab., ed. 1999. *What Have You Lost?* New York: Green-willow Books. ISBN: 0–688–16184–7. HC, 205 pp.

An anthology of poems that discuss various levels of loss, including death. Includes comments from each poet regarding something lost and found.

GRIEF RESOURCES

Association for Death and Education Counseling
342 N. Main Street
West Hartford, CT 06117–2507
(860) 586–7503
www.adec.org
A professional organization devoted to death education and research. Provides comprehensive information on death, dying, grief, bereavement, and counseling.

Bereavement: A Magazine of Hope and Healing
5125 N. Union Blvd.
Colorado Springs, CO 80918
(888) 604-HOPE (4673)
www.bereavementmag.com
Prints poetry, artwork, and stories of hope for child, adolescent, and adult mourners. It also includes research articles on death, dying, grief, and bereavement.

Death and Dying.com
www.death-dying.com
Provides adolescents with a comfortable forum for discussing and researching all aspects of grief, bereavement, death, and dying. Written at a level that is both understandable and informative for adolescents.

Grief and Loss Resources Centre
Box 1290
Golden, BC, V0A 1H0
www.selkirk-tangiers.com/~spirit/grief/grief.html
Includes a comprehensive list of links where students can research all aspects of grief and death.

REFERENCES

Abelove, Joan. (1999). *Saying it out loud*. New York: DK.
Aldrich, L. M. (1993, February). "The grieving child." *Learning* 93, no. 21: 4043.

Allen, Stephanie West. (1998). *Creating your own funeral or memorial service: A workbook*. Denver: Kite Shade.

Blume, Judy. (1981). *Tiger eyes*. New York: Bantam Doubleday Dell.

Bowlby, John. (1980). *Loss: Sadness and depression*, vol. 3. New York: Basic Books.

Brooks, Martha. (1991). *Two moons in August*. Toronto: Groundwood Books.

Bunting, Eve. (2000). *The memory string*. New York: Houghton Mifflin.

Casadagli, Penny, Francis Gobey, & Caroline Griffin. (1992). *Grief: The play, writing and workshops*. London: David Fulton.

Clifton, Lucille. (1983). *Everett Anderson's goodbye*. New York: Holt, Rinehart.

Cohen, Cindy Klein. (1997). *Daddy's promise*. Bloomfield Hills, MI: Promise.

Corr, C. A., & D. E. Balk. eds. (1996). "Adolescents, Developmental Tasks, and Encounters with Death and Bereavement. In *Handbook of Adolescent Death and Bereavement*. New York: Springer.

Dines, Carol. (1997). "Listening to my father's silence." In Dines, *Talk to me: Stories and a novella*. New York: Bantam Doubleday Dell.

Fitzgerald, Helen. (1992). *The grieving child: A parent's guide*. New York: Simon & Schuster.

Fry, Virginia L. (1995). *Part of me died, too: Stories of creative survival among bereaved children and teenagers*. New York: Dutton Children's Books.

Grollman, Earl. A. (1993). *Straight talk about death for teenagers: How to cope with losing someone you love*. Boston: Beacon Press.

Grosshandler-Smith, Janet. (1995). *Coping when a parent dies*. New York: Rosen.

Hesse, Karen. (1997). *Out of the dust*. New York: Scholastic.

Jongsma, Arthur E., & Mark Peterson. (1995). *The complete psychotherapy treatment planner*. New York: John Wiley & Sons.

Klein, Lee. (1995). *The best gift for mom*. New York: Paulist Press.

Krementz, Jill. (1994). *How It Feels When a Parent Dies*. New York: Alfred A. Knopf.

Lagorio, Jeanne. (1993). *Life cycle: Classroom activities for helping children live with daily change and loss*. Tucson, AZ: Zephyr Press.

McIntier, T. M. (1993, June). "Guiding the child through death and grief." Paper presented at the meeting of the Carondelet Management Institute, Mobile, AL.

Minuchin, Salvador. (1984). *Family kaleidoscope*. Cambridge, MA: Harvard University Press.

Nye, Naomi Shihab, ed. (1999). *What Have You Lost?* New York: Greenwillow Books.

Pastan, Louise. (1978). *The Five Stages of Grief: Poems*. New York: W. W. Norton.

Ragouzeos, Bobbe. (1987). *The grieving student in the classroom*. Lancaster, PA: Hospice of Lancaster County.

Spelman, Cornelia. (1996). *After Charlotte's mom died*. Boston: Albert Whitman.

Tyson-Rawson, K. J. (1996). "Adolescent Responses to the Death of a Parent. In C. A. Corr & D. E. Balk, eds., *Handbook of adolescent death and bereavement*. New York: Springer.

Valente, S., J. Saunders, & R. Street. (1988). "Adolescent bereavement following suicide: An examination of the relevant literature." *Journal of Counseling and Development* 67, no. 3: 174–77.

Van der Kolk, B. (1985). "Adolescent vulnerability to post-traumatic stress disorder." *Psychiatry* 48, no. 4: 365–70.

Van Eerdewegh, M., Clayton, P. & Van-Eerdeweg, P. 1985. "The Bereaved Child: Variables Influencing Early Psychopathology." *British Journal of Psychiatry, 147,* 188–194.

Webb, N. B. (1993). "The child and death." In N. B. Boyd, ed., *Helping bereaved children*. New York: Guilford Press.

Wilby, J. (1995). "Transcultural counseling bereavement counseling with adolescents." In S. C. Smith and M. Pennells, eds., *Interventions with bereaved children*. London: Jessica Kingsley.

"A Steaming Bowl of Happiness"
from *Fig Pudding*
Ralph Fletcher

It happened on October 15. At four thirty-five in the afternoon the phone rang at our house. Brad, who was eight, had been riding his bike, tearing down a hill with a bunch of other kids and talking to his best friend, Jack Wells, at the same time. The way we heard it, Brad turned his head and smashed full speed into an ambulance parked on the street.

Somebody found the ambulance driver. He rushed Brad, who was unconscious, to Good Samaritan Hospital.

Mom was in the kitchen slicing up Greek olives for a special olive-feta-cheese-and-sun-dried-tomato-over-pasta dish she made, Dad's favorite supper. The phone rang. When Mom hung up she put Josh in his car seat and drove straight to Good Sam. I came, too, and I'd never known Mom to drive so fast. We met Dr. Wentworth in the intensive care waiting room. He stood there wringing his big hands. Shaking his head. Avoiding our eyes.

"It's very, very bad," Dr. Wentworth said. "His brain stem—he practically severed it."

"Brain stem?" Mom asked.

"The part at the lower back of the head. It connects the brain to the top of the spine. It's . . ." He shook his head.

"What? What does it mean?"

For the first time he looked at her.

"Well?" she demanded.

He spoke in a croaking whisper. "There's really no hope, Lisa."

Mom stepped back, as if someone or something had just struck her in the face.

"I can't accept that," she said.

A Letter from Ralph Fletcher

When I receive letters from children about my novel *Fig Pudding*, most of them go like this: "I loved your book, but why did Brad have to die?" One young reader took it a step further: "It was sad when Brad died. But then I realized that you wrote the book. You made him die. Why did you kill him off like that?"

Tough question. My brother Bob died in a car wreck in 1974. He was seventeen years old at the time, four years younger than me. Most people assume that fiction is reality thinly disguised. Let's cut to the chase: Was Bob's death the reason for Brad's death in *Fig Pudding?* The answer is: no, and yes.

The main reason for Brad's death is an aesthetic one. Yes, it's a painful part, and I can't be cavalier about "killing off" a wonderful kid like Brad. I knew it would be painful for children to read (and who wants to bring pain to children?) but I believed then, and still believe, that the book needed it. Without Brad's death, *Fig Pudding* would have been a series of amusing family tales. This tragedy gave the book a center of gravity—it gave the book ballast. It pulled the book together, and it pulled the family together.

But that's not the simple answer. Most writers have certain autobiographical itches they scratch now and again in their work. I did that in *Fig Pudding*.

While many parts of Brad's death were invented or at least exaggerated, others were not. You may remember the part where Mom and Dad go into the bedroom of Cliff and Nate to deliver the news that Brad died. Mom does not speak. She reaches down and starts picking up dirty socks on the floor. That's exactly what happened when my parents came in to tell my brother Jim and I that Bobby had died.

Fig Pudding is a work of fiction, but there was enough "truth" to make it a painful book for my parents and siblings to read when I gave it to them. And it was painful to write. I cried when I wrote it, and I cried rereading what I'd written. I cried when I read the published book, too. But writing it helped me to heal. That tragedy scarred me as a young man, but by using it as the raw materials for a novel, I discovered that it contained not only sorrow and loss but also beauty and real power.

There's something else. When you write, you can give yourself little gifts. My parents were so devastated by Bobby's death they didn't really talk to us about it afterwards. My siblings and I were left to our own devices. In my book, I decided that the Abernathy parents would really talk to the children about Brad's death. Mom and Dad in *Fig Pudding* were emotionally available to the children in a way that my parents probably wanted to be, but could not be. Brad died in my novel but in a way, I wrote a happier ending.

Sincerely yours,
Ralph Fletcher

CHAPTER 4

Making Sense of Sibling Loss: Using *A Summer to Die* as a Guide through the Grief Journey

Kyle E. Gonzalez and Cynthia G. Clark, with assistance from Denise P. Beasley

> Children live in a world not of their own making and are subject to influences beyond their control. If as parents and professionals we are interested in improving our children's quality of life, we must concern ourselves with their relationship to death.
>
> Helen Rosen, *Unspoken Grief* (p. 75)

We don't know about you, but there was never a course in our education programs entitled The Real World 101. We learned about the teaching of literature and writing, but no one prepared us to help children accept the most basic fact of life: death. How ironic, since literature is often such a direct reflection of life. This chapter will discuss how the death of a sibling can affect a child or adolescent, how a school can respond to a student who experiences such a loss, and how to use the novel *A Summer to Die* (Lowry, 1977) in the classroom to address the issue of sibling loss.

When a child (ages six through eleven) loses a sibling, he/she may experience the grief process through dreams. Children often have feelings of guilt, can become afraid that they will die, can experience difficulty in school, and may engage in "risk-taking" behaviors, which can result in accidents or physical harm (Fanos, 1996).

When an adolescent (ages twelve through eighteen) loses a sibling, he/she may engage in "risk-taking" behaviors that are much more dangerous than those of a child. These may include alcohol and drug abuse, criminal activities, and inappropriate intimacy. The adolescent may experience a lack of motivation in school and have difficulty developing long-range goals (Fanos, 1996). In addition, adolescents who have lost a sibling to suicide may have an increased risk of suicidal tendencies.

Rabbi Marc Gellman and Monsignor Thomas Hartman (1999) interpret the grief process for young people as the Three Sadness Steps: shock, searching, and finding. The first step is *shock*, which adults identify as denial. Gellman and Hartman write that, for young people, "Shock is like a blanket for your soul. Shock keeps your soul a little warm while everything around you is turning cold" (110).

The second Sadness Step is *searching*: "You don't feel the worst pain right away, but after a little while—YIKES!—you REALLY feel the pain" (Gellman & Hartman, 1999, 111). This step is when the emotions of the child/adolescent emerge, such as anger, pain, and confusion as the surviving sibling struggles to make sense of the loss. It is common for grieving young people to feel anger toward God or authority figures at this stage.

The third Sadness Step is *finding*. During this stage the child/adolescent may find answers that enable him/her to return to some sense of normalcy. Gellman and Hartman reassure us that "Finally, you'll find a place to store the pain so that it does not keep you from feeling joy again" (116).

What does this look like in the classroom? Young people, like adults, can go through the three "sadness steps" or stages of grief repeatedly. The stages may blend into one another and will not necessarily occur in order. It may seem as if the student is doing very well one week, and then the next a new behavior may arise that causes concern. Teachers may observe the student becoming easily distracted, perhaps accompanied by a decline in academic performance, an increase in inappropriate behavior, withdrawal or isolation, and sporadic attendance.

Classroom teachers don't have to handle this alone. The student's guidance counselor, the school social worker, the school's student assistance coordinator, or other school support personnel are resources that should be contacted if a student is faced with sibling loss. These people should be able to guide a teacher in how to approach the grieving student as well as how to work with his/her peers to help them become more comfortable with the idea of death itself. The local hospice agency or hospital can be contacted for additional information and resources.

Teachers need to remember that building the communities of their classrooms is a daily process. The stronger the foundation of trust among the students and teacher, the more able the classroom community will be to nurture the healing process to support any member in crisis. The tragedy of losing a sibling is not complete once the funeral has ended. The grief process or sadness steps are just beginning, and the student will need a safe place to learn about and experience the many implications of death and grief.

Adequate support for children and adolescents who have lost a sibling may not always be present in the home. Gellman and Hartman recognize that parents or caregivers may be preoccupied with their own grief, which can lead to feelings of abandonment for the surviving sibling: "Another tough thing about the death of a brother or sister is that it can totally wreck your parents for a long time. It may seem like they don't have much time for you after the death of your brother or sister because they are so sad themselves and may need time alone to get through it" (155).

Remember that the parents or caregivers will be wrapped up in their own personal grief and may not be able to be as emotionally present as usual to the surviving sibling(s). Yet support for the surviving sibling(s) is so vital, as pointed out by Claudia L. Jewett (1982) in *Helping Children Cope with Separation and Loss*: "In about half of families that suffer the loss of a child, one or more remaining siblings will develop symptoms such as depression, severe separation anxiety, and problems with going to school. This seems clearly to be the result of the changed behavior of the parents toward the remaining children rather than the death itself" (94). It is important that the teacher or appropriate school staff act as the advocate for the child, offer condolences to the parent or caregivers, ask them how they are faring, and present opportunities for the children to gain support on their grief journey.

Student support groups facilitated by trained staff or individuals from local agencies such as hospice are beneficial resources for grieving students. It's no secret that peers are one of the most influential forces on children and adolescents, and the student support group is an excellent place to allow students to experience the effects of positive peer pressure. Students, especially those in middle school, tend to prefer the kinesthetic modality of learning, and a group is a terrific place for using art and play in the healing process. It's important for students to know that they are not alone in their grief journey, and that others are traveling with them. The student support group is a healthy place for young people to make connections and build relationships.

In addition, the school-based student support group can assist the parent or caregiver because the group meets during school. Therefore, the parent or caregiver is not asked to take on any additional responsibility for scheduling the sessions or worrying about transportation. Many students daily spend more time with their teachers and peers at school than with family members. This is all the more reason to provide students with support and appropriate resources at school.

While professional therapy is certainly beneficial to families dealing with grief, it's not always available to every child who is experiencing loss. The school can provide groups led by trained facilitators, counselors, social workers, and teachers to help bridge that gap. The key, however, is the working relationship between and among teachers, students, and school support staff, such as counselors, student assistance professionals, or social workers that creates an effective team to facilitate the teaching process and to support students who need help in their personal grief processes.

A SUMMER TO DIE

A Summer to Die, a novel by Lois Lowry, tells the story of the Chalmers family's loss of their oldest daughter, Molly, to acute myelogenous leukemia. The protagonist of the story is Molly's younger sister, Meg. Molly's illness is unexpected and claims her life in less than a year. As her parents struggle with the crisis of Molly's illness, rather true to life, Meg is left to create her own support system and come to terms with her own adolescence and Molly's loss of her adolescence.

Meg and Molly have a typical sibling relationship, which includes conflict. One of their conflicts is that they have to share a room. Molly is neat; Meg is messy. At the beginning of the novel, Molly gets angry at Meg for being so messy and draws a line down the middle of their bedroom to set a boundary. Meg is hurt by this but doesn't really express her feelings to her sister.

Unlike Meg, Molly quickly fits in at her new school. She is chosen as an alternate cheerleader and almost immediately gets a boyfriend. Meg's school experience is different. She does not even discuss her new school with the reader. Instead, she focuses on a friendship that develops with her elderly neighbor, Will Banks. She gives Will photography lessons in the new darkroom that she and her father built.

Molly gets sick in February with what the doctor labels as the flu. She is confined to the couch downstairs. On the one hand, Meg likes having her sick because it causes Molly to stay home and actually spend time with Meg. On the other hand, however, Meg also views Molly's illness as a "nuisance" because she is so grouchy. Molly starts to get a lot of nosebleeds. In fact, the rug in their room is stained with the blood from Molly's nosebleeds.

Molly seems to get better and return to her old self. One afternoon she and Meg get into a discussion about marriage: the fact that Molly wants to get married and Meg doesn't. It escalates further into an argument about Molly's beauty versus Meg's intelligence:

> "You'll be pretty, Meg, when you get a little older. . . . Look at all the talent you have. And brains. I'm so *stupid*. What do I have, really, except curls and long eyelashes?"
>
> I should have known that she meant it sincerely. . . . I can't imagine how it would feel to be beautiful; how could Molly know how it feels *not* to be? (52)

Later that evening Meg wakes up in the middle of the night with a horrible feeling. She calls Molly's name and finds her already awake. Molly is having a horrible nosebleed. Molly is literally covered in blood, an image that remains in Meg's mind long after her parents rush Molly to the hospital that night. Meg, of course, has guilt about the argument that she and Molly had earlier that day. Fitzgerald (1992) writes about this guilt in her book *The Grieving Child: A Parent's Guide*: "She will feel ashamed for having harbored such thoughts, perhaps convincing herself that this wish was the actual cause of the sibling's death" (67). Meg experiences this shame/guilt when she says, "If I hadn't fought with Molly this afternoon, none of this would have happened" (57).

Fanos (1996) warns parents/caregivers to be aware of the guilt siblings may feel when another sibling has died: "The link for many between depression and guilty feelings is quite explicit. Some siblings torment themselves with any slight thing they later regretted" (108).

Secrets are a part of all families experiencing dysfunction, whether the dysfunction is alcohol, violence, or loss. Often it is a child within the family that breaks the cycle of secrets. Meg's parents do not tell her that Molly is dying. They simply leave her with the impression that Molly will recover from her illness. Meg breaks the cycle of secrets about Molly when she and her parents begin to share their sadness and fears, "My mother . . . was crying. I looked back at Dad in bewilderment, and there were tears on his face, too, the first time I had ever seen my father cry. . . . I reached out my arms to him, and we both held out our arms to Mom" (Lowry, 1977, 117–118).

Meg finds support not from her parents or school but, surprisingly, from a wonderful neighbor named Will Banks. Will has suffered his own loss in the death of his wife and is able to offer Meg words of wisdom. Later, after she visits Molly in the hospital and realizes that she will never see her again, she shares Will's words with her father, which helps her father understand how alone Meg has been throughout the mourning process.

It's interesting to note that Meg's parents never take her to visit Molly in the hospital until right before Molly's death. They tell her that she is too young, according to hospital rules, but Meg thinks differently. Fitzgerald (1992) discusses the subject of taking children/adolescents to visit the seriously ill. She suggests that you ask your child/adolescent whether he/she would like to visit the ill person. If your child/adolescent says no, Fitzgerald suggests that you find out why, whether fear of the unknown, a strange place, or whatever. If your child still does not want to visit the ill person after you have discussed his/her fears, Fitzgerald suggests that you do not force him/her to go but be prepared to help the child later if he/she has guilt feelings about not going.

Meg does, however, decide to visit Molly in the hospital after she photographs the birth of their neighbors' son. Before Molly's leukemia led her to stay in the hospital, Molly had been thrilled to learn that their neighbor was pregnant and was very involved in the pregnancy, even helping sew clothes for the baby. Meg wants to be the one to tell Molly about the birth.

As Meg's father drives her to the hospital, he does what Fitzgerald (1992) suggests to parents by preparing Meg about the hospital room, Molly's appearance, state of health, etc. "She'll be very sleepy . . . because of the drugs. . . . she can't talk to you. . . . she can hear you, Meg. Talk to her . . . underneath all that stuff . . . our Molly is still there" (Lowry, 1977, 135).

Meg brings Molly a gift when she visits her, a little vase of pussy willows. Molly dies two weeks after Meg's visit. "She just closed her eyes one afternoon and didn't ever open them again. Mom and Dad brought the pussy willows back for me to keep" (139). Meg reaches the third sadness step near the end of the book. She returns to Will to discover the secret of the flowers Molly had found before her death. In that discovery Meg embraces the cycle of life and death and continues on her journey of self-discovery: "Nothing will be the same, ever, without Molly. But there's a whole world waiting, still, and there are good things in it" (Lowry, 1977, 140).

IN THE CLASSROOM

Before Reading

Teachers should become familiar with their students before reading a novel that deals with a real-life issue such as loss. All students have experienced loss at some level, whether it is a pet, self-confidence, or a loved one, and these experiences can be included in the development of a curriculum for a novel such as *A Summer to Die.*

- Invite a guest speaker from hospice or another agency that deals with grief/adolescent crisis to lead a discussion about loss in your classroom.
- Have students write about some form of loss that they have experienced in their lives. One of Kyle's students, Daniel Sellars, wrote about a loss in his life, the death of his sister before he was even born:

  I would have a sister today but she died when she was born. She was born two years before I was. . . . I think I would like having a sister. I always think about what would happen if my sister lived. . . . My parents never told me how they felt about losing a little girl, but I think they were really sad about it.

- Have students complete "My Experience with Loss" as follows

  My Experience of Loss
  1. A loss that I have experienced in my life is _____.
  2. This loss happened when I was _____.
  3. I felt _____ when this loss happened.
  4. Ways my life has changed since the loss are _____.
  5. What I want to know about loss is _____.
  6. I did/did not get support about this loss.
  7. What I would tell other people about loss is _____.

- If students have difficulty identifying feelings or grasping the concept of grief, brainstorm a list of possible responses.
- Read a poem or children's story whose theme is death/loss and discuss with students (see related reading for titles).
- Ask students to interview a friend or family member about their feelings or experiences surrounding death/loss.

During Reading

Meg is faced with many stressful situations throughout the book and there are plenty of opportunities for a school to step in and offer support to a student in Meg's situation. By addressing these issues as the class reads the novel, the teacher can prepare the students for the tougher issues as the plot unfolds. In the beginning of the story Meg and Molly are faced with moving in the middle of the school year, changing schools, and having to share a room. Some activities that could facilitate a connection between the reader and Meg and Molly are the following:

- Suggest that students write about what they would miss at home or school if they had to move.
- Ask students to brainstorm ways that they, their class, or their school could welcome new students. Some activities that Cindy has sponsored at her school to welcome new students include a buddy system, a new student luncheon, and a classroom welcome packet. The buddy system connects the new student with a veteran student who will not only guide the new student around the school but also offer support and introductions to other students, school traditions, cultures, etc.
- Jo Denmark, a guidance counselor that Cindy and Kyle used to work with, designed the new student luncheon. It occurs once a month and gives new students a chance not only to eat pizza and drink soda, but also offers the opportunity for new students to network and meet key staff members at the school.
- Teachers can have students design a classroom welcome packet to orient the new student to the culture of their classroom community. Items that might be included in the packet are notes of welcome from other students, classroom procedures, rules, and guidelines.

In addition to her family's move, Meg also faces the issues of sibling rivalry and personal self-discovery. This is introduced early in the novel as the reader discovers the different ways Meg and Molly view the family's move. Meg is upset that she will have to leave behind her photography and art classes. Molly is upset because she will lose her position on the cheerleading squad and her myriad of friends, while Meg wonders about the differences between her and her sibling. In order to understand the themes of sibling rivalry and self-discovery in the novel, students might complete some of the following activities:

- Comparison/Contrast: At this point in the reading of the novel, the teacher can have students complete a comparison/contrast chart of the two sisters, Molly and Meg. Students could complete individual or small-group charts, with the teacher bringing the class together to share their responses. Charts could be displayed around the classroom or kept in student notebooks for future reference during the reading of the novel. This could also extend to students completing a chart about themselves and a sibling (or close friend, cousin, etc., if student does not have a sibling).
- Another suggestion is to have students write about their own siblings (or close friend, cousin, etc., if student does not have a sibling). The

following quote could be used as a writing prompt for students: "Sometimes it seems as if, when our parents created us, it took them two tries, two daughters, to get all the qualities of one whole, well-put-together person" (Lowry, 1977, 3–4).

- Like most of us, Meg had difficulty honoring her unique special gifts and talents. Invite students to make a list of five of Meg's talents and personality traits, using a "top five list." Next, invite students to complete a "top five list" about themselves.

After Reading

"Rituals are important as the family seeks to retain a connection to the dead child," explain Arnold and Gemma (1983, 69). In the same way, the students will need appropriate closure activities for this novel unit.

Students can follow the gift-giving example that Meg gives in the story. Fry (1995) writes about two sisters whose older brother dies of brain cancer. He spends his last few months at home, in the care of his mother and hospice staff. Hospice counselors worked with the two sisters to help make gifts for their brother. Both sisters painted their brother pictures and, on his eighteenth birthday, they performed a special dance for him. These gifts helped the girls to cope after their brother died: "Throughout the overwhelming sadness of Frankie's dying, Amy and Betsy knew that the celebration and gift-giving were important. Within that tragic situation there was room for laughter and dancing. These were the gifts Amy and Betsy gave to Frankie and to themselves. The memory of those good times they will treasure proudly long after his death" (81).

Similarly, Meg makes gifts for Molly during her illness. At one point, she paints her a beautiful Easter egg. Meg's mother brings the egg to Molly's hospital room and tells Meg that it did indeed brighten up the room. Some suggestions for students that embrace the idea of giving or honoring a loved one's memory include the following:

- Invite students to make a gift for Meg, to help her get through her sister's death. Making an egg, wildflower book, or quilt would tie directly to the story.
- Brainstorm a list of activities on how the class could help a peer in the healing process following a sibling death.
- Invite students to brainstorm and create a handbook on proper etiquette for funerals and hospital visitation. See related readings for resources

for this activity. Be sure to be culturally inclusive and allow students to share rituals and customs from their cultures.

- Encourage students to create a memory book for Molly or Meg. This might include flowers, pictures, and other artifacts important to the sisters. Students could include poetry and letters written to Molly.
- Partner with a science teacher to create a cross-curricular project in which students would make a book of pressed flowers identifying their scientific names, etc., as Will did with Molly.
- Allow students to design a memorial for Molly, such as planting a flower box for the classroom. Work in conjunction with the art teacher on a photography journal that could be included in the memorial.
- Encourage students to develop a community-service project that relates to leukemia. This could be a fund-raiser or a research activity that promotes awareness of the disease.

As educators, we want to be able to support our students should any one of them find themselves on a grief journey. We want the school and our classrooms to be places of safety and security. Our hope for children/ adolescents who suffer the loss of a sibling is that, with the proper support, they can reach the place that Meg eventually did:

> Time goes on, and your life is still there, and you have to live it. After a while you remember the good things more than the bad . . . gradually, the empty silent parts of you fill up with sounds of talking and laughter again. . . . the jagged edges of sadness are softened by memories. (Lowry, 1977, 140)

RECOMMENDED READINGS

Fiction

Bunting, Eve. (1991). *A sudden silence*. New York: Fawcett Books. ISBN: 0–449–70362–2 (6–12). PB, 107 pp.

Jesse Harmon must come to terms with his grief and guilt after seeing his deaf brother being struck and killed in a hit-and-run accident. Jesse becomes determined to find his brother's killer and must learn to cope with his grief in the process.

Butler, Charles. (2000). *Timon's tide*. New York: Margaret McElderry Books. ISBN: 0–689–82593–5 (9–12). HC, 192 pp.

In this dark gothic mystery, Daniel tries to determine whether he was the cause of his older brother's death that occurred six years previously, or if Timon was murdered. As he tries to ferret out the cause of death, Daniel is wracked with guilt as the old feelings of mourning resurface.

Couloumbis, Audrey. (1999). *Getting near to baby*. New York: G. P. Putnam's Sons. ISBN: 0–399–23389–X (6–12). HC, 211 pp.

Willa Jo and Little Sister face the loss of their baby sister. They have to spend the summer with their rather stuffy Aunt Patty, as their mother is having a difficult time recovering from the loss of the baby. Willa Jo, Little Sister, and Aunt Patty learn a great deal about each other during the summer before they return home to their mother.

Egan, Jennifer. (1996). *The invisible circus*. New York: St. Martin's Press. ISBN: 0–312–14090–8 (12+). PB, 338 pp.

Eighteen-year-old Phoebe is determined to solve the mysterious death of her sister, Faith, eight years previously. She sets out for Europe to learn the truth and finds out more than she ever wanted to know. This helps Phoebe come to grips with Faith's death and allows her to put the past behind her.

Ewing, Lynn. (1996). *Drive-by*. New York: HarperCollins. ISBN: 0–064–40649–0 (6–8). PB, 96 pp.

After his older brother is killed in a gang-related shooting, twelve-year-old Tito tries to put into perspective his brother's role in the gang. To aid in the grieving process, Tito remembers all the good things that his brother did during his life.

Mead, Alice. (1998). *Adem's cross*. New York: Laurel Leaf. ISBN: 0–440–22735–6 (6–12). PB, 132 pp.

Thirteen-year-old Adem witnesses his sister being shot and killed while she is reading a poem at a political rally against the Serbs' control over Kosovo. After her death, Adem also becomes the victim of beatings and violence, and he eventually makes a journey to Albania to seek refuge.

Park, Barbara. (1996). *Mick Harte was here*. New York: Random House. ISBN: 0–679–88203–0 (4–8). PB, 89 pp.

Thirteen-year-old Phoebe remembers her twelve-year-old brother Mick, who died in a bicycle accident because he wasn't wearing a helmet. In her remembrances, Phoebe recalls Mick's sense of humor and practical jokes in order to help herself cope with his sudden death.

Rodowsky, Colby. (1988). *Remembering Mog*. New York: Farrar, Straus, and Giroux. ISBN: 03–380–72922–9 (11–12+). PB, 136 pp.

As Annie prepares for her own high school graduation, she is reminded of the similarities between her graduation plans and those of her sister, Mog, who was murdered two years previously. Annie turns to a therapist, who helps her come to terms with her grief and who helps Annie realize that it is okay to continue living out her dreams, even though Mog was not able to do so.

Smith, Jane Denitz. (1999). *Mary by myself*. New York: HarperCollins. ISBN: 0–064–40568–0 (4–8). PB, 152 pp.

Mary, a fifth grader, gets sent away to summer camp after her baby sister dies of SIDS. There she befriends Celeste, who is not a good role model, and Mary gets into trouble. When Mary returns home from camp, she realizes the depths of her grief and how to cope.

Springer, Nancy. (1994). *Toughing it*. San Diego: Harcourt, Brace. ISBN: 0–152–00008–8–9 (9–12). HC, 119 pp.

Sixteen-year-old Shawn, also known as "Tuff," witnesses his older brother's murder. He sets out to find who killed Dillon and in return finds a soul mate in his father, who helps Tuff sort out his grief.

Williams, Carol Lynch. (1996). *Adeline Street*. New York: Yearling Books. ISBN: 0–440–41206–4 (4–8). PB, 185 pp.

Eleven-year-old Leah struggles with all the changes in her life a year after her sister's death. Tom, a new friend, helps Leah see the inner strength she has and helps her put the past to rest and look toward the future.

Wilson, Nancy Hope, (1998). *Flapjack waltzes*. New York: Farrar, Strauss, and Giroux. ISBN: 0–374–32345–3 (4–8). HC, 144 pp.

Molly, a twelve-year-old, cannot get past the death of her brother two years earlier. She finds a friend in an elderly Holocaust survivor, who helps her cope and see the rebirth that springtime offers.

Nonfiction

Bluebond-Langer, Myra. (1996). *In the shadow of illness: Parents and siblings of the chronically ill child*. Princeton, NJ: Princeton University Press. ISBN: 0–691–02783–8. HC, 271 pp.

This looks at the impact of chronically ill children on parents and siblings and outlines nine family case studies.

Davies, Betty. (1999). *Shadows in the sun: The experiences of sibling bereavement in childhood*. Philadelphia: Brunner Routledge. ISBN: 0–876–30911–2. PB, 264 pp.

Uses ten different chapters to help readers understand the special bond that siblings have and how a sibling's death affects the other brothers and sisters.

Grollman, Earl A. (1993). *Straight talk about death for teenagers: How to cope with losing someone you love*. Boston: Beacon Press. ISBN: 0–8070–2500–3. PB, 146 pp.

A guide that leads adolescents through the grief process and gives them guidelines for coping, rebuilding their lives, and creating memories of their loved one.

Rosof, Barbara D. (1995). *The worst loss: How families heal from the death of a child*. New York: Henry Holt. ISBN: 0–805–03241–X. PB, 269 pp.

Helps both parents and children understand how the loss of a child/sibling affects the entire family. Offers advice and strategies to help the family members cope with their loss.

Picture Books

Cohn, Janice. (1994). *Molly's rosebush*. Morton Grove, IL: Albert Whitman. ISBN: 0–807–55213–5. HC, unpaged.

When Molly's mother has a miscarriage, her family must come to understand their grief. When they plant a rosebush outside, they realize it will become a symbol of hope for them and a remembrance of the unborn child that will help them through their suffering.

Old, Wendie. (1994). *Stacy had a little sister*. Morton Grove, IL: Albert Whitman. ISBN: 0–807–57598–4. HC, unpaged.

Stacy feels jealousy and resentment when her new baby sister is born. This makes her feel horrible and guilty when her sister dies suddenly of SIDS. Her parents help her realize her feelings are normal and that she is not responsible for her sister's death.

Rothman, Juliet. (1996). *A birthday present for Daniel*. Amherst, NY: Prometheus Books. ISBN: 1–583–92054–1. HC, unpaged.

After the death of her brother, a young girl discusses the death's emotional impact on all the members of her family and how they each grieve in their own distinct way. The story ends with a celebration of the deceased child's birthday, which helps them all come to terms with his death.

Turner, Barbara. (1996). *A little bit of Rob*. Morton Grove, IL: Albert Whitman. ISBN: 0–807–54577–5. HC, unpaged.

A month after her older brother Rob's death, Lena and her family continue a special family tradition of going crabbing. While on this journey, the family reflects on their many happy memories and this helps them ease their bereavement.

REFERENCES

Arnold, Joan Hagan, & Penelope Buschman Gemma. (1983). *A child dies: A portrait of family grief*. Rockville, MD: Aspen Publishers.

Fanos, Joanna H. (1996). *Sibling loss*. Mahwah, NJ: Lawrence Erlbaum Associates.

Fitzgerald, Helen. (1992). *The grieving child: A parent's guide*. New York: Fireside Books.

Fry, Virginia Lynn. (1995). *Part of me died, too: Stories of creative survival among bereaved children and teenagers*. New York: Dutton Children's Books.

Gellman, Marc, & Thomas, Hartman. (1999). *Lost and found: A kid's book for living through loss*. New York: Morrow Junior.

Jewett, Claudia L. (1982). *Helping children cope with separation and loss*. Boston: Harvard Common Press.

Lowry, Lois. (1977). *A summer to die*. Boston: Houghton Mifflin.

Rosen, Helen. (1986). *Unspoken grief: Coping with childhood sibling loss*. Lexington, MA: Lexington Books.

A Letter from Jan Cheripko

For the past several years I've been involved in answering the many letters from the readers of *Highlights for Children* magazine. *Highlights* receives about 1,000 personal letters each month. These are in addition to the thousands of poems, puzzles, stories, jokes, riddles, and drawings that the magazine receives each month. The policy of *Highlights* has been from the beginning that each personal letter deserves a personal response. We have a core group of people who answer letters, which includes the editors of *Highlights for Children*. My job—and I'm very honored to have this responsibility—is to be sort of a sounding board for the editors responding to some of the more difficult letters. These are letters that might deal with divorce, alcohol or drug abuse, violence or threats of violence, running away, racial problems, stealing, and a host of other problems that beset young people today.

I am particularly proud of the way that the *Highlights* editors always respond with a sense of respect for each individual child. We do not send back form letters to these personal letters from our readers. Instead, each child gets a serious, thoughtful response to his or her question or problem. I think some of the best letters we've written are those letters where we acknowledge the child's dilemma, but then offer a list of possible ways of finding a solution. Almost always that list includes talking to a trusted adult, particularly the child's parents, unless the parents are not alive or are keenly involved in causing the problem.

I think the *Highlights* philosophy, which is manifested in the letters to our readers, is synonymous with my own philosophy both as a writer for and teacher of young people. It is this; treat each person individually and with respect; offer hope; emphasize the role of the adult in a child's life. A young person doesn't magically walk from the darkness of ignorance into the light of wisdom by listening to those who are similarly in the darkness. Each of them needs adults who can guide them along the way. I'm fortunate to be associated with a publishing company and a school whose philosophies respect individual youngsters, offer hope, and see clearly the necessary roles of adults in providing that hope. The following letter is from a young girl who shares her desperation with us. My letter to her is our way of making a difference in the lives of children.

Dear   Highlights
        I want to   Die,   I
like your   issues / I have   truble
with   my   family, Thay a scrowed up.

Dear ———,

It sounds from your letter to us that you've been feeling pretty low. I'm really sorry to hear that you've been having a tough time.

In your letter you didn't give many details, so I'm a little unsure just what kind of advice I can offer you. However, I can tell you some things that I have discovered, and maybe they will be of help to you.

When I was younger, about your age, in fact, I wanted to die and I thought my family was screwed up. I'll tell you a little about my life, and maybe that will help you. My mother died when I was five years old and my father was an alcoholic. My sister and I went to live with my aunt and uncle, and my uncle was also an alcoholic. My family was pretty screwed up. Many times I felt that I wanted to die.

I think there were a couple of reasons that I didn't die. One is that in my heart I really didn't want to die, because I knew there were times when I was having fun. Maybe it was just playing by myself, running in a field, making up games to play; maybe it was playing with a special friend; maybe it was knowing that somebody did love me and care for me, though sometimes it was hard for me to see that. In the end, I didn't really want to give up the good things that I had, because, if I died, they would be gone and I didn't know what was ahead for me if I were dead.

Another reason why I didn't die was that I talked to adults whom I trusted. All through my life I found that there were adults, and some of them had had worse lives than mine, who were happy and who had advice for me that really helped me. If you're having a tough time, find some adults you can talk to about this. Maybe it's one of your parents, another relative, a teacher, a guidance counselor, or a clergy person. Whoever it is, I urge you to find an adult you can talk to about your feelings and thoughts.

Today, I have a great job here at *Highlights for Children*. I am married to a wonderful wife, and we have a beautiful six-year-old daughter. I am so happy about my life that sometimes I cannot even express my thoughts. If I had died when I was younger, none of this would have happened to me.

Please go talk to an adult and tell him or her about your problems and your thoughts. If you feel that you need to talk to someone right away, you can always call 1–800–442–4673. There are people you can talk to at this number any time of the day or night. These people are trained to talk to people who have thoughts about dying, and all of the calls are confidential.

Your friends at *Highlights* are pulling for you.

Sincerely,
Jan Cheripko

CHAPTER 5

The Legacies of Our Lives: Exploring the Loss of a Grandparent with *A Ring of Endless Light*

Anne E. Cobb and Maribeth Ekey

Go to Grandma and Grandpa, Mom and Dad and other relatives and friends. Discover and remember what they have to say about what they learned growing up. By keeping their stories alive you make them, and yourself, immortal.

Christopher Paul Curtis (2000)

Death happens. In the "normal," or at least hoped for, scheme of things, the strongest attachment of the child is to the parent. Grandparents, although potentially well loved, play a secondary role. Grandparents die first. Parents die next, but only after the child is well out of childhood. And finally, the child, having matured into a parent and then a grandparent, herself dies.

Grandparents are supposed to die. Therefore, it is not assumed to be a difficult reality with which to come to grips. It's hard; it's sad. But it's normal life, not considered tragic or traumatic. In a formal diagnostic manual for psychologists, there was actually a category for this type of loss: uncomplicated bereavement. For the adolescent, the loss of a grandparent can actually be a gracious introduction to the reality of death and of the brevity of her own life.

A RING OF ENDLESS LIGHT

Madeline L'Engle's *Ring of Endless Light* is a tale of an uncomplicated bereavement. Everything happens almost exactly as it should. Although this may trigger disbelief in the "idealness" of the protagonist's dilemmas in many teenagers who do not have as neat and clean a family background, nonetheless the book provides a nice picture of a healthy grief process (Coles, 1994). Valuable lessons on how an adolescent might grieve the loss of a grandparent are interwoven in a captivating story of one girl's growing up.

Elisabeth Kübler-Ross, one of the first to systematically study the mourning process in a dying person, observed stages that we go through in coming to grips with death: denial, anger, bargaining, depression, and finally acceptance (Kübler-Ross, 1969). We see most of these stages, as well as other aspects of the grief process, modeled in the themes of mourning throughout this novel.

Mourning

One of the principal requirements for working through loss is a capacity for mourning. This means having permission to feel the topsy-turvy, black, despairing, and unpredictable feelings that go with losing someone. No matter that you knew it was going to happen, that death *does* happen to someone we love shocks us deeply. The purpose of mourning is to allow us to let go of the person we lost so that our passion and love can be freed up to bring real life and living to people once again. The end is acceptance. But the awfulness of mourning must be endured in order to achieve acceptance.

The novel opens with a funeral. A family friend, Leo Rodney, has just lost his father. To comfort him, the teenage protagonist, Vicky, puts her arms around Leo and encourages his tears, in which she then joins him. Tears, comfort, and a little growing up, which are essential ingredients to mourning, are generously modeled here. But the mourning process is not portrayed merely in the warm decency of sadness. Leo also models for us the angry outrage of losing a father and Kübler-Ross's stage of anger. Vicky is caught off guard by his display, which will prepare her for the process she will soon endure. In mourning, we cry; we rage. We feel intensely, unpredictably, and then, just as we're getting used to the intense feelings, we go numb. In the process, the only mooring we can attach to is that of comforters: the people willing to face the blackness with us.

Comfort

Comfort is essential in coming to grips with loss, especially for children:

It is comfort that makes the difference between a loss that is overwhelming and a loss that is manageable. Children need to know their losses are real, their sadness is normal, and it won't last forever. They need to be taught there is life after disappointed wishes [even the deeply disappointed wishes caused by death], and they need to be helped to reengage in life. (Ekey, 1998, 29)

First and foremost, comfort is *being with* the bereaved person in the complex feelings about his loss as is modeled in the above interaction between Vicky and Leo. Comfort is more than empathy; it is also explanation. Especially for children, comfort involves explaining loss and helping them make sense of it. Finally, comfort involves helping the child know that the sorrow need not last forever. Children, especially younger children, have little sense of past, present, and future. They need help in knowing that there can be life after loss and help in rebuilding a future that can be different from the sadness of the present loss.

Vicky's grandfather offers her wise comfort on page 68. By explaining and normalizing her recent confusion and struggles, Vicky's grandfather points out the many losses she has suffered—leaving her home, school, and friends in New York as well as staying with him as he dies. In this he helps Vicky identify her losses, and he teaches her that suffering several losses at once raises the stakes significantly. Putting into words the reality of our losses and our feelings about those losses is comforting. Words give structure and can translate what is vague and overwhelming into something that is manageable.

In another scene of comfort (page 165), Vicky talks with a wise and caring friend, Adam, and struggles to express her feelings about the many deaths she has experienced lately. Again, Vicky receives help putting words to her feelings from someone who is willing to be with her in the feelings. The bottom line of comfort for Vicky, in the throes of her grief, is not philosophy, but the presence of another human being *with her* in her sorrow: "I wasn't sure that Adam's words were comforting. But his arm about me was. He made me feel very real, not replete with me at all, only real, and hopeful" (168).

Denial of Death

Like most of us, Vicky and her family waffle in their attitude toward their grandfather's approaching death. At times they deny it; at times they work to accept it. Asking her seven-year-old brother Rob what he was talking to their grandfather about, Vicky is jolted when he responds:

"Dying." Vickie reflects on discussing death with the dying. "But why don't you? If I had a fatal disease I'd want people to talk to me about dying, instead of getting embarrassed and pretending I was going to get well" (25). She concludes that while not denying the severity of his illness, the family isn't talking about it either.

Vicky's father, a medical doctor, has been "completely open" (20) with his children about his own inability to save their grandfather. In other ways, too, he modeled acceptance of death, such as when he instructed them about their dog, Mr. Rochester, who was aging. In spite of his wise and careful instruction, repeated in many ways throughout the novel, this family can't quite bring themselves to talk about dying head on. There is, after all, something about death that is simply unbearable.

Inwardness

Coming to grips with loss requires a time of inwardness. At first we find ourselves more passionately invested in the person we lost than ever before as we mull over the meanings of the loss and of their life and we miss them intensely (Freud, 1983).

People in mourning look and act depressed. Sometimes they enter a clinical depression that needs medication or psychological intervention. When depression is particularly severe, they may lose their appetite, they may sleep, and they may withdraw from people, which creates a downward spiral that is increasingly difficult to overcome. They cannot heal without sleep, food, and comforters. Medication or psychological intervention may help them mobilize their innate healing resources.

The real problem in mourning is not this temporary sadness and withdrawal from life. The real problem occurs when we become stuck in unresolved mourning that never becomes a place of acceptance, which ultimately allows us to rebuild our lives.

Vicky's grandfather makes a loaded statement when he tells her it should be a good summer for poetry for her (70). He does not want her stuck in unending mourning, and so he coaches her toward the soul-searching that will help her transform her loss into growth, wisdom, and renewed life. He also acknowledges their common love of poetry and tendency toward introspection, which says "I will live on in you," which frees her from clinging to him. Finally, he encourages her to freely express her own unique gifts. He does not want her to be blocked by guilt or regret as she pursues her world of poetry and creativity, which her grandfather, too, had always loved.

Regression

Loss triggers regression, which is a natural falling apart because our props have been knocked out from under us. Regression is, in part, a desperate attempt to return to a younger (safer) era. Vicky's kid brother, Rob, serves as a prime example of someone in regression. Vicky comes home to a stilled, tearful baby brother who is grief-struck because grandfather had a nosebleed and had to be rushed to the hospital. Rob's query about his stuffed elephant, long ago discarded, introduces us to the very legitimate need to regress when life gets too sad and hard.

In the midst of heartbreak we, like Rob, long to return to a younger era where lullabies and stuffed animals held magic power to soothe away hurts. It can be especially hard for the teenager to allow herself the healing and soothing of a measured regression. Peter Blos emphasizes the strange double bind of the teenager, caught in that paradoxical age between infancy and adulthood, as she wards off infantile longings (Blos, 1979). Anna Freud also comments on the "enormous fear of regression" (Sandler, Kennedy, & Tyson, 1980, 87) in the teenager. The teenager is so near the infantile longings to be taken care of by mom and dad, and is so ashamed of them, that she fights these urges. She is dead set on renouncing her dependence and tries to forge ahead into the independence of adulthood. Thus the teenager, especially, may feel compelled to "hang tough" and to remain stoic in the face of loss.

Vicky's inability to allow herself to regress like younger, more pliable Rob did triggers the more thoroughgoing regression that Vicky ultimately suffers as she nears the loss of her grandfather. She loses her ability to communicate and to perceive reality. She feels disoriented, lost in darkness, and desperate. In response to her mother's words, we hear Vicky's inner thoughts, "Her words were a dim roar against my eardrums. I was lost in a cloud of terror, with dim pictures transposing themselves one on top of the other. . . . There was no light. The darkness was deep and there was no dazzle" (318).

Ultimately, Vicky is able to regroup. Images of life call her back: café au lait; baby swallows flying; her special kindred spirit, Adam, appearing with uncanny timing at the screen door, then taking her back to the dolphins—and her grandfather's ever-present voice of (loving) reality confronting her with her responsibility to *choose and value life*—in spite of its inherent heartbreak (325–326). Her temporary psychosis serves as an apt reminder of how difficult loss is, no matter how "ideal" the circumstances surrounding the loss.

Acceptance and Internalization

At one point in the novel, Vicky is caught up in life as she enjoys new experiences with her budding romance, Adam. Watching him turn cartwheels along the shore, she pauses to recognize that she is truly happy. She enjoys the moment, basks in a healthy idealizing of Adam, and masters the world in new and exciting ways.

The task in acceptance is to embrace life fully, becoming open to its wonder, and getting lost in the enjoyment of the moment in spite of death. In Vicky's case, her task of acceptance is to mourn and to work her way through her current attachment to her grandfather, to the point that she can imagine the world without him and even revel in it.

Vicky would eventually need to do some of this mourning even if her grandfather had lived. She would need to divest her grandfather of some of his strength and wisdom and take it in as her own; and she would need to take away some of her grandfather's wonder and give it to a young man like Adam. This internalization process works by taking on another person's strength, wisdom, and other attributes as our own, which aids in the mourning process. It frees us up to let go of the person we've lost and gives us a sense that they really do live on inside us.

Grandfather talks about the choice to respond to life's losses with love and acceptance or with resentment, and by addressing Leo, he highlights Leo's mother's life-affirming choices after the loss of her husband, Leo's father. To drive home this lesson, he draws from his vast reservoir of literature as well. Citing Elie Wiesel, grandfather reads: "It is possible to suffer and despair an entire lifetime and still not give up the art of laughter" (82).

ROLE OF AND LOSS OF A GRANDPARENT

Erik Erikson was the first psychologist to theorize about the entire lifespan of man. His rich statement, "healthy children will not fear life if their elders have integrity enough to not fear death" (1963, 269), provides a unique insight into the potential interplay between a teenager and her grandparent, and into the magic of Vicky's interactions with her grandfather. Vicky's grandfather did not fear death. He embraced it and modeled embracing it for Vicky in a way that enabled her to relish living.

In their foreword to Kübler-Ross (1975), Braga and Braga put well the rich benefit that can come as we face death:

> All that you are and all that you've done and been is culminated in your death. When you're dying, if you're fortunate enough to have some prior warning (other than that we all have all the time if we come to terms with our finiteness), you get your final chance to grow, to become more truly who you really are, to become more fully human. But you don't need to nor should you wait until death is at your doorstep before you start to really live. If you can begin to see death as an invisible, but friendly, companion on your life's journey—gently reminding you not to wait till tomorrow to do what you mean to do—then you can learn to *live* your life rather than simply passing through it. (1975, x)

Guided by her grandfather's wise words, Vicky also takes in this lesson from her friend, Zach. Many authors have tried to illustrate the high cost of getting too much, of being spoiled, of suffering too little loss. Psychologically speaking, the cost is narcissism, being lost in our own wishes and dreams in a way that blocks our capacity for closeness with another human being.

This is Zach's plight. He is a budding narcissist. He has always gotten whatever he wanted and has experienced very few limits in life. The tragic result is that he values no one and nothing. The novel begins with his suicide attempt and unfolds around his ongoing death wishes. Rather than loving people, he compulsively uses them as objects. He has learned to see people only as a means of fulfilling his cravings. Zach echoes in a negative way what Vicky's grandfather is earnestly trying to teach her. Vividly he illustrates how sterile and empty life can be when we try to avoid mourning. He highlights the gift there is in sadness because sadness means that we loved someone enough to miss them deeply.

The loss of the grandparent can have many meanings. What is pivotal is to allow the teen the room to explore the particular meanings of the loss. Techniques for helping teens explore the meaning of the loss may include asking about early memories with the grandparent, about favorite and least favorite traits, about what they wished they could have said before the grandparent died or what they think the grandparent would like to have said to them, and about what they miss most now that the grandparent is gone.

Grandfather consistently teaches this lesson: hold life as precious . . . get on with living . . . don't let the despair of losing make you fold. He encourages his loved ones to use their talents, to love and to laugh—

all marks of the person who has freed up her passion from someone who has died in order to bring that passion to real life and real people once again. Under good circumstances, perhaps the most gracious introduction that real life can offer us is the loss of a grandparent, such as the one that takes place in Madeline L'Engle's *Ring of Endless Light*.

IN THE CLASSROOM

Michael walked into our sixth grade English class without his usual strut. He bypassed his classmates' high-fives, merely uttered an inaudible mumble. As the other students tried to catch up on weekend exploits and readied themselves for some morning writing, Michael remained still and silent. Typically, Michael would be at the hub of weekend storytelling. Writing, however, was not his forte. Forever unprepared to take pen in hand, he would need to borrow supplies from the classroom Writer's Corner. This trip was the consummate writing avoidance he had mastered.

Topics for writing were not Michael's problem. He was a storyteller; writing any of his stories down was just a waste of his time. But on this Monday, there were no stories, no trip to the Writers' Corner, and no desk-hopping writing-avoidance. On this Monday, Michael pulled out a pencil, wrote for about thirty seconds, and first put his pencil down on his desk, then his head. His classmates seemed to notice something missing from their Monday morning routine. Several looked up at me questioningly during their writing, then glanced at Michael. Several shrugs shifted about the room and I wondered, too, what Michael's untold story was that day. As he left class that morning, I found out. His paper said simply, "My Grandpa is dead."

For students who have experienced the loss of a grandparent and for those who haven't but will, bringing this life experience into the classroom affords several benefits. Through story, we can identify the roles grandparents play in adolescents' lives, what is lost upon their death, and what our students can gain from their grandparents and the death experience. As the themes of grandparents, their roles in our lives, and our losing them to death are addressed in the classroom community, students may be given the necessary permission to grieve. Sharing that grief lets students know they're not alone. Identifying the grief stages through story and life experience may not only benefit the already bereaved student but help prepare those who've yet to meet death, up close and personal.

L'Engle's story affords the opportunity to delve into the significance of our students as individuals and help them define themselves through their personal histories. What better way to discover this than through their grandparents? The story offers other discoveries, particularly the relevance of death to life. While filled with pain and sorrow, death and mourning serve the purpose of bringing the living back to the wonder and joy of life. Who better than grandparents to provide the vehicle for this journey? Not all our students will have had the benefit of the ideal grandparenting Vicky experiences in the novel. Through a whole-class shared reading of *A Ring of Endless Light*, students can share Vicky's grandfather as they make their journey toward self-discovery and, ultimately, life discovery. Dr. Ekey (1998) notes that "words give structure and can translate what is vague and overwhelming into something that is manageable" (68). L'Engle's words, together with student writing, will help students "make death manageable."

Before Reading

Active readers make connections when they encounter unfamiliar text in order to delve deeper in their search for meaning. Adam would call this "digging for gold." To prepare for our "dig," I would begin with reading aloud a poem by jo carson from her collection of poetry, *stories i ain't told nobody yet* (1989). In number 54, we hear the voice of an old woman appealing to her child or grandchild to return home before she dies because she wants to give him her stories. After reading the poem once for fluency, I would read it a second time, interjecting my thoughts as I read the text. For example, the ailing mother explains, "I've got whole lives of stories that belong to you." I was reminded of my Aunt Myrtle. She was like a grandmother—she told stories, she let me play teacher in the school where she would be the principal for 50 years, and her chest was fluffier than the down pillows on the creaky beds upstairs. She had "whole lives of stories," some of which she shared with me. I'd share this memory with the students as I read the line. Not only are you modeling your thinking as you read, but you're sharing yourself and your stories with your students. This may clear the way for students to share theirs.

Poetry plays a central role in the bond between Vicky and her grandfather. The excerpts woven through the text include Sir Thomas Browne, a seventeenth-century English physician and author, Henry Vaughan, a seventeenth-century Welsh poet and mystic, and Vicky's own efforts with various poetic forms; fugue, sonnet, and rondel. While the works cited are beautiful and central to the themes of the novel, they may be difficult for some students to connect with because style and language may act as barriers to independent understanding. Introducing more contemporary selections provides an invitation to the rhythms and concise language of poetry and helps "scaffold" the students' reading experience (Graves & Graves, 1994).

The following poems and brief essay offer effective prereading tools for introducing the theme of grandparents, their roles in adolescents' lives, and the connections between generations: "The Little Boy and the Old Man" by Shel Silverstein (1981), "The Picture" by Jeff Moss (1989), "My Grandmother Is Waiting for Me to Come Home" by Gwendolyn Brooks (Giovanni, 1994), "Grandpa's Hand" by Juli Peterson (Kulpa, 1995), "Martine Provencal, Period 5, Room 206" and "Jonathan Sobel, Period 5, Room 206" by Mel Glenn (1988). Silverstein's poem humorously depicts the similarities between the old and the young. In "The Picture," Moss describes a young boy's realization that he can't reverse his grandfather's aging. Moments shared between grandmother and grandchild, the security and impact of this bond, are concisely illustrated in Brooks's piece. "Grandpa's Hand" is a very short narrative written by a student about lessons passed on through the wrinkles in grandpa's hands. Mel Glenn's two poems begin to introduce the inevitability of life—death.

Record the poems on transparencies and ask students to read silently along with you while you read each piece aloud. At the end of each poem, ask students to write down any connections they made to the text: memories of their grandparents, the stories they've shared, or the history they've experienced through their grandparents. These can be brief descriptions or even a list of key words that are clear enough that they'll be able to decipher them later. After recording their connections to the poems, have as many students as wish to share a brief grandparent memory orally with the class. Collect these brief writing pieces. You'll use them later on to drive home the significance of the work you'll be asking of them.

Just before beginning the novel, read aloud to the class the afterward from Christopher Paul Curtis' novel, *Bud Not Buddy* (2000, 237–243). Mr. Curtis does a wonderful job driving home the significance of our grandparents' stories and our privileged role as recorder of those stories. After these reading and writing connections have been made, the novel can be introduced as a continuation of their exploration of grandparents and death. Explain that you're going to be reading the novel together and that perhaps more than any other story you read, this book will guide them toward becoming the authors of their own stories, the stories of their heritage. Ask them to imagine that only they can be the connection between past and future for their family's legacy. They are the chosen messengers between generations. Their mission? To carry their ancestors' stories and pass them on to their descendants. Their tools? A Legacy Log, a tape recorder (optional but helpful), and a pen or pencil.

The Legacy Log

At the end of chapter 1 (pages 40–41), Vicky tells Leo about her grandparents' work with an ancient African tribe, recording the tribe's language and history, which were at risk of dying with the elders of the tribe. L'Engle provides an excellent opportunity to introduce the students to the Legacy Log and interview process.

The Legacy Log is the students' record of discovery through the novel, a place to record their connections, their ideas, their questions, and their writing experiments. It is the diary of their days as they become the messenger between generations and of the journey through loss to living. Ultimately, it will lead to the products of this journey, in the form of multigenre pieces of writing. In teacher preparation for fostering and nurturing multigenre writing, I recommend two books, Murray (1996) and Romano (1995). Each offers not only helpful insights into the process but provides inspiration to writers. Two sections that speak directly to the goals and could be read aloud to the class from Murray's book are "I Write to Discover Who I Am" (3) and "I Write to Slay My Dragons" (5). Romano shares his own and his students' ups and downs on a semester-long multigenre writing journey, giving the reader the chance for a "virtual teaching" experience.

Throughout the text, samples of multiple genres will be introduced: poetry, newspaper articles, letters, narratives, picture books, songs, and art. Your students may even make suggestions for genres they'd like to experiment with as they tell the stories of their personal histories. Perhaps the greatest source will be their grandparents.

The Interview

In addition to the writing prompts, class discussions, and novel readings, students will go to the source: their grandparents. While the interview won't be introduced until the end of the first chapter, it is included here for preparation purposes. In the event a student's grandparents have already died, or are otherwise unavailable, help students determine who the next best source might be for an interview: older relatives or family friends who knew the grandparent, parents, or older siblings.

Ask students to share the formats of interviews they've seen or read, such as talk show hosts interviewing famous guests, sports writers speaking with amazing athletes, news reporters questioning victims of crime. Explain that each of these interviewers has a purpose. The students' purpose is to learn about themselves and their place in the generations through their family histories.

Rief (1992) highlights the importance of primary source connections, "Few opportunities exist in schools for students to gather information from primary sources. Students don't realize that people often give them more useful information for writing than do books or encyclopedias" (71). She also offers guiding questions specific to our topic: "How often do you speak to your grandparents long enough to find out what memories they hold dear? What life was like for them as a teenager? What life is like for them now? How they feel about growing older" (71). Rief advises students to take the time to know their grandparents and learn from them. After losing his father, Leo admits having been too absorbed with himself to have ever asked his father much about himself. These references help justify the importance of the work the students are about to undertake.

These questions can help students brainstorm their own questions for their interviews. Not everyone's interview needs to be, nor should it be, the same. The list the class brainstorms simply provides ideas. Students should be reminded that a tape recorder comes in handy when conducting the interview, because it allows the interviewers to introduce questions based on their grandparents' responses and frees them to concentrate on the flow of the interview rather than recording freehand. If recorders are not available, have students prepare the interview in writing beforehand so that they only have the responses to write down. The completed interview, together with the collected pieces from their Legacy Logs, serve as the sources for their published works.

During Reading

Writing Prompts for Quick Writes

Writing prompts can generate thinking and can help students find focus for class discussions. Students record responses in their Legacy Logs, being sure to note the page number for each response. Each prompt offers an opportunity for reflection on the themes of study and provides a playground for writing experimentation and crafting of their final writing products. While I have included some guiding questions with each quote, it is important to encourage students to respond with their own questions.

Chapter	Page	Excerpt
1	24	"Thou art all replete with very thou" What does Browne mean here? Are you ever "all replete with very thou?"
2	50	"When one tries to avoid death, it's impossible to affirm life." Can we avoid death? How do you affirm life?
4	98	"All life lives at the expense of other life." Can you give several examples?
4	116	"It's hard to let go anything we love. We live in a world which teaches us to clutch. But when we clutch we're left with a fistful of ashes." Have you ever had to let go of something/someone you love? Have you ever clutched and been "left with a fistful of ashes?" Tell me the story.
5	123	Grandfather says, "I thought I could die with you around me, and I didn't realize how much it would hurt you and that I cannot stand that hurt." His son, Vicky's dad responds, "Perhaps you ought not deprive us of that hurt." Dad is suggesting that this pain is important. Can you make sense of this?
6	155	"Every death is a singularity." Consider Grandfather's belief that a butterfly's death can cause an earthquake in another galaxy. Do you believe it? Explain your response.
6	164	Adam tells Vicky about Jeb's losses two years ago and adds, "But he still isn't over it." Is death something we can "get over"?
7	172	"And nothing loved is ever lost or perished." The last line of Vicky's poem to Ynid's dead baby—what do you make of it?
9	241	"A lot of discoveries come through teamwork, with two completely different types of imagination working together and being far more than either one alone." Agree? Disagree? How might this statement affect your work with your grandparent in recording and publishing your family legacy?

Writing Extensions—Not-So-Quick Writes

Quick writes are excellent discussion prompts, where writing plays a secondary role. These "not-so-quick" writes afford students the opportunity to extend their thinking as well as their writing process as they explore more deeply the challenging concepts of legacy, loss, and death. In chapter 2, on page 47, Vicky thinks about what happens after someone dies, what's left behind and the significance of making a mark on the world. As students work independently, ask them to look through the newspaper to find articles describing individuals' accomplishments, mistakes, contributions—how they leave a mark. The obituaries provide excellent information, as well as feature articles and crime reports. Have the students pair up and share their selected articles and their reactions with their partners. As an entire class, discuss these questions: In what ways do people leave their marks on the world after they die? Is it important to make a mark with your life? What mark has your grandparent left on the world? What mark would you like to leave? After the discussion, allow time for students to make personal connections in their Legacy Logs.

In chapter 3, grandfather shares some words on death and dying from Elie Wiesel, a Holocaust survivor and author. Fleischman (*Whirligig*, 1998) writes one chapter about a Holocaust survivor and her granddaughter (102–114). This grandmother, very near death, asks her granddaughter to drive her to an old section of town, one which holds dear memories for the dying woman. In sharing these memories and places with her granddaughter, she makes a gift of her legacy. The writing is incredibly moving and this chapter stands alone for modeling short-story writing.

By the completion of chapter 7 in *A Ring of Endless Light*, the students have been exposed to quite a bit of "deep thoughts" poetry in likely unfamiliar styles. By introducing some poetry that is more accessible to them with some of the same themes, students may find models for their own poetry writing. Nye (*Salting the Ocean*, 2000) offers an ideal selection of powerful poetry written by student writers. The seven selections that address grandparents come from her chapter "My Grandma Squashes Roaches with Her Hand—Twenty-three Poems about Anybody's Family." Poetry selections which address the life cycle are "The Most Important Time" (Dakos, 1993), "Translating Grandfather's House" by E. J. Vega (Carlson, 1994, 6–8), and "Last Visit to Grandmother" by Enid Shomer (Martz, 1987). These poems can be read aloud to the class as points of extension for the themes in the novel.

Keeping copies of any extended reading selections in a notebook or file folder helps create a Legacy Building section in your classroom. In addition, texts can be copied and added to a bulletin board or hung so that students can refer to them for modeling their own writing. Books, tapes, and videos can be displayed so that students have access to them throughout the unit.

Whole-Class/Small-Group Activities

As they progress through adolescence, students increasingly seek comfort and support from their peers. As adolescents attempt to attain independence, peers provide the testing ground for becoming an adult. A good book also provides a testing ground as the students interact with the characters and events of the story. Group activities around books provide safe places for trying out new and developing under-standings.

In chapter 2, Zachary talks with the Austins about his mother's death and the science of cryonics. The discussion (pages 47–50) highlights several options for and philosophies of death rituals such as funerals, freezing, and cremation. After reading this chapter, students can work in small groups with each group reading one of the following picture books: Kroll (*Fireflies*, 1995), Thomas (*Saying Good-bye*, 1988), Zalben (*Pearl's Marigolds*, 1997), Polacco (*The Keeping Quilt*, 1988), and Ross and Ross (*Cemetery Quilt*, 1995). These stories introduce a variety of death ceremonies and rituals from several cultures. Students can conduct a mini literature circle which provides an opportunity to "share our re-sponses to books, [which] is so automatic that we don't recognize its insistent power. . . . Readers need to talk" (Daniels, 1994, 8). Each group needs to designate someone to read the book, someone to record the comments and questions generated in the group discussion, and someone to share these with the whole class. Students should record any textual connections they make with the books.

Upon completion of the literature circle discussions, take the oppor-tunity to start making text-to-text connections (Keene & Zimmermann, 1997). Text-to-text connections can be modeled using some of the poems and stories previously shared. They allow students to draw comparisons and contrasts between the texts they have just read by analyzing the characters, the setting, and the stages of grieving being depicted. As with all activities, time for whole-class activities and recording their re-sponses, questions, and ideas in Legacy Logs is necessary.

Also in chapter 2, Vicky thinks about how confusing it is when her grandfather refers to her mother as "daughter," when Vicky sees herself as the daughter. This moves her to reflect on a world without death. To introduce the concept of immortality and the resulting complications, any one of the following picture books could be read to the whole class: Anderson (*The Key*, 1994), Bruchac (*Fox Song*, 1993), Miles (*Annie*, 1971), Walker (*To Hell with Dying*, 1988). These books poignantly il-lustrate the eventuality of death and explain death's role in life. Have students respond to the story in their Legacy Logs after a class discussion. Encourage them to include their questions about the themes in their responses and to experiment with their writings.

At this point, students should have a variety of writing in their Legacy Logs. It would be critical for students to reread their writing periodically. Have students ask themselves writerly questions such as What images do these thoughts and reflections create? What pictures do they paint? Would those images work best in a poem? Is there a story I want to tell about this memory? Whose voice would tell the story? Which characters would I include? Who is my audience for this piece of writing? Would the story make a good picture book or a short story? Encourage their questioning about their writing and the end-of-life themes being explored.

Chapter 4 offers a prime opportunity to justify the benefits of the students' information gathering to produce finished, publishable work, by way of creating a family legacy. Adam addresses the issue for us when he notes the significance of writing things down—recording history: "without history there isn't any future" (99). Ask students to remember the activity around the poem, "stories i ain't told nobody." With the briefly recorded grandparent memories in hand, ask students to share a memory they recall. Clearly, you'll want to let several days pass between the oral history sharing and this revisitation. This activity punctuates the fact that oral history has a rich place in many cultures, but when words aren't recorded, they can become lost or forever changed.

Adam provides yet another teaching moment in chapter 4 (page 111) when he's comparing Vicky's depth of thought and her sister Suzy's superficiality. Help the students understand the analogy between Adam's words comparing the sisters and their efforts at writing. Encourage them to "dig for gold" in their interviews and in their writing to delve beneath the surface.

The compare/contrast Grieving Graph (see Figure 5.1) helps students discover what grieving looks like, how to communicate about it, and how to distinguish between healthy and unhealthy mourning. Vicky offers some insight into the three characters in question on page 139 that should help the students compare and contrast Zack's, Leo's, and Adam's grieving processes. Introduce the graphic organizer and complete column 5 as a whole class. Brainstorm the types of things people say when someone has died, such as "his time had come," "she's in a better place," "how will I live without her?" Discuss and define euphemisms. Include some of the euphemisms people use to avoid saying someone is "dead," such as "passed on," "on the other side," "kicked the bucket." Have the students complete the graphic organizer individually or in pairs

Figure 5.1
Grieving Graph—Comparison/Contrast

Character	Reaction to Death: What did he do?	Emotions Demonstrated: How did he feel?	Your Assessment: Helpful? Hurtful?	What People Say	What could you say?
Leo					
Zachary					
Adam					
List any questions you have:					

or groups to promote further discussion and an exchange of ideas. Take time to discuss their findings and to assess their identification and understanding of the stages of grief. This could be accomplished in a group discussion after your review of their completed Comparison/Contrast Charts. Ask the students to keep their charts in their Legacy Logs.

Later in chapter 6, Vicky talks about the role music plays in her life. She says, "Sitting there in the gathering twilight, I was lifted up on the music, soaring with almost the same freedom and joy as Basil leaping into the sky" (149). Vicky shares the places and sounds that lift her spirit, that make her less "replete with very me." Ask students to note what places and sounds, including music, lift them. Play some of the classical songs mentioned in the book, some of your own favorites, and some of the students' choices. Note the healing, writing, and "getting outside ourselves," music can accomplish. Suggest song lyrics and music as a genre for their writing products and as a question topic for their interviews.

You can revisit analogy as an effective tool for their own writing. Read Vicky's comments, at the end of page 234, which compare our lives to going to school. Explain that Vicky is considering the similarities between two things that are unlikely things to be compared. To further illustrate the cycle of life, read the picture book Fox (*Sophie*, 1994). Ask the students to review books and poetry that have already been shared to consider what analogies have been used for the life cycle with Anderson (1994), for example. Challenge the students to draw their own analogies for the life cycle. Have them list these in their Legacy Logs.

Publishable Products

At this point, the students should have a cache of writing gems in their Legacy Logs. The rich discussion you've shared in groups, their individual journey through the story, and the whole-class activities will prepare them for determining what genres they hope to include in their publishable works. At this point, students should begin concentrating on their finished writing pieces, and they should be given the opportunity to simply experience the end of the book more completely.

In addition to poems, short stories, narratives, articles, and letters, another publishable idea is to create their own picture books. Their books could focus on their grandparent as a source of information about history or their perspective on ages past. Helpful titles for modeling include Aliki (*The Two of Them*, 1979), Egger (*Marianne's Grandmother*, 1986), Khalsa (*Tales*, 1986), Mitchell (*Grandaddy's Gift*, 1997), and Russo (*A Visit*, 1991). Another focus might be the gifts of personal history that grandparents share, whose titles for modeling include Capote (*I Remember*, 1985), the illustrated poem in Lindbergh (*Grandfather's Lovesong*, 1993), Martin and Archambault (*Knots*, 1987), and Russo (*Grandpa Abe*, 1996). Each of these stories helps the reader move through the mourning process toward the goal of acceptance. Memories seem to be the common thread running through all these tales, the means by which we come to living with dying. It is vital to make this explicit to students as they consider their audience. Will the book be for their own family members? Would it be a book to share with young children to help them understand death? For students whose grandparents have been ill, or who experienced illness before death, the following picture books might be helpful: de Paolo (1973), Delton and Tucker (1986), Nelson (1988), and Sakai (1990). For those students who'd like to include epic poetry, longer poems covering a grandparent's lifetime, Paul Janeczko's (1993) collection has two helpful selections, "Family Portrait" (107) and "Family" (126).

Art projects are encouraged as tools for grieving. In addition to illustrating their picture books, students create a collage of images with central themes of the life cycle, family history, or their grandparent. Several picture books center on collected artifacts handed down through the generations for holding memories. Several favorites are Bahr (*Memory Box*, 1992), Scheller (*Grandfather's Hat*, 1992), Miles (1971), Polacco (1988), Ross & Ross (1995), and Thompson (*Looking*, 1993). Each offers ideas for creative projects for individual students or the entire class. For example, students could create a quilt to memorialize all the students' grandparents who have died; a sculpture or collection of artifacts that represent symbolic items significant to each member of the class; a photo album with pictures of the students and their grandparents at similar ages and in the present; or an illustrated collection of letters written by the students in the voices of their grandparents.

A quick perusal of the Internet reveals another opportunity for student writing toward family legacy. Several web pages serve as memorials to grandparents. The authors range from 7 to 77 years of age and writing styles range from poetry to essay. Any search engine can reveal any number of such memorials by using the keywords "death of a grandparent."

After Reading

The teacher's primary function at this point is to assist students as they polish their final pieces. Peer editing gives students opportunities to share their writing, exchange ideas, and conduct self-assessments. Some students might use these peer groups to express more feelings on death and dying or for coming to terms with losing a grandparent. The related readings offer short-chapter books, which could provide models for yet another genre of writing for students interested in taking on that reading/ writing challenge.

Each student should provide a reflection that they turn in with their final writings. These reflections are helpful for assessing their understandings about death and the grieving process, about their own experiences with loss, and about what they've learned. Questions you might pose: What have you learned that you didn't know before about your grandparents, your family legacy? Has this knowledge changed how you view yourself? In what ways? Do you feel better prepared to face the death of a loved one? Perhaps the most important question, asking students to reflect on their completion of the mission, is, How have you served as a messenger of your family's legacy, and how will you continue to do so? Do you feel yours is an important mission? Why?

These culminating reflection papers help you assess not only the students' achievements, but the strengths and weaknesses of the unit itself. Our students are the truest test of our teaching efforts. Listen to them. Ask them to share what worked and what didn't. This assessment will help inform your teaching for future grandchildren, the messengers of the legacy from generation to generation.

RECOMMENDED READINGS

Fiction *(Short chapter books are indicated by *.)*

Brooks, Bruce. (1990). *Everywhere*. New York: HarperCollins. ISBN: 0–06–440433–1 (4–8). PB, 70 pp.*

Love heals all, even grandfathers, in this story of a young boy ready to try anything to save his grandfather after a heart attack. A visiting nurse's nephew attempts a "soul switch," convincing Peanuts of its lifesaving forces. Peanuts discovers, however, that his special words of love were the true cure and that Dooley is a special friend. The strong bond between Peanuts and his grandfather is depicted in the times they've spent together making things in the garage. He worries there'll be no more creating, no chance to share his secret place, no one to appreciate the beauty of a well-tied bowtie if grandfather dies. Instead, he grasps the time left to grow a little and love a lot.

Clifford, Eth. (1985). *The remembering box*. Boston: Houghton Mifflin. ISBN: 0–688–11777–5 (4–8). PB, 59 pp.*

Joshua and Grandma Goldina celebrate the Sabbath weekly with blessings and traditional delicacies. It's her magical remembering box, though, that makes these visits events of wonder and celebrations of family heritage. Her memories are unleashed as Joshua reaches into her "remembering box" and emerges with peculiar artifacts. Each item represents a story and brings "remembering tears" to his Grandma Goldina's eyes. The stories culminate in a gift—a picture of Goldina. She gives Joshua a picture of herself as a young girl, one he's long cherished. "Why are you giving this to me now?" "It's time for you to have it. For *your* remembering box." With this gift, Grandma Goldina dies. And Joshua is prepared, thanks to the guidance of his precious Goldina and her stories.

Fleischman, Paul. (1998). *Whirligig*. New York: Laurel Leaf. ISBN: 0–440–22835–2 (6–12). PB, 133 pp.

This is a wonderful book for addressing death and dying with adolescents. The story opens with Brent, a rather narcissistic teen, upon his move to a new school. Brent's failed attempt to fit in at a party leads to a drunken drive, culminating in the death of a young girl, Lea—Brent is at fault. The young girl's mother asks only one thing of Brent—that he make a mark for her memory. Brent travels the country constructing and placing whirligigs to share Lea's joy for living—her legacy. Several chapters are then dedicated to this legacy—the joy the whirligigs bring to new generations.

Forward, Toby. (1992). *Traveling backward*. New York: Puffin Books. ISBN: 0–14–037875–8 (4–8). PB, 123 pp.*

Fanny's grandpa is dying and she wants him to live forever, to keep her laughing with his funny antics. Fanny's magical friend, Mrs. May, offers a green solution in a strange bottle. The potion sets grandpa's clock in reverse and so begins a youthful journey for grandpa and one of wisdom for Fanny. She soon realizes that grandpa wasn't always old. She sees grandpa as a young man and hears his personal accounts of wartime bombing. She pulls playful pranks with him as he slides into adolescence, and, as grandpa approaches infancy, wonders where his growing younger will end. The author's true craft lies in the use of fantasy and humor to bring readers face to face with the realities of death, offering understanding and comfort to the bereaved.

Gilbert, Barbara Snow. (1996). *Stone water*. Arden, NC: Front Street. ISBN: 1–886–91011–1 (9–12). HC, 169 pp.

Fourteen-year-old Grant is faced with an issue straight from today's newspaper headlines—euthanasia. His grandfather, closer to him than his own father, suffers a catastrophic stroke and is moved to the intensive care unit of a nursing home. A letter, left in the old man's desk for just such an occasion, asks Grant to abide by his wish not to be put on life support. Discreetly, Grant researches the legal, ethical, and moral implications of withdrawing life support, euthanasia, and assisted suicide. Juxtaposed with Grant's ongoing life at school, the struggle for understanding and thoughtful resolution make this a great tale for discussing the consequences of an issue receiving more and more national attention.

Henkes, Kevin. (1997). *Sun and spoon*. New York: Greenwillow Books. ISBN: 0–688–15232–5 (4–8). HC, 135 pp.

Ten-year-old Spoon is bereft with the loss of his gram. He needs something to hold on to, something of his grandmother. Her solitaire cards are the answer, so he takes them from her bedside table, leaving his grandfather worrying and wondering about the missing deck. Henkes's characters are touching in their eccentricities as they cope with guilt and loss. Metaphors are abundant in the story, making for effective teaching of writing strategies.

Koertge, Ron. (1994). *Tiger, tiger, burning bright*. New York: Orchard Books. ISBN: 0–531–06840–4 (6–12). HC, 179 pp.

Jesse lives in the hot, dry desert of California with his mom and pappy. Survival is tough in this barren landscape, but Jesse's been given the gifts of his pappy's knowledge. From tracking the indigenous wildlife of the desert to knowing how to wear a cowboy hat in just the right way, Jesse has learned it all from pappy. But pappy is slipping; cigarettes left burning, pots left on the stove, and memories coming in illogical sequences. Mom, concerned for their safety, wants to take pappy to Golden Acres and Jesse isn't about to have it. Together, the three face the challenges of living with dementia by preserving pappy's legacy through humor and love. Ultimately, Jesse grows to understand that it's his turn to carry the torch of pappy's wisdom, just as pappy has carried it for him.

MacLachlan, Patricia. (1991). *Journey*. New York: Bantam Doubleday Dell. ISBN: 0–440–40809–1 (4–8). PB, 83 pp.*

Eleven-year-old Journey and his sister, Cat, have been abandoned by their parents and are left with their grandparents to care for them. Journey is desperately seeking his family, who he is, and where he came from. Mom left nothing behind but a box of photos she'd ripped into bits. In an attempt to rebuild what he's lost, Journey is determined to "make everything right again" by piecing together his history from the fractured glimpses. It is his grandparents who guide him toward redefining family. Through photography, his grandpa helps Journey construct a renewed sense of family, teaching that love and memory bring discovery and connection. Neither grandparent dies in this story, but the roles of grandparents as family historians, providers of security, mentors, and guides are warmly illustrated.

Mazer, Norma Fox. (1987). *After the rain*. New York: Avon Books. ISBN: 0–380–75025–2 (8–12). PB, 249 pp.

Rachel is fifteen, frustrated, stubborn, and fearful. While she's experiencing typical adolescent concerns—embarrassing parents, a potential boyfriend, what she'll do with her life—Grandpa Izzy is diagnosed with terminal cancer. Izzy's always been a part of Rachel's life, but he's such a grouch. He never really talks to her, mostly barks orders at whoever's nearby. Fiercely independent and strong, Izzy insists on continuing his long daily walks. Over the course of the last three months of his life, Izzy and Rachel learn about one another as they walk together. As they cross bridges Izzy built in town, together they build a bridge between their generations' differences, over their shared stubborn streaks, to love, understanding, and growth. A Newbery Honor Book, *After the Rain* is powerful and bristles with realism. Mazer has a knack with the grandparent/grandchild relationship.

Mazer, Norma Fox. (1973). *A figure of speech*. New York: Dell. ISBN: 440–04374–095 (6–12). PB, 159 pp.

This one's an oldie, but definitely a goodie. Jenny's grandpa lives with her family and has been her best friend all her life. They both share the feeling of being in everyone's way; Jenny because she's the overlooked middle child and grandpa because his pace is too slow for the busy, active family. Only Jenny enjoys his told and retold stories of life on the farm, but she doesn't enjoy the family's lack of patience and respect for the old man she so loves. Together, grandpa and Jenny escape the family's decision to move grandpa to the "home" by journeying toward independence and grandpa's final escape.

Rylant, Cynthia. (1992). *Missing May*. New York: Dell. ISBN: 0–440–82131–2 (4–8). PB, 89 pp.*

Summer spent her early life being passed from relative to relative, "treated like a homework assignment somebody always had to do." At age six, her Aunt May and Uncle Ob visited from Deep Water, West Virginia, and left with Summer. Elderly and not in the best of health, May and Ob gave Summer what she'd not had since her mother died—a loving, nurturing home. Six years later, Aunt May is dead. And so this story begins. While it's about an aunt and uncle, the relationships mirror those of adolescents and grandparents and offers keen insight into the grieving process. In their efforts to live with missing May, Ob and Summer journey from disbelief and denial to meaningful memories and hope.

Schmidt, Gary D. (1996). *The sin eater*. New York: Lodestar Books. ISBN: 0–525–67541–8 (8–12). HC, 184 pp.

After his mother's death, Cole and his father move to New Hampshire to live with his grandparents. Dad increasingly isolates himself from Cole, his grandparents, his life. Cole relies on his grandparents for connection, and the connections are many; learning the history of the town of Albion, of the Emersons in the family graveyard, and stories of his mother as a young girl. Through these shared stories, Cole discovers much about dying, death, and ultimately, living.

He is twice more bereaved during the course of the book and learns about the mysterious sin eater, a historical character of the town. From him, he learns forgiveness. While neither of his grandparents die in the story, family legacy, death, grandparent roles, and history are richly illustrated.

Williams, Carol Lynch. (1998). *If I forget, you remember*. New York: Bantam Doubleday Dell. ISBN: 0–440–41420–2 (4–8). PB, 201 pp.

Twelve-year-old Elyse plans to write a novel the summer following sixth grade. She's got plenty of material with all the changes that seem to be happening around her. Her grandfather has died, leaving her beloved granny alone. Her friend, Robert A., wants to hold her hand. Her sister, Jordyn, is way too beautiful and her mom is starting to date. In the midst of it all, granny is moving in because she's suffering from Alzheimer's disease. Elyse wants to help granny hold onto her memories and she wants to hold onto granny. Williams develops strong characters as she takes a tough look at the disease's process and this family's foibles and challenges along the way. Love and humor may not provide a cure for the disease, but they combine to bring Elyse and her family a long way over a short summer.

Winthrop, Elizabeth. (1973). *Walking away*. New York: Dell. ISBN: 440–08676–095 (6–12). PB, 192 pp.

"Everybody dies sometime, Emily. I'm not afraid of it," grandfather had said. "Well, I am," Emily thought. "I'm afraid for you, Grandfather." Emily has spent every summer with her grandparents on their farm. She works hard at her grandfather's side, and they share everything. Until her friend, Nina, comes to visit. Nina and Emily are very different, which has been their attraction for one another. But for her grandfather, the differences are difficult, and he responds with remoteness. And this summer is different—more than Nina's presence and the resulting distance created between Emily and grandfather. It's different because grandfather is dying, a knowledge he has but keeps from Emily. He will work through it alone, because work is what he knows. But, in his own way, he tries to prepare Emily through story. "If nothing ever died, Emily, the world would be in pretty awful shape. There would be so many chickens over at Joe's place that there wouldn't be any room for him."

Nonfiction

Elkind, David. (1984). *All grown up and no place to go: Teenagers in crisis*. New York: Addison-Wesley.

Erikson, Erik H. (1963). *Childhood and society*. New York: W. W. Norton.

Kornhaber, Arthur, with Sondra Forsyth. (1994). *Grandparent power! How to strengthen the vital connection among grandparents, parents, and children.* New York: Crown.

Rofes, Eric E., and the Unit at Fayerweather Street School. (1985). *The kids' book about death and dying.* Boston: Little, Brown.

Westheimer, Ruth K., and Stever Kaplan. (1998). *Grandparenthood.* New York: Routledge.

Picture Books

Aliki. (1979). *The two of them.* New York: Mulberry Books. ISBN: 0–688–07337–9. PB, 30 pp.

A wonderfully written story that begins with all the things a grandfather does for his granddaughter—share stories of long ago, provide support and security, and teach about the seasons and growing. As the story progresses, it is the granddaughter who does these things for her ailing grandfather and, after his death, comes to understand the nature of life through his lessons and her own discoveries.

Anderson, Janet S. (1994). *The key into winter.* Morton Grove, IL: Albert Whitman. ISBN: 0–8075–4170–2. HC, 32 pp.

Clara has lived with the stories of the keys that hang above her grandmother's hearth, each one a key into one of the four seasons. As the seasons pass, it is the job of the eldest woman to turn the key into the upcoming season. As a child, Clara's mother, Mattie, once stole the key into winter in hopes of keeping her dying grandmother alive. But Mattie learns that holding her grandmother means losing something more. A "seasons of life" story, this tale provides solid solutions for accepting loss and change.

Bahr, Mary. (1992). *The memory box.* Morton Grove, IL: Albert Whitman. ISBN: 0–8075–5052–3. HC, 32 pp.

During a fishing trip, gramps tells his grandson, "It's a memory box day." It is through the memory box that gramps tries to teach his grandson about death and Alzheimer's. "It's a special box that stores family tales and traditions. An old person and a young person fill the box together. Then they store it in a place of honor. No matter what happens to the old person, the memories are saved forever." No one dies in this story, but it provides a wonderful source for introducing family tradition, history, and legacy as we prepare for loss.

Bruchac, Joseph. (1993). *Fox song*. New York: Philomel Books. ISBN: 0–399–22346–0. HC, 32 pp.

With each page of this beautifully written story, Grama Bowman shares with her grandaughter the nature of life. Grama Bowman has died, and so Jamie is walking with her in memory—memories of walks through the forest, each one sharing a lesson about nature. In the autumn, Grama tells her "the leaves love to dance. But they can only do their best dancing when they are ready to give themselves to the wind." The tale is derived from Bruchac's own Abenaki family, where he gathered the stories of the elders about animals, nature, and the cycle that is life, death, and renewed life.

Capote, Truman. (1985). *I remember grandpa*. Atlanta: Peachtree. ISBN: 0–934601–22–4. HC, 38 pp.

After living with his grandparents in a little wooden cottage in West Virginia, Bobby moves with his parents to a city in Virginia because Bobby's father wants Bobby to be able to go to school. In the Allegheny Mountains, Bobby's teacher has always been his grandfather. With a promise to return, Bobby leaves with his memories for comfort. The longing and love he and his grandfather shared help Bobby come to terms with the inevitability of change. The story is based on Capote's uncle and was written as a gift for his aunt in 1946, before he met with fame. This offers a unique text-to-world opportunity through extended reading of the famed author. Although only 38 pages, the amount of text puts this picture book on a par with a typical younger reader's chapter book.

Coville, Bruce. (1996). *My grandfather's house*. Mahwah, NJ: Bridgewater Books. ISBN: 0–816–73804–1. HC, 32 pp.

"Where do people go when they die?" Ahh, the ultimate question. While this picture book doesn't offer conclusive answers, it does achieve a starting point for consideration and discussion. The grief stages of anger and confusion are well illustrated as the main character grapples with the question of death, making his way toward acceptance through the comfort of memory. Honesty and explanation surrounding death are the story's strong points.

de Paolo, Tomie. (1973). *Nana upstairs and nana downstairs*. New York: G. P. Putnam. ISBN: 0–698–11836–7. PB, 32 pp.

Tommy's weekly visits to nana (nana downstairs) and grandfather's house include a visit with his great-grandmother whose weakness keeps her in her room on the second floor (nana upstairs.) Great introduction to the concept of generations. Story of loss and understanding, sharing and love.

Delton, Judy, & Dorothy Tucker. (1986). *My grandma's in a nursing home*. Niles, IL: Albert Whitman. ISBN: 0–807–55333–6. HC, 32 pp.

Jason undergoes a transition from hating the nursing home where his grandmother now lives with Alzheimer's to the joy he feels and brings to both grandmother and her fellow residents. Very realistic view of the drawbacks associated with nursing homes, as seen through a young boy's eyes and the humor and surprises inspired by a young boy's heart. Text-to-world connection to the questions surrounding nursing homes as alternative care facilities. No death occurs in the book.

Egger, Bettina. (1986). *Marianne's grandmother*. New York: E. P. Dutton. ISBN: 0–525–44335–5. HC, 26 pp.

Marianne's grandmother has died. The story recounts the wonderful times they had together as Marianne remembers baking cookies together, her always encouraging words, and, most of all, her stories about long ago. As she shares her memories, she is moved to paint a picture of grandmother so that she might always remember her.

Fox, Mem. (1994). *Sophie*. New York: Trumpet Club. ISBN: 0–590–06581–5. PB, 32 pp.

This is by far the easiest read listed here, but in simple, concise, phrase-a-page language, this book says it all. "Once there was no Sophie," the story begins. With that a journey through the lifespan unfolds, taking Sophie and her grandfather through the joy of living and loving. "And then there was no Grandpa, just emptiness and sadness for a while, till a tiny hand held on to Sophie's and sweetness filled the world, once again," the story ends.

Khalsa, Dayal Kaur. (1986). *Tales of a gambling grandma*. New York: Clarkson N. Potter. ISBN: 0–517–56137–9. HC, 32 pp.

Grandma shares the family history in her stories about escaping the Cossacks in Russia and supporting the family playing poker. She gives her grandchild "laws of life," teaches her card games, and shares the treasures hidden in her bedside table drawer. Upon her death, the grandchild inherits one of those treasures, a ring won in a poker game. Makes the text-to-world connection of Russian history and offers numerous text-to-self connections through artifacts handed down from generation to generation.

Kroll, Virginia. (1995). *Fireflies, Peach Pies and Lullabies*. New York: Simon & Schuster. ISBN: 0–689–80291–9. HC, 32 pp.

Great-granny Annabel doesn't remember family and often speaks strangely. Francie overhears family saying all the good memories will be swept away because of granny's behavior. When Granny Annabel dies, Francie vows to remember her differently—the smell of her dress, the sound of her wind chimes, the warmth of her handmade afghan. As funeral preparations are made and folks gather, Francie decides to gather the special memories. She has each person write down his or her own special memory and Father John reads the list at the funeral. "Soon the church was buzzing like a hive full of bees while sweet golden memories spilled over the pews and into the aisles."

Lindbergh, Reeve. (1993). *Grandfather's lovesong*. New York: Puffin Books. ISBN: 0–14–055481–5. PB, 32 pp.

A poetic journey through the seasons and spectacular landscapes with a grandfather and his grandchild. The poem shares the love unique to this intergenerational relationship. No death, just a rhythmic poem great for introducing the role of grandparents in grandchildren's lives.

Martin, Bill Jr., and Archambault, John. (1987). *Knots on a counting rope*. New York: Scholastic. ISBN: 0–590–99448–4. PB, 32 pp.

A young Native American boy loves to hear his grandfather tell him stories about himself growing up and about the times they've shared. With each telling, the boy remembers more and more of the tales, joining in the telling. With each telling, grandfather ties another knot in the counting rope. When the rope is full, the young boy will know the stories by heart. In poetic language for two voices, this book reveals the value of shared family story—passing on knowledge, reinforcing love, and understanding the cycle of life. Text-to-world connections to Native American traditions and oral histories.

Miles, Miska. (1971). *Annie and the old one*. New York: Trumpet Club. ISBN: 0–440–84258–1. PB, 44 pp.

Annie's grandmother, the Old One, shares stories of the earth, of generations, and of Navajo tradition. One day she announces that with the removal of the new rug from the loom, she will go to Mother Earth. Annie understands this to mean she will die and attempts to halt time by keeping the rug from completion. It is once again the Old One who explains the wonder of life and the cycle of time. Annie takes up the Old One's weaving stick to make her mark on the tapestry that will be her own. Text-to-world connection to Navajo traditions and spirituality.

Mitchell, Margaree King. (1997). *Grandaddy's gift*. Mahwah, NJ: Bridge Water. ISBN: 0–8167–4011–9. PB, 32 pp.

Grandaddy Joe Morgan taught his granddaughter many important lessons, particularly to stand up and make your voice heard. He does what it takes to register to vote in a time when African Americans faced threats and prejudice to do so. No death in this story, but grandparent as mentor and caregiver is poignantly depicted. Great text-to-world connections to the civil-rights movement.

Polacco, Patricia. (1988). *The keeping quilt*. New York: Trumpet Club. ISBN: 0–440–83170–9. PB, 32 pp.

A beautiful story about generations, tradition, and the passing of the "keeping quilt" through the ages of a Jewish Russian family. From their immigration to the United States, through marriage ceremonies, funerals, and births, the quilt plays the role of keeping the rich heritage of one family's story alive and well. Each piece of the quilt represents memories of the homeland, the new land, and carries with it the hope for future generations. Text-to-world connections to immigration, Russian history and culture, and Jewish tradition.

Ross, Kent, and Alice Ross. (1995). *Cemetery quilt*. Boston: Houghton Mifflin. ISBN: 0–395–70948–2. HC, 32 pp.

Josie doesn't want to go to her grandfather's funeral and she doesn't want to be on grandmother's cemetery quilt. The quilt reflects the family's births and deaths, each depicted by a "coffin" which is moved to the "cemetery" in the center of the quilt upon death. Josie thinks it's terrible, "Like something Dracula would do!" Gradually, Josie comes to embrace the family heritage, the quilt, and her place in the cycle of life. Facing the fears associated with loss while celebrating the progression of life is uniquely dealt with through the cemetery quilt.

Russo, Marisabina. (1996). *Grandpa Abe*. New York: HarperCollins. ISBN: 0–688–14097–1. HC, 32 pp.

Sarah's first eight years of life were filled with Grandpa Abe. Gifts, magic tricks, shared likes and dislikes, and dancing were memories she had when Grandpa Abe dies in her ninth year. Simple, tender tale of life and loss.

Sakai, Kimik. (1990). *Sachiko means happiness*. San Francisco: Children's Book Press. ISBN: 0–89239–065–4. HC, 32 pp.

Sachiko shares her grandmother's name, but her grandmother no longer shares her attentions with Sachiko. Alzheimer's has changed grandmother, and Sachiko is angry with this stranger who denies being her grandmother and claims to be "Sachiko, five years old!" During an evening's sunset, Sachiko comes to an understanding and accepts her changed grandmother as someone who can be her friend. This story could help adolescents recognize that anger is understandable in the face of life's changes in the sunset of our years. In a note from the author at the end of the story, Sakai shares her reason for writing the book: "I just kept looking at her, not knowing what to do. I was a child then. But now I am an adult and now I feel I could do something for [my grandmother] if she were here."

Scheller, Melanie. (1992). *My grandfather's hat*. New York: Macmillan. ISBN: 0–689–50540–X. HC, 24 pp.

After Jason's grandfather dies, his hat is passed on to Jason. Rich memories come with this worn hat, and Jason learns that though his grandfather is gone, his memories live on with him. Great introduction to artifacts and their ability to trigger memory, capture the past, and aid in the continuity of living life.

Thomas, Jane Resh. (1988). *Saying good-bye to grandma*. New York: Clarion Books. ISBN: 0–395–54779–2. PB, 48 pp.

Thomas investigates the sorrows and joys surrounding the grieving process of one family's loss by discussing a youngster's point of view of the rituals surrounding death: funeral, church dinner, family support, and loss. The young girl gains understanding for her grieving grandpa's tears, often torn because of her own joy in living in the face of such sorrow. Bonding with grandpa brings comfort and guiltless joy to them both.

Thompson, Colin. (1993). *Looking for Atlantis*. New York: Alfred A. Knopf. ISBN: 0–679–88547–1. PB, 30 pp.

"Shut your eyes and open your heart." Grandfather gives his treasure chest from years at sea to his grandson. "Everything you could ever want is in that chest if you know where to look for it." Speaks magically to the legacy held by grandparents and the beauty of passing it on to grandchildren. Grandson keeps grandfather in his heart through the wonder of his grandfather's imagination and story.

Walker, Alice. (1988). *To hell with dying*. Orlando, FL: Harcourt Brace Jovanovich. ISBN: 0–15–289075–0. HC, 32 pp.

Mr. Sweet is one of those folks who was always old, diabetic, drunk, and well loved by the nearby children. He's one of those adults who could cross over the line between adult and child successfully. Periodically, he'd go through the dying times, but a quick rousting by his princess and her brother would revive him once again for more good times. Beautifully illustrates the unique bond between the old and the young as well as the reality of death's ultimate triumph.

Zalben, Jane Breskin. (1997). *Pearl's marigolds for grandpa*. New York: Simon & Schuster. ISBN: 0–689–80448–2. PB, 32 pp.

Pearl can't understand the eating and laughter at home after grandpa's funeral. How can they have a party without grandpa? She's forgetful. She's grieving.

"Who will I play checkers with? Who will read me stories for as long as I want? Who will send me marigold seeds this spring?" Her father will—and so Pearl plants marigolds in memory of grandpa, hearing his words of wisdom as she tends her garden. Simple description of the cyclic nature of life. The book includes the section "Burial and Mourning Customs from around the World." Great discussion-prompting story about death, tradition, and family.

ADDITIONAL RESOURCES

Places to Find Additional Help

Center for Grieving Children
www.cgcmaine.org
A wonderful site which offers excellent bibliographies for literature dealing with death and dying.

Department of Elder Affairs
(800) 96-ELDER
Funded under the Older Americans Act, each state has a Department of Elder Affairs which could be useful in conducting research and in providing resources for intergenerational activities.

Family Planet Grandparent's Gateway
www.thirdage.com
A web site that is part celebration of the importance of grandparents, part advice on the sometimes thorny byways of family politics. It includes a photo album of happy grandfolks and precious babies, a question-and-answer column, as well as parents' and grandparents' discussion groups.

Grandloving: Grandparenting with Activities and Long-Distance Fun
www.world.std.com
This web magazine by Sue Johnson and Julie Carlson includes tips and book reviews. See also their book, *Grandloving: Making Memories with Your Grandchildren* (Fairview Press), which contains tips on long-distance grandparenting, visits, holidays, family traditions, and over 200 inexpensive and innovative activities.

Journeys—Adolescent Issue for Kids by Kids
Hospice Foundation of America
2001 S St. NW, Suite 300
Washington, DC 20009
(202) 638–5419
www.hospicefoundation.org
The Hospice Foundation of America provides numerous resources to assist adolescents dealing with death and dying. In addition to *Journeys*, they offer

the pamphlet, "Living with Grief at School: A Practical Guide for Schools," by Kenneth J. Doka, Ph.D.

KIDSAID
www.griefnet.org/KIDSAID
KIDSAID is part of GriefNet. GriefNet is a place where anyone dealing with grief or major loss can come for help. KIDSAID is where kids can come to get help and to help each other.

Parent Council
www.parentcouncil.com
Another excellent site for mourning issues and annotated bibliographies of literature and nonfiction materials on death and dying.

Publishing Student Work

Merlyn's Pen
P.O. Box 1058
East Greenwich, RI 02818–0964

Stone Soup: The Magazine by Young Writers and Artists
Published by Children's Art Foundation
765 Cedar Street, Suite 201
Santa Cruz, CA 95060
(800) 447–4569
(Grandparent story in vol. 24, no 2, November/December 1995.)

The 21st Century: Written Entirely by Teens for Teens
Box 30
Newton, MA 02461
(800) 363–1986
(Grandparent focus in Vol. 11, No 2, October 1999.)

REFERENCES

Aliki. (1979). *The two of them*. New York: Mulberry Books.
Allen, Janet. (2000). *Yellow brick roads: Shared and guided paths to independent reading*. Portland, ME: Stenhouse.
Anderson, Janet S. (1994). *The key into winter*. Morton Grove, IL: Albert Whitman.
Bahr, Mary. (1992). *The memory box*. Morton Grove, IL: Albert Whitman.
Blos, Peter. (1979). *The adolescent passage: Developmental issues*. New York: International Universities Press.
Bruchac, Joseph. (1993). *Fox song*. New York: Philomel Books.
Capote, Truman. (1985). *I remember grandpa*. Atlanta: Peachtree.

Carlson, Lori M., ed. (1994). *Cool salsa: Bilingual poems on growing up Latino in the U.S.* New York: Henry Holt.

carson, jo. (1989). *stories i ain't told nobody yet.* New York: Theater Communications Group.

Coles, Robert. (1994). *Books that build character: A guide to teaching your child moral values through stories.* New York: Simon & Schuster.

Curtis, Christopher Paul. (2000). *Bud, not Buddy.* New York: Scholastic.

Dakos, Kalli. (1993). *Don't read this book, whatever you do! More poems about school.* New York: Trumpet Club.

Daniels, Harvey. (1994). *Literature circles: Voice and choice in the student-centered classroom.* Portland, ME: Stenhouse.

de Paolo, Tomie. (1973). *Nana upstairs and nana downstairs.* New York: G. P. Putnam's Sons.

Delton, Judy, & Tucker, Dorothy. (1986). *My grandma's in a nursing home.* Niles, IL: Albert Whitman.

Egger, Bettina. (1986). *Marianne's grandmother.* New York: E. P. Dutton.

Ekey, Maribeth. (1998). *Shattered hopes, renewed hearts: What to do with wishes that don't come true.* Ann Arbor, MI: Servant Publications.

Erikson, Erik H. (1963). *Childhood and society.* New York: W. W. Norton.

Fleischman, Paul. (1998). *Whirligig.* New York: Laurel Leaf.

Fox, Mem. (1994). *Sophie.* New York: Trumpet Club.

Freud, Sigmund. Willard Gaylin, (ed.), (1983). "Mourning and Melancholia." In *Psychodynamic understanding of depression: The meaning of despair.* New York: Jason Aronson.

Giovanni, Nikki, ed. (1994). *Grand mothers: Poems, reminiscences, and short stories about the keepers of our traditions.* New York: Henry Holt.

Giovanni, Nikki, ed. (1999). *Grand fathers: Reminiscences, poems, recipes, and photos of the keepers of our traditions.* New York: Henry Holt.

Glenn, Mel. (1988). *Back to class: Poems by Mel Glenn.* New York: Clarion Books.

Graves, Michael, & Graves, Bonnie. (1994). *Scaffolding reading experiences: Designs for student success.* Norwood, MA: Christopher Gordon.

Janeczko, Paul B., ed. (1993). *Looking for your name: A collection of contemporary poems.* New York: Orchard Books.

Keene, Ellin Oliver, & Zimmermann, Susan. (1997). *Mosaic of thought: Teaching comprehension in a reader's workshop.* Portsmouth, NH: Heinemann.

Khalsa, Dayal Kaur. (1986). *Tales of a gambling grandma.* New York: Clarkson N. Potter.

Kroll, Virginia. (1995). *Fireflies, peach pies and lullabies.* New York: Simon & Schuster.

Kübler-Ross, Elisabeth. (1975). *Death: The final stage of growth.* Englewood Cliffs, NJ: Prentice-Hall.

Kübler-Ross, Elisabeth. (1969). *On death and dying.* New York: Collier Books.

Kulpa, Kathryn, ed. (1995). *Short takes: Brief personal narratives and other works by American teen writers*. East Greenwich, RI: Merlyn's Pen.

L'Engle, Madeleine. (1980). *A ring of endless light*. New York: Bantam Doubleday Dell.

Lindbergh, Reeve. (1993). *Grandfather's lovesong*. New York: Puffin Books.

MacDonald, George. (1980). *The wise woman: And other fantasy stories*. Grand Rapids, IA: Wm. B. Eerdmans.

Martin, Bill Jr., & John Archambault. (1987). *Knots on a counting rope*. New York: Scholastic.

Martz, Sandra, ed. (1987). *When I am an old woman I shall wear purple: An anthology of short stories and poetry*. New York: Papier-Mache Press.

Miles, Miska. (1971). *Annie and the old one*. New York: Trumpet Club.

Mitchell, Margaree King. (1997). *Grandaddy's gift*. New York: Bridge Water Books.

Moss, Jeff. (1989). *The butterfly jar: Poems by Jeff Moss*. New York: Bantam Books.

Murray, Donald M. (1996). *Crafting a life in essay, story, poem*. Portsmouth, NH: Boynton/Cook.

Nelson, Vaunda Micheaux. (1988). *Always gramma*. New York: G. P. Putnam's Sons.

Nye, Naomi Shihab. (2000). *Salting the ocean: 100 poems by young poets*. New York: Greenwillow Books.

Polacco, Patricia. (1988). *The keeping quilt*. New York: Trumpet Club.

Rief, Linda. (1992). *Seeking diversity: Language arts with adolescents*. Portsmouth, NH: Heinemann.

Romano, Tom. (1995). *Writing with passion: Life stories, multiple genres*. Portsmouth, NH: Boynton/Cook.

Ross, Kent, & Alice Ross. (1995). *Cemetery quilt*. Boston: Houghton Mifflin.

Russo, Marisabina. (1996). *Grandpa Abe*. New York: HarperCollins.

Russo, Marisabina. (1991). *A visit to Oma*. New York: Greenwillow Books.

Sakai, Kimik. (1990). *Sachiko means happiness*. San Francisco: Children's Book Press.

Sandler, Joseph, Hansi Kennedy, & Robert L. Tyson. (1980). *Discussions with Anna Freud*. Cambridge, MA: Harvard University Press.

Scheller, Melanie. (1992). *My grandfather's hat*. New York: Macmillan.

Silverstein, Shel. (1981). *A light in the attic*. New York: Harper & Row.

Thomas, Jane Resh. (1988). *Saying good-bye to Grandma*. New York: Clarion Books.

Thompson, Colin. (1993). *Looking for Atlantis*. New York: Alfred A. Knopf.

Walker, Alice. (1988). *To hell with dying*. Orlando, FL: Harcourt Brace Jovanovich.

Zalben, Jane Breskin. (1997). *Pearl's marigolds for grandpa*. New York: Simon & Schuster.

From *Tenderness*
Robert Cormier

His case had drawn national attention when authorities attempted to try him as an adult for the murders of his mother and stepfather. It was two months after his fifteenth birthday. He had remained silent during the frenzy of publicity, granted no interviews, made no statements. When he allowed himself to be photographed, he was careful to smile for the camera, not the smile of The Charmer but a sad, wistful smile that he calculated would soften his image. The clincher came when he faced the cameras outside police head-quarters after his arrest. Slowly and deliberately, he pushed up his sleeves and revealed the scars from the cigarette burns on his arm, the bruise that remained from his broken arm. The wounds were silent and compelling evidence of the abuse he had received from his stepfather, abuse that, he told his interrogators, his mother had not only condoned but encouraged.

Support for him came immediately, not only from the freaks who sent him letters and gifts but from college professors, newspapers as far away as Boston. They had played right into his hands. None of those who supported him cared to look deeply into his case, letting a few scars on his arm and a sad smile convince them that he had been done wrong. *Kill Your Parents and Become the Victim. What a wonderful country*, he thought.

CHAPTER 6

Pencils, Books, and Guns: Violence Goes to School

Julie Joynt and Patricia H. Fedor

We have failed our children. They live in a world where danger lurks all around them and their playgrounds are filled with broken glass, crack vials, and sudden death. And the stuff of our nightmares when we were children is the common reality for children today. Monsters are out there and claiming children in record numbers. And so we must stand up and be visible heroes, fighting for our children. I want people to understand the crisis that our children face and I want people to act.

Geoffrey Canada, *fist stick knife gun* (1995, 178–179)

250,000 or more weapons are brought to school each year by children and teens (Dwyer, 1999, 1).

About half of all American teenagers feel that a mass school shooting, such as occurred in Columbine High School in Littleton, Colorado, could happen in their own school (Silent March Campaign, 2000).

Between 1985 and 1994, the risk of dying from a firearm related injury more than doubled for teenagers 15 to 19 years of age (Silent March Campaign, 2000).

In addition to the massacre at Columbine High School, eight other mass shootings have occurred in U.S. schools between 1996 and 1999 (Grapes, 2000, 9).

Nearly a third of teens say they have witnessed a violent situation at school (Morse, 2000, 1).

In a poll conducted by *Time* and the Discovery Channel in conjunction with the National Campaign Against Youth Violence about half of the teens said that they had been insulted or threatened in the past year (Morse, 2000, 1).

These statements are anything but calming, and they probably don't make many people anxious to spend much time in schools. However, the *Journal of the American Medical Association* determined that "between 1991 and 1997, U.S. high school students became less likely to carry weapons, to engage in physical fights, and to be injured in physical fights" (Grapes, 2000, 9). So, how do we explain so much violence, especially in our schools?

One possibility is that although the probability of a school shooting in most communities is remote, the recent school shootings have almost all involved multiple deaths and have had a high profile in the media. Advance planning occurred in most of the shootings; persons other than the perpetrators knew the possibility of the upcoming event; and the ease with which these adolescents obtained their weapons was frighteningly real.

School boards across the country have responded to the threat of violence in a multitude of ways: metal detectors, armed security guards, razor-wire fences, frequent searches of lockers or the elimination of lockers, transparent purses and backpacks only, and an increased awareness of clothing, language, and antisocial behavior. In the American Psychological Association's (2000) "Warning Signs" brochure, the authors listed twenty-two signs that might indicate a "serious possibility" or "potential" for violence. President William Clinton directed the secretary of education and the attorney general to prepare a guidebook of "early warning signs" for potential school violence, hence the creation of *Early Warning, Timely Response* (*Frontline*, 2000, 2). These documents are helpful, but even the writers of these guides warn that they are only a rough draft of a solution to a more complicated problem.

So, what *is* the problem? Why is so much violence occurring in our schools? Is there any one thing that can be blamed for this growing epidemic? Most experts who have been studying the issue say that there isn't any one thing but rather a combination of things that have been changing in our society over the past few decades:

- Breakdown of the family structure
- Violence in the media (TV, movies, music, video games)
- Alcohol and drug abuse
- Easy access to guns

- Increased number of children being raised in poverty
- Violence as a learned behavior—abused children become abusive teens, then adults (Day, 1996, 15–30)

Is society to blame? Is there too much bad parenting going on? Too much TV violence, Hollywood violence, and violent music lyrics? Or could it be something biological? No one knows for sure, and researchers are struggling for answers. Meanwhile, educators everywhere are wondering, what else can be done?

Hoping to aid the schools with their safety issues, the Secret Service created the National Threat Assessment Center to see whether their method of analyzing assassins might also prevent attacks on schools. They have been analyzing forty attacks on schools for the past twenty years, not simple schoolyard violence, but organized, planned assaults in which the school was the target. All the shooters were boys, nearly all of them white, and together they killed 59 people and wounded 124 (Phynchon, 2000, 2). Though there is no definitive list of characteristics to come out of this body of work, several common threads have emerged, and these may be the factors that schools can address in trying to prevent violence and to equip students with the necessary tools to deal with the conflict that occurs in their lives.

ROOTS OF VIOLENCE

A large majority of the shooters were bullied, teased, and threatened throughout much of their schooling. Many of them never felt they had someone to go to for help. They felt they had no adult who could intervene. Suicide or homicide became, for some, the only way to stop their torment. For others, homicide was chosen because they wanted others to suffer as they had.

Aggressive youth usually lean toward acting impulsively, have values that support the use of violence, and lack problem-solving skills for behaving or reacting otherwise. Certain individuals are carefully selected as victims, and many youth who are victimized also develop habits that put them at risk for violence.

Finally, the majority of youth, who are neither aggressors nor victims, play an important role as bystanders. They may unknowingly support the violence through their passivity or active encouragement. Others may try to stop the violence through preventive actions. Behavioral science research findings show that behavior leading to violence is guided strongly, and sometimes automatically, by an individual's habits of thought. Individuals develop habitual ways of thinking early in life about how to solve social problems and what role violent or nonviolent actions might play (Slaby, 1994, 10).

Another interesting finding from this study is that the shooters communicated their plans to somebody. Many told a friend or multiple friends, or they hinted at their plans inadvertently through something they had written in school or through drawings they had created. Did any of their friends relay the plans or alert someone in a position of authority so that it could be stopped? No. In fact, in the Bethel, Alaska, shooting on February 19, 1997, Evan Ramsey's two friends who helped him plan his attack called several friends the night before so that they would be on the mezzanine around the courtyard to witness the attack. This situation highlights the need for students to realize that it is critical to inform someone in a position of authority. Typically, students would see this as "ratting" on a friend.

Metal detectors and security cameras certainly help prevent violence, but those measures alone won't always prevent the violence. On October 1, 1997, Luke Woodham walked into his high school in Pearl, Mississippi, with a rifle, killing his ex-girlfriend and another student. In an interview with Secret Service agents afterward, he said that even a metal detector wouldn't have stopped him.

Luke Woodham had easy access to guns, as have many of the other school shooters. The availability of guns, especially handguns, continues to be a volatile issue. One side defends a person's right to bear arms while the other side reels from the staggering statistics. "Protect Children Instead of Guns" (Grapes, 2000, 1) reports that in 1999, 3,761 children and teens were killed by gunfire; 2,184 of those were homicides; 1,241 young people took their own lives with a firearm; and, 262 died in accidental shootings. The issue of gun control is rapidly becoming one that students need to be aware of, if numbers like these are ever going to decrease.

EXPLORING SUDDEN VIOLENT DEATH

When death occurs from sudden, unexpected circumstances such as a school shooting or any kind of homicide, bereavement reactions are usually more severe, exaggerated, and complicated. The mourner, whether directly or indirectly involved, may be so overwhelmed that the capacity to cope with his grief can be nonexistent. This is not to minimize the pain of any kind of death, but several other factors complicate the bereavement process in sudden violent deaths. Redmond (1996) highlights the major factors that make the process more exaggerated and difficult by noting critical response factors:

- Cognitive dissonance
- Murderous impulses and anger
- Conflict of values and belief system
- Withdrawal of support due to the stigma of murder
- Fear and vulnerability
- Guilt and blame
- Intrusions by law enforcement, the criminal justice system, and the media (53)

In a school setting, not only do the above factors complicate the bereavement process, but school counselors or outside grief counselors must also devise ways to address groups of students, not just individuals. The first step for counselors is getting the students to talk. Letting them dump their thoughts, feelings, fears, and anger through a group discussion is often necessary before any kind of therapy can begin. Counselors should attempt not to stifle, offer advice, or become judgmental with the students.

When counselors form groups of students with whom they will work more closely, they attempt to select students with similar relationships or interests to make them feel comfortable, and therefore more likely to share. Athletes, surfers, friends of the deceased are examples of how groups might be formed. Counselors may also choose to guide students in other forms of therapy such as art therapy, journaling, or drama therapy.

The complicating factors of violent death can be addressed in a very realistic manner when literature is used. Stories and their fictional characters allow students to "trial and error" their way through conflicts and problems, eventually reaching productive, effective, and nonviolent coping mechanisms.

Schools and teachers cannot be expected to eliminate the violence issue on their own. Teachers can, however, make an important contribution by helping their students develop resources to aid them in solving social problems in productive and nonviolent ways. One powerful resource is literature in the classroom. Through literature, students can learn safe and nonviolent ways to deal with conflicts they face in their lives.

IN THE CLASSROOM

Todd Strasser's novel, *Give a Boy a Gun*, closely resembles many of the incidents and events in several of the recent school shootings. Two boys, Gary Searle and Brendan Lawlor, endure years of being bullied, intimidated, and made fun of by the school jocks, with no help from teachers. They devise a plan to get revenge on all of them. They decide to take them all hostage at a school dance, block off the exits with homemade pipe bombs, and use a stolen semiautomatic rifle to torture and kill them.

The story is told in the voices of the students, teachers, friends, and the gunmen themselves. It starts in the early years of middle school when Gary and Brendan become friends and continues through and after the night of their violent rampage. As the story progresses, Strasser includes facts about guns and school violence that keep the reality of the problem in the forefront of the readers' minds.

Before Reading

The following strategies focus on three key issues for discussion and teaching with the novel *Give a Boy a Gun*. They are designed to plant the initial seeds of awareness in the students' minds about bullying, gun control, and dealing with a sudden, violent death.

Bullying Awareness

Many students engage in bullying behavior and are not aware of it simply because they do not have a clear definition of what it is. One way to increase this awareness, and the devastating impact that it can have on others, is to divide the students in small groups and have them come up with a definition and examples of what they think bullying is and what it is not. Encourage them to give specific examples with quoted comments that a student might make to another student. Also, have each group come to consensus on the following questions:

- Why does bullying happen?
- What effects does it have on people?
- What can students who are bullied do?
- What can students who witness the bullying do?
- How can bullying be stopped?

Groups should then present their definitions, quoted comments, and answers to these questions to the rest of the class. No judgments should be made about any one definition at this time, because a wide range of opinions is needed for students to understand the complexity of the issue. It would be best to have students do their work on large chart paper to be displayed in the classroom throughout the reading of the novel.

This activity can be extended by examining different bullying behaviors. Miklowitz's "Confession" (1997) is an excellent read-aloud highlighting this problem. This short story is told through the confession of a teenage boy who ends up being in the wrong place at the wrong time. Bullying behavior is present but in a subtle form. After reading, students can discuss why JJ went along with his friends. They can predict the consequences he would suffer if he didn't. Students can then look at these choices and discuss whether they think this is a form of bullying.

Gun Control

Gun control is a very volatile issue, on which many people take a strong stand. Students can debate the issue by examining how they would react in any situation where someone is holding a loaded gun.

Because these issues are so emotionally charged, opinions could be solicited by conducting an anonymous survey with the class. The following questions would highlight the students' beliefs on these issues:

- Does anyone in your home own a gun (or guns)? Who?
- What kind of gun is it (are they)?
- Have you ever been taught to shoot the gun? By whom?
- Have you ever taken a gun-safety course?
- Do you think people who want to buy a gun should have to have some kind of license before they can purchase a gun?
- The Brady Bill mandates a five-day waiting period before you can buy a gun. Do you think this is a necessary or unnecessary law?
- Do you think the government should be allowed to control who can buy a gun as well as what kinds of guns can be purchased (other than by the military), and how many guns a person can own?

The tabulated results can become points of discussion throughout the reading.

During Reading

Keeping Track of Bullying Behavior

In *Give a Boy a Gun*, it becomes apparent to the reader early on that Brendan and Gary were frequently picked on, harassed, and bullied by many of the other students and that other students didn't seem to realize their wrongdoing. Neither boy really had a parent he could turn to for help, nor did the teachers at Middletown High seem to place much emphasis on stopping the torment. Everyone had excuses for what went on, and no one made an effort to stop it. It is this lack of awareness and involvement that adds to Brendan's and Gary's unhappiness, as well as their hatred toward their tormentors. Teaching students about bullying, its effects, and how to avoid or stop it would be instrumental in improving many of the relationships that occur in schools, and could possibly avoid another Columbine incident.

One activity that would facilitate this discussion could begin by brainstorming the three roles associated with bullying: the victim, the aggressor, and the bystander. Explain to students that roles can change when the level of conflict changes, but normally, people fall into the same role again and again. This may have to do with patterns of behavior that are developed during childhood, but patterns can be changed as children learn how to respond to conflict in new ways.

Students need to keep track of bullying in the story and who is involved. They can do this by turning a piece of notebook paper horizontally and dividing it into four columns. Label the columns in this manner:

Event and Page Number   Victim(s)   Aggressor(s)   Bystander(s)

As they read, students record the bullying incidents that happen, to whom, by whom, and who witnessed them. After several days, conduct a class discussion with the students by sharing their findings and by looking for common characteristics of each role. The three roles can be listed on the board or overhead, and the characteristics can be recorded. Students can be asked if they can think of, or can find, reasons why the characters have fallen into these roles in relation to the bullying. Also, students can study the locations of where the incidents took place to see if there are any patterns. When students discover that most bullying takes place in a public place with others around, this may lead them to the heart of the bullying issue.

The role of the bystander as active or passive should also be explored.

Do bystanders help to instigate the bullying, encourage it, or passively accept it? How often do they try to stop it, and what happens if they attempt to stop it? If they decide to do nothing, can that still lead to negative consequences? As students explain and defend their views, some clear lines of thinking will emerge.

At this point, the different kinds of bullying behaviors can be explored, including physical aggression, verbal aggression, social alienation, and intimidation. Based on their new understandings, students can generate examples of each, record these on chart paper, and post them in the classroom. This can lead to a discussion of why these should be considered examples of bullying (Are they harmful to someone? Could they damage a person's self-esteem?).

Role Plays

Many times adolescents just don't have the knowledge or experience needed to help them out of a tough situation. They are given a broad solution to a very specific problem and it just doesn't work. Gary and Brendan had very little knowledge about how to deal with the bullying they encountered every day at Middletown High. Consequently, they had little knowledge of how to deal with the way it made them feel about themselves and their place in the school. If they had been aware of alternative methods or responses to use when the bullying was directed at them, they wouldn't have resorted to violence.

This strategy is designed to aid students in learning nonviolent ways the victim or bystander can deal with conflict and bullying. The class is divided into groups of three or four students, and each group is assigned one of the four kinds of bullying to enact. Certain criteria should be met in each role-play:

- The conflict must be resolved in a nonviolent way
- The bystander(s) should have an active role
- Communication between all involved is critical

As each role-play finishes, discuss how the conflict was resolved and other ways it could have been handled. Were the situations portrayed in a realistic manner? Why might many students have difficulty with nonviolent conflict resolution? Also, students can generate reasons why it is so difficult for bystanders to intervene and identify ways they think it could have been made easier to react. These discussions can lead to local connections. Are there any other things they can think of that might help to eliminate incidents of bullying at school?

Anti-Bullying Policy

In the aftermath of Brendan's and Gary's rampage, the school must make a conscious choice to improve how each and every student is treated, as well as the general acceptance level for each student. The entire school needs to recognize, treat, and prevent this kind of behavior from continuing or happening at all. Designing a schoolwide or even a classwide anti-bullying policy can make people aware of the problem, as well as get a large number of students involved in finding solutions.

Bringing students into the process by asking them to design an anti-bullying policy can begin the conversation. Divide students into small groups who will be responsible for designing an anti-bullying policy for the classroom and school. Each group's policies should cover the following features. Each has definitions and cited examples, but students should be encouraged to expand the policy.

1. The school's stand in relation to bullying. This should be a clear state-ment on the unacceptability of bullying in the school.
   Example: (Name of school) does not tolerate bullying of any kind. Everyone here is committed to providing a safe and caring environment where students can learn and be accepted for who they are.

2. A clear, concise definition of bullying with a complete set of examples.
   Example: Bullying is . . . and some examples of bullying are. . . .

3. The rights of students. This should be a statement having something to do with the rights of students to feel safe at school or that the school has an obligation to ensure the safety of its students (and staff).
   Example: When students are bullied (cite examples of how it might make students feel and what it can make them do—feel sick, have no friends, etc.).

4. The responsibilities of students who witness bullying. This might in-clude some reasons why students should take an active part in trying to prevent bullying and where/to whom they can go for help.
   Example: We plan to prevent bullying at (school name) by . . . (here students should cite what they can do if they witness bullying in and around the school).

5. What the school will do to counter bullying. Students need to realize prevention is everyone's job and can include how teachers, adminis-trators, and parents can help.
   Example: The staff at (school name) needs to (1) be role models in

how they act and what they say at all times; (2) actively supervise the campus and report incidents to the appropriate staff member.

Each group should present its policy to the rest of the class. Posters could be made, a name given to the policy, and an anti-bullying slogan developed. When all the presentations have been made, discuss the possible problems that could be encountered in implementing these policies and how students would address those problems. How would they get students, staff, and even parents to support these policies?

Gun-Control Debate

The issue of handguns, their availability, and their deadly consequences is presented through the facts that Strasser lists in *Give a Boy a Gun*, such as numbers of adolescents killed, quotes from real students that have witnessed violent incidents, and quotes from students who committed violence against others. He mentions again and again how quickly and easily most of the handguns were obtained.

These can be the beginnings of research that students use as they prepare to have a debate on whether there should be more or less handgun control. The class can be divided into four groups: two groups will be for more handgun control, and two groups will be against. Students should brainstorm and record what things they might want to know if they are going to be debating the issue. They will probably generate a list that includes statistics on how many handguns are currently in the U.S., regulations on purchasing a handgun, etc. Students should be given at least a week to gather information to support their arguments.

Before the actual debate begins, students should develop some rules to follow in order to ensure a fair and orderly debate. They should decide on what to do if a stalemate occurs. Each group could be given several index cards, in order to write questions to ask the opposing side in the debate. Select and use these during the debate, as well as any questions you may have. For the actual debate, the groups can debate in their original groups, or a random selection of students from the two sides can be selected to form new debate groups. By debating the issue, students become informed about the views and beliefs of the opposing side. As each debate finishes, students could reflect on the relationship between gun control and the events in *Give a Boy a Gun*.

Public Service Announcements (PSAs)

Even though the students just debated both sides of the gun-control issue, in keeping with the ideas presented in *Give a Boy a Gun*, students should write public service announcements only *for* gun control. With the large number of adolescents that are killed each year by guns, understanding the need for reducing the numbers of guns, as well as access to guns, should be a need they acknowledge.

Explain to the students that they are going to be writing public service announcements for the radio. PSAs are a form of advertising that tries to involve the listener in a persuasive message, while delaying the presentation of information that identifies the message as persuasive. In other words, a PSA is a message that tries to manipulate without the listener being aware of the manipulation. There is a claim that people are less likely to be manipulated by a message when they are aware of its persuasive intent. PSAs have the following characteristics:

- Short (30 or 60 seconds)
- Goal is to change attitudes or behavior
- Use of emotion and clear voice (listener needs to be able to hear and understand message)
- Identifying tag for the organization or cause comes at the end

Students may be paired, or may write individual PSAs, and deliver them in a 30- or 60-second format, such as the following 30-second PSA:

We all know prevention works. So if you agree not to leave your handgun lying around your house, I'll agree not to leave mine lying around my house. Then I'll know my kids are safe when they are at your house, and you won't have to worry when yours are at my house. Let's take a stand to prevent accidental deaths of our children by gunfire. Friends don't let friends play with guns—or their kids play with guns either.

After Reading

Murderous Impulses and Anger

It is normal to feel anger and even fantasize about acting out rage after being a witness to a violent death. Plans of torture and desires to see the murderer suffer are normal reactions for bereaved survivors. What is difficult is that the survivors are afraid of telling anyone their thoughts, which leads them to feeling they are no better than the murderer. "I must be going crazy" is a common response of survivors and, the survivor must be reassured that he is not "going crazy," that such thinking is typical (Redmond, 1996, 56).

If these thoughts are verbalized and vented, the anger behind them begins to lose its intensity, and the survivor can begin the healing process. The discussion of the violent imagery serves as a way to talk about, but not actually act upon, that violence. Most survivors are able to release anger, bitterness, helplessness, and frustration, as they become aware of what can be accomplished by channeling their anger in more productive directions. As they gain knowledge of the circumstances surrounding the event, the aftermath, and their conflicting feelings of powerlessness and frustration, they can begin to transform this negative trauma into some kind of positive accomplishment.

Role Play

In *Give a Boy a Gun*, several of the survivors acted upon their murderous rage and anger by kicking and brutalizing Brendan to death. The consequences for these boys would need to be addressed by the reader. Some people would consider them heroes for saving lives and others would consider them nothing more than a lynch mob. As an entry into this discussion, the class could role-play these possibilities: groups representing the boys that attacked Brendan and law-enforcement officials or citizens concerned about the violent actions of the boys. Students would need time to gather examples from the story to defend their actions. When, or if, the role-play stalemates, students should describe their perceptions of what happened. This activity should enable students to see the importance of dealing with violent situations in a nonviolent way, which leads to fewer lives being drastically affected by the event.

What If?

Most people have a time in their lives that they would like to be able to live over again. They might want the opportunity to see an event or situation end differently or to say something to someone in another way. The ending for *Give a Boy a Gun* provides an excellent opportunity for engaging students in this kind of thinking. What if Beth Bender, the guidance counselor, had spent more time with Brendan when he first came to Middletown High? What if Sam Flach hadn't given Brendan such a hard time? What if he had befriended him instead? What would have occurred in the gym that night? Would anything have happened at all?

The graphic in figure 6.1 can facilitate students' "what if" discussions. Students can work together by selecting one pivotal event in the story. They should briefly describe the event in the "situation" and determine two other options for what could have happened instead of the actual

Figure 6.1
No Easy Answers

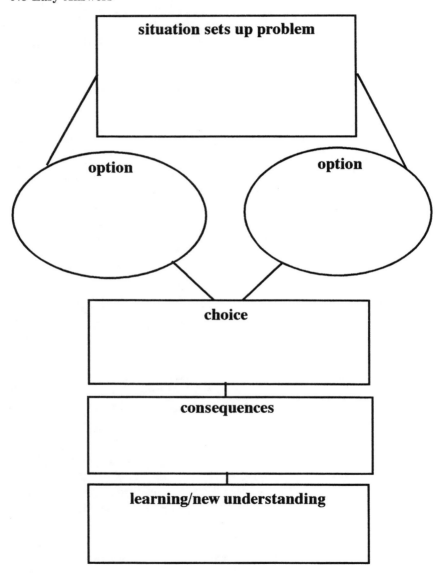

outcome. They can then select one choice they see as the better option and detail that solution. As students infer possible less violent consequences, they extend their knowledge of how to peacefully resolve a conflict and learn why peace is a more viable solution than violence.

Time Line

Giving students the opportunity to explore Gary's or Brendan's life by creating positive and negative timelines provides another opportunity to explore alternative choices.

Students can be organized into groups, with each group receiving a 4- to 6-foot strip of butcher paper. The activity is more effective if students are allowed to tape their pieces on the walls around the classroom. Each group should draw a line, horizontally, about halfway down and along the entire length of the paper, in order to chart events in either Gary or Brendan's life. They should note the positive things that happened to the character on the top half of the paper and the negative things on the bottom half. For each of the negative events, however, they must also make up one positive that could have counteracted it. These can be written on self-stick removable notes and stuck to the timeline as they chart. This gives students yet another chance to focus on nonviolent ways to deal with conflict, as well as seeing times when an outside person could have stepped in and made a difference.

Guilt and Blame

When people are directly or indirectly involved with a sudden violent death, they often have feelings of guilt because they survived, while their friends or loved ones were killed. People are taught to be responsible for their lives, activities, careers, and families, which creates a sense of power over those responsibilities. This belief is shattered after the murder of a loved one, and the result may be the loss of power and control needed to carry out daily functions. Survivors blame themselves or look for others to blame, and when no satisfying answers arise, the guilt they feel may intensify, which may trigger withdrawal and strained communications. Survivors need to talk about their feelings, come to terms with whether they could have done anything to prevent the incident, or decide whether blaming others will change what happened. Finally, they need to understand that while nothing can be changed about what *has* happened, their attitudes, behaviors, or beliefs can be altered to help them move forward, get on with their lives, and possibly learn from the event.

If Only . . .

In many of their final comments in *Give a Boy a Gun*, the survivors wondered how things would have been different if only they had intervened during certain incidents, or if only they had paid closer attention to comments made by Brendan and Gary. Rarely in life does the chance to do or say something over again, in order to set things right, happen. But, looking at that "if only" possibility, after reading *Give a Boy a Gun*, could help students realize the necessity of thinking through their actions and decisions before carrying them out, so that they can get it right the first time.

Begin by having students think back to incidents in their lives, not necessarily violent incidents, they wish they could go back and relive so the outcome would be different. Each student can write about an incident, describing when it happened, where, how old they were, who else was involved, what the outcome was, and what would have happened if only he/she had done something differently. Students should also include what the "something else" would have been. This can lead students to explore opportunities to make a difference.

To extend this concept in literature, Werlin's short story, "War Game" (1997) can be read aloud. A class discussion can lead students to the answers to questions such as if only Jo had; what would have happened to Lije instead; how would his life have been different/the same; and how would it have affected Jo's life? With both personal and literary connections to the "if only" concept, students can transfer their understandings to *Give a Boy a Gun* by examining guilt, blame, responsibility, and moving forward.

• Copy a statement the character says at the end of the book and then decide whether it is a guilt statement (they feel guilty about what happened); a blame statement (they are blaming others and feel they had no part in causing what happened); or a taking-responsibility statement (they acknowledge they had something to do with what happened.
   Example: [as said by Sam Flach from *Give a Boy a Gun*]: "My pastor say I have to try and forgive them for what they did to me. Meanwhile I'm still on crutches with two knees that'll never be any good again. Why? Did I do anything that a thousand other guys at a thousand other schools haven't done? Sorry, folk, I'm not forgiving them. Ever." (124)
   This is an example of a blame statement because Sam doesn't think he did anything wrong and that it was completely Gary and Brendan's fault.

- Next, students need to come up with moving forward statements. These address some change the characters know they need to make in their behavior toward others, their attitude toward others, or the way they would react in the future should they be in a similar situation.
Example: I guess I should have been a little easier on them. It bothers me sometimes when kids don't have any school spirit and get involved with stuff at school but I guess that doesn't give me the right to pick on them and make fun of them. I need to work on accepting kids that don't like sports and just leave them alone, kind of like minding my own business.

  Sam still doesn't like the idea of having no school spirit and kids that don't think like he does, but this statement shows that he has at least increased his level of awareness about his part in the event.

As volunteers share their work, the class can discuss the difficulties associated with people accepting guilt or blame. In Sam's example, his level of awareness may have increased, but he still has a long way to go. During the discussion, students may need to be reminded that beliefs don't change overnight, nor do people's reactions. This can lead to a discussion of the kinds of problems this can create for people as they work through their grief.

Garbage In, Garbage Out

Linda Cunningham, founder/director of Teen Age Grief, Inc. (TAG), an organization designed to offer support to the bereaved teenager, created the following activity to help students get rid of negative thoughts they might be experiencing as they grieve. These "garbage thoughts" can be triggered by many things, and during a time of grieving they surface and can affect how we look at or deal with life.

First read an introduction and examples, such as the following:

Picture yourself walking into a room and there, in the middle of the room, you find a large container of garbage. This garbage looks bad and smells bad. What do you think you would do? If you had a need to be in the room, my guess is that you would get rid of the garbage before you did anything else. The sight and smell of the garbage would be a real distraction, and it could keep you from getting things done. Isn't it interesting— most of us would have very little tolerance for staying in a room full of garbage; but the garbage we hold onto in our mind is something we often hold onto with a vengeance, as though it had great value. Let me give you some examples of garbage thoughts:

- "I hate my teacher. She's ugly and boring. I wish I wasn't in her class."
- "I had a fight with my friend Jane and now she's dead. I'll never forgive myself."
- "I'll never be anything in this life. Life's just too hard."
- "I hate my body. I'll never get a date looking like this."

After discussing the concept of garbage thoughts, students can select one of the surviving characters in *Give a Boy a Gun* and list four negative thoughts they think that character might be holding. After writing down the negative thought, ask students to write explanations of the benefit in getting rid of that thought. Share the following example to clarify:

"I had a fight with my friend Jane and now she's dead. I'll never forgive myself."

Benefit: Sometimes, when someone dies, we feel guilty for being alive or for experiencing any feelings of happiness. By never forgiving ourselves, we have found a way to punish ourselves for being alive and for having had a fight with a good friend. Another question you might ask yourself: "Do I need to punish myself because of Jane's death, or is there something else going on? Punishing ourselves will not bring Jane back or erase the past, but it can get in the way of our healing process.

After discovering the garbage thoughts in *Give a Boy a Gun*, students can discuss other ways that they could help the characters with their grief, fears, or anger. You might explore the differences in how people deal with their grief as well as the length of time involved in the healing process. Can they think of kinds of personalities as well as outside influences that might cause some people to grieve longer than others? What ideas do they have about ways that Middletown High or any other school could help students deal with their grief? What kind of support might the school offer?

Final Reflections

Students need to be aware of the fact that though the likelihood is slim, an incident such as the one presented in *Give a Boy a Gun* could happen in any school. By paying attention to how each and every student is treated and accepted at school, we may be able to eliminate some of the possible causes for these incidents. When differences are accepted, they serve as a point of learning and provide an opportunity to expand each other's horizons.

A point of closure for students reading this book can happen if they write an epilogue to *Give a Boy a Gun*. They can pretend it is one year later at Middletown High School. They are returning seniors who were present in the gym the previous year when the rampage took place. Now, however, as they walk down the hallways, they not only see signs of differences, they feel them when they encounter students. Describe what they see. Describe what they feel. How do the students treat each other? How aware are the teachers about what is going on during class changes? How are things different in the school cafeteria? They should write so one can really feel what it is like *now* to be a student at Middletown High.

Todd Strasser shares some suggestions at the end of the novel for things that could be changed to reduce the probability of school violence. The statement that he makes, which should be emphasized to students, is that their generation is the one that may have the power to make real changes that will save young lives. On October 21, 1999, over two million students signed the Student Pledge against Gun Violence, which might be a place for you and your students to begin:

- I will never bring a gun to school.
- I will never use a gun to settle a dispute.
- I will use my influence with my friends to keep them from using guns to settle disputes.
- My individual choices and actions, when multiplied by those of young people throughout the country, will make a difference. Together, by honoring this pledge, we can reverse the violence and grow up in safety (http://www.pledge.org/).

RECOMMENDED READINGS

Fiction

Arrick, Fran. (1991). *Where'd you get the gun, Billy?* New York: Bantam Books. ISBN: 0–553–07135–1 (6–12). HC, 104 pp.

Crestview Senior High School seemed like your normal everyday high school until one of its female students was murdered by her boyfriend. Though everyone knew the couple had their problems, and Lisa's friends had tried to convince her to leave Billy, now it was too late; Lisa was dead. A classroom acquaintance, David, can't get the murder out of his mind, and so he and another friend, Liz, decide to search for some answers. The story unfolds along with a hypothetical journey of getting possession of a gun.

Cormier, Robert. (1979). *After the first death*. New York: Dell. ISBN: 0–440–20835–1 (9–12). PB, 233 pp.

Multiple perspectives are presented when a busload of small children is hijacked by terrorists seeking the return of their homeland; a high school girl who was simply driving the bus that day as a favor to an uncle, an army general whose loyalty to his country outweighs his love for his son, and the son, a young man wanting desperately to win the love and respect of his father. The content is harsh, but valuable lessons in family relationships, cultural differences, and the loss of innocence are addressed. Reads and ends like real life, not always happily-ever-after.

Glenn, Mel. (1997). *The taking of Room 114*. New York: Lodestar Books. ISBN: 0–525–67548–5 (9–12). HC, 182 pp.

Seniors have everything on their mind but school as they near graduation day. One thing they certainly never thought about was being taken hostage by their senior history teacher, Mr. Wiedermeyer. The story is told in poems, and each senior speaks five times—chronicling their years in high school and ending with their thoughts as they sit in class staring into the barrel of Mr. Wiedermeyer's gun. A great story and written in a compelling and accessible manner that gives the reader the opportunity to reflect on high school years as well as mortality in the face of possible death.

Glenn, Mel. (1996). *Who killed Mr. Chippendale?* New York: Lodestar Books. ISBN: 0–525–67530–2 (9–12). HC, 100 pp.

In light of the recent real-life school shootings, this fictional account of a teacher's murder remains relevant and revealing. Mr. Chippendale is shot and killed on the school's track, and as his murder is investigated the reader will meet students and teachers whose lives he touched—and not necessarily in a positive way. The story is told in the form of free verse, and it is an insightful journey into the lives and minds of those who attend Tower High School.

Mazer, Harry, ed. (1997). *Twelve shots*. New York: Bantam Doubleday. ISBN: 0–385–32238–0 (7–12). HC, 229 pp.

A collection of short stories about guns. The right and wrong ways they are used and how they can affect the life of an adolescent. Some of the stories are funny, some are sad, but all will make the reader think about the issues surrounding guns and possibly challenge some beliefs about the world.

McDonald, Joyce. (1999). *Swallowing stones*. New York: Laurel Leaf. ISBN: 0–440–22672–4. (9–12). HC, 245 pp.

Imagine getting a gun for your seventeenth birthday! Then imagine finding out that the first bullet fired into the air came down a mile away and killed a man.

This is what Michael Mackenzie must deal with or should deal with, but instead, he buries the gun, pretends he knows nothing about the incident, and tries to go on with his life. Fate, however, has different plans when Michael meets the daughter of the man he killed. The story is told from both points of view— Michael's and Jenna's, going back and forth as they struggle to cope.

Nonfiction

Bernall, Misty. (1999). *She said yes*. New York: Pocket Books. ISBN: 0–7434–0052–6. PB, 163 pp.

Cassie Bernall was one of the twelve students killed in the Columbine High School shootings. This memoir, written by her mother, traces the struggle, confusion, and pain that Cassie and her family endured as Cassie struggled to find her way through adolescence. An almost "tough love" approach from her family, their continual love, and finally, Cassie's newfound faith gave her the courage to embrace her life and convictions. Many students will be able to identify with Cassie's struggles yet finish the book learning some valuable lessons about life and love.

Canada, Geoffrey. (1995). *fist stick knife gun*. Boston, MA: Beacon Press. ISBN: 0–8070–0423–5. PB, 179 pp.

This autobiographical account begins when Canada is four years old and becomes aware of violence. An amazing and shattering look at what growing up in the South Bronx was like. Rituals of fighting just to stand on a certain part of the sidewalk—graduating from using your fist, to a stick, a knife, and finally a gun. Canada also discusses the gun-manufacturing industry and how they have aided in the increase of adolescent deaths by guns. This is an eye-opening account of the violence and fear that many of America's youth live with day in and day out. For many students, this book would provide insight into a kind of life they know nothing about and don't understand but certainly need to.

Curwin, Richard L., & Allen N. Mendler. (1997). *As tough as necessary: Countering violence, aggression, and hostility in our schools*. Alexandria, VA: ASCD. ISBN: 0–87120–280–8. PB, 145 pp.

Starting with a chapter on how violence, aggression, and hostility have affected society and schools, this book then offers strategies for schools and teachers to use to help students change the way they perceive and respond to aggressive feelings. It gives some sound approaches that can be adopted in any school that is experiencing violence or has an increasingly aggressive student body.

Day, Nancy. (1996). *Violence in schools: Learning in fear*. Springfield, NJ: Enslow. ISBN: 0–89490–734–4. HC, 128 pp.

Day examines the issue of school violence and all the factors that may be contributing to it. From the causes of violence to the victims and perpetrators she looks at the issues outside schools that may be contributing factors in the increase of school violence: racial and ethnic fighting, vandalism, sexual harassment, gangs, biological factors, poverty, alcohol and drug abuse, and most important, access to guns. SAVE (Students Against Violence Everywhere), a North Carolina organization, is detailed with the efforts it has made in getting students involved with combating the problem of youth violence. Readable and a great resource for teachers and students alike.

Grapes, Bryan J., ed. (2000). *School violence*. San Diego: Greenhaven Press. ISBN: 0–7377–0332–6. HC, 156 pp.

This collection of essays discusses the many issues surrounding school violence. Historical background and current statistics are given and related to the most recent school shootings. The varying viewpoints and discrepant information in the essays make one wonder if school violence is on the increase as the media portrays or if it is on the decrease. Portions of an extensive interview that the *New York Times* conducted with eight Columbine students are included. A great resource to use in exposing students to both sides of an issue and to decide whether there are "rights" or "wrongs."

Kellerman, Jonathan. (1999). *Savage spawn: Reflections on violent children*. New York: Ballantine. ISBN: 0–345–42939–7. PB, 134 pp.

Kellerman, a clinical child psychologist, focuses on antisocial youth—kids who kill without remorse. The impulse to blame violent movies or society's lack of morals and the nature–nurture debate are discussed. A few case studies are presented which offer the reader an inside look at these kids and can leave you with a feeling of unease. Students would probably be fascinated with the information Kellerman presents and his doubts about rehabilitation for these kids.

Rigby, Ken. (1998). *Bullying in schools and what to do about it*. Markham, ON: Pembroke. ISBN: 1–55138–097–8. PB, 160 pp.

A detailed look at bullying, how to define it, the process it follows with a passive or resistant victim, the consequences of bullying, and finally, measured steps that schools can take to combat it. Rigby gives suggestions on how to run a school meeting with students, parents, administrators, and community members to discuss the issue and how to go about getting the backing needed to implement preventive measures within a school. Several strategies are presented for aiding the victims in becoming more assertive as well as teaching the bullies to become more aware of how the victims feel. Resources on bullying are also provided that can aid educators, parents, and children.

Romain, Trevor. (1997). *Bullies are a pain in the brain*. New York: Free
   Spirit. ISBN: 1–57542–023–6. HC, 112 pp.

Blending humor with serious, practical suggestions, this book uses cartoons to
help kids understand, avoid, and stand up to bullies while preserving their own
self-esteem.

Schleifer, Jay. (1998). *When someone you know has been killed*. New
   York: Rosen. ISBN: 0–8239–2779–2. HC, 64 pp.

This is a book from the "Everything You Need to Know" series and gives clear
and concise information about handling the death of a loved one who is suddenly
killed. The book cites the disappearance and murder of a teenager in a small
town and uses it to discuss the death issue. Schleifer goes through the stages of
grief and how to handle them and stresses an adolescent's need to talk about
the incident, which is what should be done. He states that often adults want to
pretend that it didn't happen or just say we need to move on. Adolescents often
are prevented from moving on by the intensity of the feelings they may be
experiencing. Simple, direct text relating some of the challenges that a sudden
and violent death can impose on the survivors.

INTERNET RESOURCES

Blueprints for Violence Prevention
http://www.colorado.edu/cspv/blueprints/model/ ten_bully.htm
Details the premise behind the Bullying Prevention program, and provides further sites on bullying prevention.

Kids and Violence: A Resource Guide from MSNBC
http://www.msnbc.com/news/297184.asp?0nm=-268
Provides information for parents, students, and teachers about the warning signs
of violence and how to prevent its outbreak.

National Campaign Against Youth Violence
http://www/ncayv.org
This site contains a variety of information, including basic facts and definitions
related to youth violence, stories written from the perspectives of young people,
and ten things all of us can do to prevent youth violence.

REFERENCES

American Psychological Association. (2000). "Warning signs. Fight for your
         rights: Take a stand against violence." Washington, DC: the Association.
Canada, Geoffrey. (1995). *fist stick knife gun*. Boston: Beacon Press.

Cunningham, Linda. (2000). "Garbage Thoughts." Drug Prevention and School Safety. Titusville, FL: Teen Age Grief.

Day, Nancy. (1996). *Violence in schools: Learning in fear.* Springfield, NJ: Enslow.

Dwyer, Kevin. (1999). "Children killing children." National Association of School Psychologists, *Communique*, Spring Special Edition.

Frontline. (August 2000). "The killer at Thurston High." www.pbs.org/wgbh/pages/frontline/shows/kinkel/profile

Grapes, Bryan J., ed. (2000). *School violence.* San Diego, CA: Greenhaven Press.

Miklowitz, Gloria. (1997). "Confession." In Don Gallo, ed., *No easy answers.* New York: Bantam Doubleday Dell.

Morse, Jodie. (2000). "The perception gap: School violence." Time.com.

Phynchon, Marisa. (2000). *Secret Service school shootings.* National Threat Assessment Center, May 18. http://www.cbsnews.com

Redmond, Lula M. (1996). "Sudden violent death." In Kenneth Doka, ed., *Living with grief after sudden loss: Suicide homicide accident heart attack.* Washington, DC: Hospice Foundation of America.

Silent March Campaign. (2000). *What we believe: Kids and guns.* http://www.silentmarach.org/noguns/data/what.html

Slaby, Ronald. (1994). *Aggressors, victims, and bystanders.* Washington, DC: Educational Development Center.

Strasser, Todd. (2000). *Give a boy a gun.* New York: Simon & Schuster.

Student Pledge against Violence. (2000). *Student Pledge against Violence.* http://www.pledge.org/.

Werlin, Nancy. (1997). "War Game." In Harry Mazer, ed., *Twelve shots: Outstanding short stories about guns.* New York: Delacorte Press.

A Letter from Sharon Draper

I've been a public school teacher for more than 25 years. I know what kids like, what they will read, and what they won't. Although I have nothing against Charles Dickens, teenagers would rather gag than read him. Dickens wrote for his contemporaries—young people of a hundred and fifty years ago. Young people today need to know about the world of London in the 1860s, but they would much rather read about their own world first. Not only will they read about recognizable experiences with pleasure, but they will also be encouraged to write as well.

Five years ago my short story, "One Small Torch," was selected as the first place, $5,000 winner of the *Ebony* magazine short-story contest. I had always loved to write—but the publication of that story gave me validation. I had been working on a novel for young people, so I decided to see if I could get it published. *Tears of a Tiger* is written for high school students—on their level, in their style, about their world. The characters are just ordinary kids trying to get through high school. The book does not deal with drugs or gangs or sex. It does, however, deal with parents, girlfriends, and homework. It also discusses the problems of drinking and driving, racism and teen suicide.

Suicide is a very delicate issue to discuss in a novel for young adults. Several companies were afraid to publish the book because of the subject matter, but I purposely tried very hard to make sure that it was clear to all readers that Andy's decision was not the right choice and that lots of options for help existed for him. I tried to show, through the voices of the other characters, that although they were saddened by Andy's death, they were angry with him and disappointed as well that he did not turn to them who would have and could have helped him through his crisis. The very last scene, when Monty visits Andy's grave, shows him leaving to live his life, a life of hope and potential and many tomorrows. Andy would never have that.

Below is an excerpt from a letter I sent to a student who wrote to me on her despondency about living, as well as an excerpt from her response to me.

I was really pleased to get your letter. It's always a pleasure to receive a letter from a reader who really likes your work. I tried very hard to write something that young people could identify with and understand. I was also a little concerned when I read your letter. It always concerns me when young people feel that they have no reason to live. That's one reason I wrote the book—to show that what Andy did was to choose the WRONG decision. He chose to make a permanent solution to what was a temporary problem. He could have solved his problems and gone to the prom! But he will never go to prom or a party or talk on the telephone, or see the sky ever again. That's sad. If you were not in the world, Mary, I would be very sad. The world needs you, and your smile, and your talents and abilities.

You know what else? I have been an English teacher for 25 years, and I can tell a good writer when I see one. You are a VERY good writer—you expressed yourself excellently! Keep on writing, OK? You have the talent! Do you know I started writing because I like to read? I didn't have many friends, but I knew lots of people from stories I read. Later I made up friends as I started to write.

Her response to me:

All I needed was for one person to believe in me, and to tell me I had possibilities. Thanks for taking the time to save my life.

She saved her own life. I just helped her see that her life had value and potential. *Tears of a Tiger* can be a powerful teaching tool.

Sincerely,
Sharon Draper

"Bandaids and Five-Dollar Bills"
Sharon Draper

My students wrote essays for homework this week,
The usual stuff for grade ten,
I asked them to write how they'd change the world
If the changing was left up to them.

His name was Rick Johnson; he was surly and shy,
A student who's always ignored.
He'd slouch in his seat with a Malcolm X cap,
Half-sleep, making sure he looked bored.

His essay was late—just before I went home,
It was wrinkled and scribbled and thin,
I thought to reject it . . . (Why do teachers do that?)
But I thanked him for turning it in.

"You can't cure the world," his essay began,
"Of the millions of evils and ills,
But to clean up my world so I could survive,
I'd cut bandaids and five-dollar bills.

"Now bandaids are beige—says right on the box
'Skin tone' is the color inside.
Whose skin tone? Not mine! Been lookin' for years
For someone with that color hide.

"Cause bandaids show up, looking pasty and pale,
It's hard to pretend they're not there,
When the old man has beat me and I gotta get stitches,
Them bandaids don't cover or care.

"And now, you may ask, why would anyone want
To get rid of five-dollar bills?
Cause for just that much cash, a dude's mama can buy
A crack rock, or whiskey, or pills.

"She smokes it or drinks it, and screams at her kids,
Then passes out cold on the floor,
By morn she remembers no pain, just the void,
And her kids wish the world had a door.

"So my magical dream is not out of reach,
Like curing cancer or AIDS, or huge ills,
All I ask from my life is a little respect,
And no bandaids or five-dollar bills."

CHAPTER 7

The Year without Michael: Exploring Unresolved End-of-Life Issues

Charlie Aubuchon and Melanie Weber

A family member who disappears and is never found is an unresolved loss. It is the end of life, as everyone connected with the missing person knew life, yet there is no end to mourning the loss because no resolution is found. Every week at school we are reminded of these unresolved losses when we receive postcards showing photographs of children. Each card asks, "Have you seen us?" Thousands of children are missing in the United States and all over the world; these families and friends suffer extended and unique stages of grief because the loss is unresolved.

THE YEAR WITHOUT MICHAEL

A book that explores this issue is *The Year without Michael*, by Susan Beth Pfeffer. This book can be read with the whole class, in a book club group, or as an individual reading choice. For our writing purposes, we are assuming the novel will be read by an entire class. In this young adult novel, the protagonist is Jody, a junior in high school. One day, her brother Michael leaves the house to play softball and does not come back. The story revolves around the disappearance's effects on family members and chronicles the reactions of friends and the community. Unlike death, a missing person is an unresolved issue. All the family can do is wait and grieve.

We really don't know how anyone will react in a crisis. What would we do if this happened to a member of our family? There would undoubtedly be problems for the members of any family, should one of them disappear without a trace and never be found. In this book we see how Michael's family reacts. The Chapmans are not prepared for bad things to happen. Michael's parents seemed to be on the verge of divorce when their son disappears, and they are unaware of how their problems affect their children. Jody is ready to enjoy being a junior but suffers when her friends draw away from her, because nobody knows how to talk to her. Kay, the youngest child, becomes defiant, rebellious, and angry with her parents' and sibling's behavior.

This family is on the edge with no coping skills whatsoever. When the crisis appears, they fall apart. The family borders on the brink of extinction. Kay is threatened with boarding school, Jody has only her senior year of school before leaving the family, and there is no way of knowing whether the issues that drove the parents to consider divorce will reemerge.

Psychological Implications

Over time, social groups, such as families, develop a way of relating to each other and solving their problems. A functional family develops solutions to problems, and if they are not successful, they discuss the outcome and try something new in order to achieve the desired goal. A dysfunctional family, on the other hand, continues to perform the same behaviors over and over, without ever solving the problem. At the root of the dysfunctional family is a faulty belief system.

All families tend to follow a distinct belief system that is unique to their individual family. It is important for students to understand how families function by exploring the belief system at work in the Chapman family. They can begin by determining the following about the Chapmans: what rules they follow; whether family members' roles are traditional or modern, rigid or flexible; are the rules and roles assumed or discussed openly, and consciously or unconsciously? Jody realizes, early after Michael's disappearance, that the family needs for its members to continue with their familiar roles:

> If her father broke down, she wouldn't be able to stand it. She could handle everything else, she thought, everything she had to, but only if she knew her father was all right. Without him, she would have to take care of her mother and Kay and her grandparents and the neighbors and the strangers and the pain. And she couldn't do it alone. Nobody should expect her to, she thought, feeling resentment. She wasn't the grown-up, why should she have to handle things? (31–32)

In this sudden flood of feeling, Jody expresses the family belief system: everyone has an assigned role regardless of changing situations. Instead of sharing her feelings with her father or mother, she hides behind the false belief that "It's okay. It has to be" (32). What does this tell us about how easily the family can change?

American families tend to have difficulty dealing with their feelings in times of stress. This novel provides the opportunity to examine how the Chapman family handles emotions and models how families break down if they do not sustain themselves in a time of crisis. The stubborn refusal of this family to share individual, intense feelings leads them into deeper conflict as they cope with Michael's disappearance. When family members cannot share feelings, opportunities abound for miscommunication and misinterpretation. It may be helpful to ask students why they think the family members are so unwilling to share their feelings. Of course, the reasons are as varied as the students who are answering. An insightful teacher may be able to determine what is happening in the lives of the students by the answers they offer.

Typical reactions to the story may include sadness and tears when discussing loss. More subtle reactions to dealing with abandonment or loss issues might come in the form of withdrawal, laughter, or irritability. Students and their families might find it beneficial, during initial contact, if the teacher provides a list of local agencies to which they could turn for personal therapeutic work. If the list is given early to every family member no one will feel singled out as "needing help." A therapist works at establishing a safe environment in which to work out troublesome issues. Due to the nature of the classroom setup, this cannot be done and should not be attempted. This allows students the opportunity to distance themselves from certain topics that are too sensitive for them to handle alone.

Understanding how a family creates hardship for itself is the first step to undoing the harm done. By working vicariously through the Chapmans' struggles, students gain a greater understanding of how a family can work effectively toward meeting life's challenges.

IN THE CLASSROOM

Students may react strongly to material presented in this book, but the classroom should provide safety for a discussion of their reactions. For this reason, it is important to notify other teachers and parents that students are studying the topic of unexplained loss. Teachers may notice that some students may be unable to express their feelings on the topic with language. These students might prefer drawing or creating music in order to express their feelings. Because of the difficult nature of this topic, it would be beneficial for all students to keep a journal for their exploration of the novel.

Before Reading

Understanding Grieving

Explaining the five stages of grief is an important first step to prepare students for reading the novel. For students facing death or loss, reading the novel could help them examine grieving behaviors, since the characters in *A Year without Michael* clearly demonstrate the behaviors of these stages. The five stages are clearly explained by Bode (1993). The value of this explanation is that people often feel there is something wrong with them as they experience the emotions associated with the stages. Students need to be reassured that those feelings are normal.

Five Stages of Grief

- Shock, disbelief
- Bargaining: "If only it could have been me."
- Denial, refusing to believe the person died
- Buying time to get emotionally caught up with what's happened
- Depression, energy falls as the feelings settle in
- Acceptance, coming to terms with the loss and moving forward

Making a chart of the five stages of grief and putting it up in the classroom for students to refer to during their reading of the book will give them a common point of reference. Students can then copy the chart into their notebooks so that they can refer to it as they work independently. It should be explained to students that these are not neat, tidy periods of time where a person is in shock for a week and then moves on to bargaining, and so on. Healing takes time. Also, a person might feel all these stages at once, or in a different order. The lesson for each of us to remember is that these emotions are normal reactions to death.

The intent of the following activity is to provide students with concrete examples of the stages of grief. They can then transfer their understanding to their reading of *A Year without Michael*. You might begin by providing students with an example of a forgotten item that must be in their possession for class, such as a project that is forgotten at home.

Ask students to write down each of the five stages in a column and to record their lost-item responses next to them. For example:

Stage of Grief	Lost-Item Responses
1. Denial	Look for it again in backpack, although it isn't found the first time.
2. Anger	Outburst about self being stupid or it's someone else's fault
3. Bargaining	"If you let me turn in my project late, I promise . . ."
4. Depression	"I'll never pass this class, I'm so helpless."
5. Acceptance	"I left it at home. I need to become more organized."

Students should be given another example of loss, such as losing a friend or family member, and once again they should write the stages in, and suggest what possible responses someone might have. It is important here to ask students to consider what happens if acceptance is not reached. In which stage do they think a person might stay? Discuss the responses the students suggested.

To help students experience how grief and emotions can be expressed in print, we can read a variety of literature as read-alouds. Before exploring poems about death, you might read aloud the sections of the picture book, *Good Answers to Tough Questions about Death* (Berry, 1990), which deals with the five stages of grief. Poems about loss and fear, such as Alfred, Lord Tennyson's "Griefs" and W. H. Auden's "Stop"—both in Haddon (1997)—provide an opportunity to discuss where the character might be in the stages of loss. Sharing a book such as *The Memory Box* (Bahr 1995) also provides an opportunity for students to view the process of grieving through literature. As you discuss how the boy and his grandmother deal with the grief for Gramps's Alzhiemer's, you provide students with an opportunity to think about other situations of loss. During such discussions, students will often generate a range of personal loss examples: losing a girlfriend, running away, the death of a pet, a missing parent. Looking at how all losses impact our individual lives helps us examine the resources we have when we experience loss.

Understanding Process

Merely giving students this vocabulary will not be enough for them to understand that grief occurs in stages. Even explaining that grief is a

Figure 7.1
Möbius Strip for Grief and Writing Processes

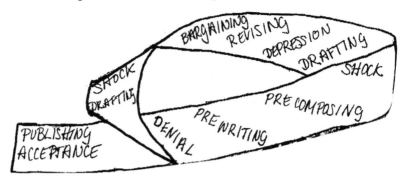

process may still not clearly communicate to them. One way to help students understand is to compare the process of grief to the process of writing. Students who have experienced writers' workshops come to understand that writers gather information, write, go back to gather more information, write again, share, and rewrite. Writing is not a series of steps in a straight line that lead to a finished piece of writing. Many drafts may be written and revised before writers are satisfied they have communicated their message in the best possible way to their readers.

Grief, much in the same way, is not a series of linear steps. People can experience anger and depression at the same time. When discussing and finding examples of the stages of grief, it may be helpful to use this familiar, concrete example of process.

In order to help students understand that both grief and writing occur as a process, and not in a series of neat steps, they can create a Möbius strip (see figure 7.1) to help them see this abstract concept as more concrete. In a conventional Möbius strip, there is no beginning and no end. However, it is important to make the distinction for students, so that they will not be caught in an endless loop of writing or of grief.

Making a Möbius Strip

1. Cut a strip of paper measuring 1 inch by 24 inches.
2. Using black felt-tip pens, write the titles of the grief process and writing process onto the paper, using both sides.

DENIAL	PREWRITING/PRECOMPOSING
SHOCK	DRAFTING
DEPRESSION	REVISING

BARGAINING   EDITING
ACCEPTANCE   PUBLISHING

3. Grasp the paper by the ends, and twist one end 180 degrees.
4. Bring the ends together and glue them so that part of one end sticks out.

The strips can then be hung in the classroom and referred to during novel reading, the related writing, and the projects which follow, in order to serve as a visual reminder for students of both the grief process and the writing process.

During Reading

Focus Questions

The novel should be read together during class in order to give students the opportunity to respond and extend their reading with questions and predictions. The following questions are beginning suggestions for this book, but teachers should create questions based on their reading of the text and the composition of their classes. These questions can be adapted for any text. Asking students to respond to questions in their journals before bringing them to class discussion gives them the opportunity to write their way into and through sensitive topics.

- Have you ever known anyone who disappeared?
- Have you ever wanted someone you know/someone in your family to just go away and never come back?
- Have you ever felt you were responsible for your parents?
- Have you ever experienced the loss of someone you cared about?
- Have you ever felt that none of your friends really understood you?

Students' responses to these prompts can help them make personal connections to events and characters. Remind students that they may refer to these questions during their reading of the novel. Another source for writing, to help students focus their feelings, stems from the unfinished-sentence journal prompts found in Grollman (1993).

Journal formats are excellent ways for students to respond to their reading, because they provide a structure for response and discussion. Journals could be completed at the end of each chapter or at the end of sections of chapters. Recorded class discussion of student responses, on chart paper, will provide a visual record of the reading of the novel. At the end of each section/chapter, students are asked to respond in both journal formats shown below. They can then be asked to share their responses, and the discussion recorded. It will be very important to allow plenty of time for students to discuss the events of the book. Two formats for journal responses are suggested here, each with a different but connected focus.

One five-column journal will focus the response on recognizing the stages of grief experienced by the characters. Do the characters respond in identifiable ways? This response would be done throughout the reading of the novel.

Denial	Anger	Bargaining	Depression	Acceptance

As students read, they look at the responses, actions, and dialogue of each character, in order to record how those responses fit into the stages of grief. Alternatively, students could concentrate on one character for this journal and record his/her process throughout the story.

The second journal format focuses on the way characters respond to the tragedy in their lives. In a three-column journal students record an event in the text, a character's reaction to that event, and an explanation of what they would have done if they had been that character in that situation. This problem-solving journal encourages students to focus on the question "Now that this has happened, what shall I do about it?"

Event	Character's Reaction	What I Would Have Done

Another way for students to fully understand a character's grief continuum would be for the students to follow one character throughout the entire book. Students could use a page of their journals to explore the character's personality and how that person reacts to the loss of Michael. After each reading, students return to the text and look at what the chosen character has said or done; what other characters' descriptions are of him/her; other characters' opinions; and the character's own thoughts. Encourage students to create a graphic organizer for their character, on which they can take their notes.

The following questions can be used to provide students with ways to explore their character and to help them create their scrapbook at the end of the novel. Students need to answer these questions as the character would:

- Your favorite food to eat for a snack is. . . .
- If you were alone on a Friday night, what would you most like to do?
- What kind of reading material are you most likely to curl up with and read?
- Give three adjectives that help to describe you.
- You wish you could. . . .
- If you had to eat at the same fast-food restaurant for every meal for one week, where would you eat?
- Nike has a great slogan, "Just do it!" Coca-Cola's slogan is "Things go better with Coke." Make up a slogan or motto that best describes you.

After Reading

Extending the Text

After reading the novel, students can write poems for a character in *A Year without Michael*. The poems can focus on the process of grieving or on the characters themselves. Their poems can be drawn from their journal responses, from class discussions, or from their detailed notes on the character they chose to follow through their reading. Found poetry is one way to help students create poetry directly connected to their response journals and the text. Student writers take words and phrases directly from their notes and journals and then turn their prose into poetry. Concrete poetry would be another choice for a character poem, using the name of the character as the form of the poem. Patterned poetry such as the I-Am poem can also help students gain insights and provide closure for the characters.

Legacies

When people we are close to die, or are lost, we often collect objects that remind us of them. The mother in this novel left Michael's room exactly as he had left it. The boy in *The Memory Box* kept his collection of memories. While we each might choose to memorialize in unique ways, most people like to keep some kind of mementos of the loved one. A scrapbook provides a way to collect these mementos of our lives, and memories of others in our lives.

Students can select a character from the story and create a scrapbook of memories that character would have collected during the course of the year. This is an ongoing project that should be finalized at the end of the reading. Students can refer to their character notes, poems, and journals for guidance. Ask students to do some real-world writing that will help them create their scrapbooks. For example, grocery lists, phone messages, to-do lists, notes to family, letters, postcards, and diary entries can be written from the perspective of the character. These real-world writings can be organized in the scrapbooks, along with physical artifacts that symbolize the character, such as photographs, report cards, or key rings.

Having read the novel and created their character scrapbooks, students can gain a sense of involvement by writing advice to the characters. Based on the scrapbook and their collection of impressions about the characters, students might give advice to the characters about living their lives. Ask students to write letters to their characters, asking them to consider the stages of grief the character has reached by the end of the book.

Moving On

For those students experiencing unresolved issues of loss, perhaps the best support they can be given is a strategy for remembering *and* moving on. Kushner (1982) gives us a model for beginning that journey, a journey that allows survivors of loss to begin again.

> The question we should be asking is not "Why did this happen to me? What did I do to deserve this?" That is really an unanswerable, pointless question. A better question would be, "Now that this has happened to me, what am I going to do about it?"
>
> We need to get over the questions that focus on the past and on the pain—"why did this happen to me?"—and ask instead the question which opens doors to the future: "Now that this has happened, what shall I do about it?" (85)

RECOMMENDED READINGS

Fiction

Disappearances

Cadnum, Michael. (1998). *Zero at the bone*. New York: Penguin Books. ISBN: 0–140–38628–9 (9–12). PB, 218 pp.

Cray narrates the story of how his older sister didn't come home from work one day. At first the family doesn't worry, because she's always been independent and strong. However, when she still doesn't return, they contact her school, her friends, and finally, the police. This novel connects closely with *The Year without Michael* in its handling of a child's disappearance. Readers learn with Cray that everybody has secrets they don't share with family members, no matter how close they may seem.

Cooney, Caroline. (1991). *The face on the milk carton*. New York: Bantam Doubleday Dell. ISBN: 0–440–22065–3 (6–12). PB, 184 pp.

When Janie sees a picture of a missing girl on the back of a milk carton, she realizes that she is that little girl. She is suddenly full of questions. Who is she? Who is her real family? Where does she belong? Coming to terms with these questions carries the reader along with Janie. Very popular with middle-grade readers, as is its sequel, *Whatever Happened to Janie?*

Mazer, Norma Fox. (1981). *The taking of Terri Mueller*. New York: William Morrow. ISBN: 0–380–79004–1 (9–12). PB, 189 pp.

Fourteen-year-old Terri lives with her father. She has no memory of her mother and no pictures and wonders how this can be. Terri finally discovers that her father kidnapped her after her parents' divorce.

Pfeffer, Susan Beth. (1996). *Nobody's daughter*. New York: Bantam Doubleday Dell. ISBN: 0–440–41160–2 (4–8). PB, 153 pp.

Emily's last known relative, Aunt Mabel, dies. Emily is sent to live in an orphanage. Alone and grieving, Emily makes friends with the local librarian and begins to search for her younger sister, who was adopted at birth.

Pfeffer, Susan Beth. (1996). *Twice taken*. New York: Bantam Doubleday Dell. ISBN: 0–440–22004–1 (6–12). PB, 199 pp.

Brooke is sixteen when she figures out that her father abducted her from her mother when she was small. She is ordered to live with her mother and a family she does not know, and Brooke must then come to terms with her father's choices and actions and learn to live with a new family.

Unsolved Sibling Murders

Bunting, Eve. (1991). *A sudden silence*. New York: Fawcett Books. ISBN: 0–449–70362–2 (6–12). PB, 107 pp.

After seeing his deaf brother struck and killed in a hit-and-run accident, Jesse embarks on a mission to find his brother's killer.

Butler, Charles. (2000). *Timon's tide*. New York: Margaret McElderry Books. ISBN: 0–689–82593–5 (9–12). HC, 192 pp.

Daniel's older brother, Timon, died six years previously, and Daniel tries to determine whether he was the cause of his brother's death, or whether Timon was murdered.

Egan, Jennifer. (1996). *The invisible circus*. New York: St. Martin's Press. ISBN: 0–312–14090–8 (12+). PB, 338 pp.

Phoebe is determined to solve the mysterious death of her sister, Faith, who died eight years earlier. When Phoebe arrives in Europe, she uncovers more information about her sister than she ever wanted to know.

Rodowsky, Colby. (1998). *Remembering Mog*. New York: Farrar, Straus, and Giroux. ISBN: 03–380–72922–9 (11–12+). PB, 136 pp.

Annie and her parents try to cope with the murder of her sister Mog and try to understand why it had to happen and who could have committed such a crime.

Springer, Nancy. (1994). *Toughing it*. San Diego: Harcourt Brace. ISBN: 0–152–00008–8–9 (9–12). HC, 119 pp.

When sixteen-year-old Shawn, also known as "Tuff," witnesses his older brother Dillon's murder, he tries to determine who killed him.

Absent/Missing Parents

Bond, Nancy. (1996). *A string in the harp*. New York: Aladdin Paperbacks. ISBN: 0–689–80445–8 (6–12). PB, 365 pp.

Fifteen-year-old Jen Morgan flies to Wales to spend Christmas with her family, but she doesn't expect the trip to be much of a holiday. A year after her mother's sudden death, her father is preoccupied, her brother Peter is hostile and sullen, and her young sister Becky can only tell Jen how much she misses her. The family exists in separate orbits, and all Jen wants to do is go home to America. Her brother, Peter, finds a harp key that shows him pictures of the life of Taliesin, a legendary Welsh bard. Combining fantasy with reality, the novel takes the reader through the alienation of the family and discusses how they pull together.

Creech, Sharon. (1996). *Walk two moons*. New York: HarperCollins. ISBN: 0–064–40517–6 (6–8). PB, 280 pp.

Thirteen-year-old Sal travels across the Midwest with her grandparents in order to trace her mother's final steps, and Sal learns about how her mother died.

Curtis, Christopher Paul. (1999). *Bud not Buddy*. New York: Delacorte Press. ISBN: 0–385–32306–9 (4–8). HC, 245 pp.

During the Depression, and after his mother's death, ten-year-old Bud goes on a mission to find his father, who he believes is a famous musician. Newbery medal winner.

Ishiguro, Kazuo. (2000). *When we were orphans*. New York: Alfred A. Knopf. ISBN: 0–37541–054–6 (12+). HC, 320 pp.

When the main character, Christopher Banks, becomes a private detective in England in the 1930s, he travels to Shanghai to find his parents, who disappeared when he was a young boy.

Maguire, Gregory. (1998). *Oasis*. New York: Hyperion Press. ISBN: 0–786–81293–1 (6–8). PB, 170 pp.

After Hand's father's death, he must learn to live with his mother, who had previously abandoned the family.

Myers, Walter Dean. (1993). *Somewhere in the darkness*. New York: Scholastic. ISBN: 0–590–42412–2 (9–12). PB, 168 pp.

Fifteen-year-old Jimmie has never known his father. His dad suddenly appears on Jimmie's doorstep one day, after escaping from jail, and takes his son on a journey to clear his name of a crime.

Paterson, Katherine. (1989). *Park's quest*. New York: Penguin. ISBN: 0–140–34262–1 (4–8). PB, 148 pp.

Park, an eleven-year-old boy, goes to live with his grandfather in order to learn about his father. He discovers he has a family he has never known, and he learns how his father lived and died serving his country in the Vietnam War.

White, Ruth. (1998). *Belle Prater's boy*. New York: Bantam Doubleday
Dell. ISBN: 0–440–41372–9 (6–8). PB, 196 pp.

Two cousins, Woodrow and Gypsy, help comfort each other as Woodrow tries
to accept his mother's disappearance, and Gypsy learns to cope with her father's
death.

Nonfiction

Flook, Maria. (1999). *My sister's life: The story of my sister's disappearance*. New York: Random House. ISBN: 0–767–90315–3 (12+).
PB, 352 pp.

This nonfiction account details the story of Maria's fourteen-year-old sister
Karen's abduction. It shows how the two sisters lead destructive parallel lives.

Grollman, Earl A. (1993). *Straight talk about death for teenagers*. Boston: Beacon Press. ISBN: 0–8070–2501–1. PB, 145 pp.

Written for teenagers in middle and high school and based on conversations
with them. Each chapter contains suggestions for dealing with grief and loss.
Contains an address for support groups and a journal section, which could be
used before reading *The Year without Michael*.

Poetry and Picture Books

Bahr, Mary. (1995). *The memory box*. New York: Albert Whitman.
ISBN: 0–807–55053–1. PB, 32 pp.

John's grandfather has Alzhiemer's, and John spends the summer gathering
memories for the two of them.

Berry, Joy. (1990). *Good answers to tough questions about death*. Chicago: Children's Press. ISBN: 0–516–22952–4. HC, 48 pp.

This nonfiction picture book is set in a classroom where children ask questions
about death. The easy-to-understand format offers questions and information at
the top of each page, while the rest of the page is filled with beautiful illustrations of children offering their thoughts and questions. Questions range from
what causes death to what dying people are entitled to.

Duffy, Carol Ann. (1996). *Stopping for death: Poems of death and loss*.
London: Viking. ISBN: 0–670–85416–6. PB, 126 pp.

An anthology of poems by well-known contemporary poets includes lesser-
known pieces both old and new. The poems highlight the various emotions death

can inspire. The anthology makes an excellent companion to the study of the five stages of grief, reflecting how our emotions battle within us.

REFERENCES

Bahr, Mary. (1995). *The memory box.* New York: Albert Whitman.

Berry, Joy. (1990). *Good answers to tough questions about death.* Chicago: Children's Press.

Bode, Janet. (1993). *Death is hard to live with.* New York: Bantam Doubleday Dell.

Grollman, Earl A. (1993). *Straight talk about death for teenagers.* Boston: Beacon Press.

Haddon, Celia, ed. (1997). *Love remembered: A book of comfort in grief.* London: Michael Joseph.

Kushner, Harold S. (1982). *When bad things happen to good people.* Boston: G. K. Hall.

Pfeffer, Susan Beth. (1987). *The Year without Michael.* New York: Bantam Doubleday Dell.

A Letter from Sara Holbrook

Sometimes life (and death) just don't make sense to me. Why now? Why that person? Why me? My brain becomes a chaotic whirlwind of questions and it's hard for me to get my thoughts straight. I know the healthy thing is to grieve over a loss and then let go of it, but how does one do that with a hurricane roaring in her head?

The way I make sense out of things is to write. Sometimes I am so mixed up, all I can manage is to throw a list of words or feelings on a page. It's like magic to see a poem emerge from this rubble. And what's even more amazing, is that sometimes the poem that rises up and walks away isn't about what had me in chaos to begin with at all, but some deeper issue—a pain I was unable to identify or too scared to write about.

The poem, "One Taken to Heart," for Wendy, was written for an assignment. The hardest writing assignment of my life. My daughter was a senior in college and I picked up the phone in the kitchen to hear her voice, made small from grief on the other end, "Mom, could you write a poem for my friend Wendy? She shot herself on Tuesday, the memorial service is next week."

Immediately, my head began to swirl. "How could this happen? Why didn't Wendy see that she had many friends and other choices?" And finally, "How can I write a poem about the suicide of a girl I don't know?" Kelly told me two facts about Wendy, that the weekend before she died, she had been teaching the girls in the dorm country line dancing and that she had a smile that would light up a room. I began sorting through the confusion by writing down these two facts—along with the questions that were making my head spin, a few of which made their way into the poem which Kelly read at Wendy's memorial service the next week.

Love,
Sara

"One, Taken to Heart . . . for Wendy"
Sara Holbrook

A book,
so much a part of our lives,
seems lost.
Fallen,
somewhere,
out of place.
We drag about the house
in heavy shoes,
examining the empty room.
We open the blinds,
wash our eyes
and search the shelf for answers.
Thinking,
what could we have done
with that book?
Where did we see it last?
Could a book just
wander off
like that?
Questions to throw at the moon,
while standing,
rooted in the shadows,
remembering the story.

The story.
Remember the time?
the page?
the chapter?
Remember?
Remember the smile?

A book can get lost,
disappear,
or simply fall to pieces,
but a story plays forever
once we've taken it to heart.

And for the rest
of what each of us will know
of eternity,
whenever we drag about the house
in heavy shoes,
wash our eyes
and search the shelf for answers,
that story will survive
to coax us from the empty room,
and back into the moonlight.
A sister,
Teaching us to dance.

CHAPTER 8

Remembering the Good Times: Making a Life Memorable after Suicide

Joanne Ratliff and Maureen McGarty

Finding an answer to the riddle of self-murder is not like tracing the origins of a disease to a single genetic marker. Suicide is more akin to a multicolored tapestry whose yarn must be unraveled strand by strand.

Jessica Portner (2000)

For families who have experienced suicide, the statistics carry little meaning. For the classroom teacher, however, the statistics are, and should be, staggering. The American Psychiatric Association (1997) reports the following:

- Suicide is the third leading cause of death among youth aged fifteen to twenty-four, and the sixth leading cause of death for five- to fourteen-year-olds.
- Experts estimate that each year nearly 5,000 teenagers commit suicide.
- For every teenager who commits suicide, 100 more will try.
- The ratio of male to female suicides is four to one, however, females attempt suicide twice as frequently.
- A family history of suicide is a significant risk factor. Biological relatives of a suicidal person are six times as likely to attempt or succeed in suicide as are adoptive relatives.
- 53% of young people who committed suicide had a principal psychiatric diagnosis of substance abuse.
- More than 67% of boys and 52% of girls ages ten to nineteen use firearms to kill themselves, 23% use hanging or suffocation. A small

percentage die by drug overdoses, drowning, falling, or slitting their wrists.

WHAT TO LOOK FOR

The strongest risk factors in attempted suicide in youth are depression, alcohol or substance abuse, and aggressive or disruptive behavior. Behavioral signs may include changes in sleeping patterns such as taking a lot of naps, a change in appetite, including sudden weight loss or gain, restlessness, withdrawal from friends and family, lack of concentration, extreme boredom, lost interest in activities, changes in personality or appearance, or sudden mood changes that continue for several days. Many of these signs are obvious but overlooked in busy lifestyles.

Less visible signs are feelings of sadness, hopelessness, rejection, loneliness, or guilt. In addition, young people who have attempted suicide in the past or who talk about suicide are at greater risk of future attempts. Listen for comments such as "I'd be better off dead" or "I won't be a problem for you much longer," or even "Nothing matters" or "It's no use," however, most people who are depressed or who are thinking about suicide won't talk about how they are feeling. This may be a result of feeling that their emotions will be a burden to others, or even that no one cares. It makes listening for single comments much more important. These feelings can be generated by abuse, recent humiliation in front of family or friends such as a breakup, or doing poorly on a test.

Parents with alcohol or drug problems, divorce in the family, or parental discord can also contribute to suicidal thoughts. However, it is important to note that it is certainly possible for a youth to be suicidal without any of these conditions being present. Suicide is the ultimate degree of depression, and the rationale is when the anger that goes with depression is turned inward, then there is self-destruction.

HOW DO I DO SOMETHING?

The most important thing is *to do something* if you have any evidence or feelings of concern. Trust your instincts. Be a friend and reassure the suicidal person that they do have people who care. Don't lecture; listen and reassure. Offer help. Depression can be successfully treated by health-care professionals. Adolescents need to know that with treatment, depression often ends. Sometimes teens who are experiencing depression may not be able to focus on that and can't see a way out.

As classroom teachers, we are not expected to treat youth with suicidal tendencies, but it is expected that we are aware and approachable. Accepting adolescents as they are, removing the taboo of talking about suicidal feelings, and telling children that it is all right to feel bad greatly reduces the distress and may help them see other options. Caring could save a young life. Suicide victims are not trying to end their lives, they are trying to end the pain.

Perhaps one way of helping adolescents with the issue of suicide is through literature. There are many books and short stories that deal with the issue of suicide for young adults. Some focus on the death of a parent, others with the death of a teen. The books have in common the people left behind and how they cope with the guilt, the loss, and the pain of not realizing what was about to happen. Exploring the incidents both before and after a suicide may give teens a voice for their own frustrations, guilt feelings, and losses. Including this literature in the curriculum could also provide some life-saving information for all students. It might even pull an adolescent back from suicide, or help those left behind by a suicide deal with the feelings that are ever present. *Remembering the Good Times* by Richard Peck is one novel that deals with these issues of suicide.

REMEMBERING THE GOOD TIMES

Three teenage friends, Buck, Trav, and Katie, are all trying to cope with attending a new high school, feelings of jealousy, and their different families. Buck lives with his father in a trailer behind a gas station. Katie lives with her grandmother in a house with an orchard that becomes a haven for the trio. Trav is the new kid who comes from a wealthy professional family with both parents at home, but who ultimately turns out to have the most dysfunctional family of the three. When Trav commits suicide, the two friends left have to come to terms with the loss and the guilt of wondering what they could have done.

An Educator's Observations

It has been interesting to discuss the differences between the signs I as an educator observed leading up to Trav's suicide and those a health-care professional observed.

I came to this topic, and to this book, many years after the suicide of my mother. It was easy in retrospect to see signs after her death that either weren't noticed or were ignored before. The same signs were apparent to me in this book, but mainly after the second reading. Perhaps the lesson is to become careful observers of behaviors, attitudes, comments, and actions as we work with students.

As early as chapter 3, there is dialogue that reflects Trav's depression. At the first meeting with Buck and Kate, Trav says that the world is a big, scary place and that he has to watch himself so he doesn't get too keyed up. When he hears a comment that a teacher is running out of luck, Trav responds that he knows the feeling. He often says things that when taken together send a signal, but individually they may be hard to pick up on. For instance, he notes that the world is deteriorating and that nothing can be done about it. When he grows up, it will be too late, and that it is already too late. Buck even found it funny for Trav to make these comments because of the three of them, he was the one with the nice home, brand-name clothes, and both parents living at home. Kate does notice that he is very serious, worries constantly about school, takes fast-track classes, and pushes himself too hard.

Kate's grandmother Polly seems to be more intuitive. When Kate comments that Trav's parents have programmed him, Polly observes that he is programming himself. Kate also thinks Trav is in a hurry to grow up, but Polly says not only is he not in a hurry, but that he dreads growing up. Several other references are made to Trav's failure to lighten up or smile very often and his need to be right at all times. Kate notes that Trav takes things harder than anyone else and is "skinned and raw inside" (61). She thinks he is "quietly out of control" (71) and "alone inside of himself" (73), which may seem to be additional signs of Trav's depression. When Buck suggests that maybe Trav needs to talk to someone like a counselor, Kate says he can talk to her, but she does admit that she doesn't know if it helps.

Trav does make at least one comment that foreshadows his suicide when he directly says, "I have to get out of here. I've got to get out of all this" (99). Unfortunately at this point, Buck doesn't know if Trav means school, going to a boarding school, or some other place. They have just begun high school, and after a summer in Bermuda with his parents, Trav has come back pale, thin, and angry at the world. He is often frustrated and says things like "Why can't I make people hear me?" (121). There is a second reference to suicidal thoughts when Buck comments that someday they would be able to say they "knew Kate when" because she got the lead in a school play. Trav comments to Buck, "You will. I won't be here" (134). Buck once again isn't sure whether he is referring to being out in the world or at Harvard.

Another behavior that may have been a signal of suicide was that Trav got picked up for shoplifting and called Buck's dad to come to the police station, even though his father was an attorney. When Kate and Buck discussed the issue, they felt he needed to be caught and had set himself up to get back at himself. "Trav's a big burden for Trav to carry around all on his own. I think he just wanted to shift the burden, to stop having to be responsible" (144).

The final event that echoed a frequent occurrence before a suicide was Trav giving away his possessions to Kate and Buck, things that he had valued. After doing that, he was more relaxed, even about the new school year starting. It was the end. Trav hung himself and Kate and Buck were left to try to figure out why. As with my mother, the signs were clear when looked for in retrospect.

Perhaps using this book in class would help both the teacher and students understand suicide and be able to recognize the signs of depression before another life is lost. Many other books are available and detailed in the related readings, which deal with the theme of suicide, whether of a peer, a parent, a sibling, or a grandparent. The signs, however, seem to remain constant.

A Therapist's Observations

In contrast to the signs that may have been observed by an educator, I would like to focus on the parental difficulties that may have contributed to Trav's suicide. Trav was a typical picture of a male adolescent suicide as the perfectionist who isolates himself. The most salient part of the picture is the family dynamics of his very narcissistic parents, which are played out in the book in very interesting ways. Kate and Buck seemed to have abnormal families, yet it was Trav's family that was really pathological. They were the upper-middle-class traditional family and the others were single parents. Everyone seemed somewhat dysfunctional, although Buck's father turned out to be what Trav was craving. The drama of Trav's narcissitic parents wanting to form the emotional life of their talented child, and the notion that they wanted everything to be cheerful seemed to contribute to his depression. He knew what they expected and wanted to be what they expected, but it led to depression, narcissism, a false self, and not knowing who he was.

There were several references in the book to things being "changed again"—which is difficult for Trav, who is always trying to figure out how to fit in. One reference of his is during the town's homecoming event, when students at the school are to dress in period costumes. Trav says they are trying to give us instant roots so that it seems as if we have a history. He has been moved around a lot and keeps his toys because he thinks every time they move he has his things taken away from him and he needs a sense of belonging, of history. "They tear up your roots. They get more and more successful, and they just expect you to walk away from everything. You have to move on to a new place, a bigger house. You want something that's yours, so you can remember yourself" (46).

To Buck, Trav always seemed to have everything together and Buck is sort of envious of Trav's intelligence and preppiness. What Trav says is that he knows he has problems and has to watch himself. Kate notes that Trav seems to resent his parents and thinks it is because he is exactly like them. She says, "When you're as uncomfortable with yourself as Trav is and you see the very same traits in your parents, then you just turn on them. You want to shift the blame onto them and get out from under it yourself" (47).

Suicide doesn't happen in isolation. There is always a history there. It plays out over and over in the book. Trav feels everyone's pain too much. That's the sign of a child whose ego boundaries are fragile. They overidentify with all the victims and feel too much pain, and that is an indication of someone who really can't handle too much stress or pressure. Trav would talk about how the situation was deteriorating in general: the world, school, the town. He had a sense of hopelessness and no boundary about what he could control and what he couldn't control. He could rage against a teacher about the curriculum, but he couldn't rage against his parents. He had learned to accommodate to parental expectations. If Trav had tried to show rage to his parents, to separate from the parental expectations, he would have felt he was risking the loss of their love. When he took the toys from the store, it was a cry for help right before the suicide. The parental reaction was to hide and seal over the incident. They dealt with it from a power vantage point, from the father's position as a lawyer. The solution was to take Trav away for a while to blow off steam. When they returned, Trav felt his father had betrayed him, and his special place in Polly's orchard, by being involved in the sale of the orchard.

Also, the kind of school that these adolescents were in was extremely conducive to overlooking Trav. It wasn't a community, because they kept bringing children into the schools without building relationships among students. The school conveyed a sense of dislocation and alienation. Neither did students have sense of intimacy with the faculty, and so the school culture had no continuity. There was no one for Trav to go to for help. Trav felt that every choice was extremely significant whether it was the electives he took in school or getting ready for the SATs; there was a sense that everything was just deadly serious. In contrast, Buck felt his brain was in neutral, which is more typical, almost healthy, for a child that age. He didn't worry about the consequence of what elective he took and lived in the present. For Trav, there was no present.

IN THE CLASSROOM

Before Reading

Before beginning a study of *Remembering the Good Times*, it may be beneficial to assess your students' knowledge of suicide and depression. One excellent way of doing this is through the use of an anticipation guide (Readence, Bean, & Baldwin, 1998). Figure 8.1 is an example of a guide with four statements that students can respond to and prompt discussion of their opinions, experiences, and beliefs. Responding to the guide prior to any reading of the text should generate a student discussion, which could serve as a transition to the introduction of the novel. The anticipation guide could be used prior to the reading of any of the novels on the related readings list. It could also be used again as a reaction guide after reading the novel to see whether their beliefs have changed.

A second suggestion before beginning *Remembering the Good Times* is to read aloud Garland's *I Never Knew Your Name* (1994). This picture book provides an excellent introduction to the topic of teen suicide. It is written from the perspective of a young boy who has a teen neighbor who commits suicide and he hadn't even bothered to find out his name. He realizes the tragedy of missed friendships and the importance of reaching out to others.

During Reading

Opportunities for writing could be used during the reading of this novel. One writing suggestion is to create a monologue for the characters just before Trav committed suicide. Ask students to imagine each of the story characters' feelings and how they saw their own situations. Reading aloud and comparing the monologues could prompt an open class discussion of how a friend's depression affects the people around him.

Another writing activity could be having students keep journals as they read each chapter of the novel. It may be easier for students who are either depressed, or see signs of depression in a friend, to respond to

Figure 8.1
Anticipation Guide

SUICIDE: AGREE OR DISAGREE?

Carefully read and consider each statement. Place a check next to each statement with your response. Do you agree or disagree?

AGREE	**DISAGREE**	
_____	_____	Nothing can stop a person once they decide to commit suicide.
_____	_____	When someone talks about suicide, ignore the person. The person is just looking for attention.
_____	_____	It's usually old people who commit suicide.
_____	_____	Suicide occurs out of the blue.

Factual Information Related to Anticipation Guide Statements:

- Talking often helps because they don't really want to die; they want to get rid of the pain.
- Open threats are made by 80 percent of teen suicides.
- Suicide is the third leading cause of death in teens.
- Usually a person contemplates and plans suicide for a long time.

their reading. As a teacher, responding to the journals may provide an opportunity for opening lines of communication with students and could provide some insight into your students' feelings. Using a double-entry journal, with what the author said, and what the student has to say (or feels), would lend itself particularly well to this text activity.

Another activity to use during reading could be a checklist of suicide signs developed from the list given at the beginning of this chapter. It could be used to gauge the characters' motivations. Were the signs evident in the text? Were there any solutions for Trav? Who should have seen the signs? Could anyone in the book have done or said anything?

A final suggestion is to read aloud sections of the text using the "say it like the character" strategy (Opitz & Rasinski, 1998). In this activity, students are expected to read passages the way they think a character might speak, in order to convey feelings or meaningful messages. First, allow students to silently read a passage, such as page 179, when Buck describes his feelings at Trav's funeral. Then, students silently reread it the way they think the character might make it sound. Students should then orally read the passage, and the teacher should lead a discussion asking questions such as, "What emotion were you trying to convey for the character?" or "What in the text made you think it should be read that way?"

After Reading

After brainstorming the pros and cons of suicide, students could examine the feelings of those left behind. This discussion could lead naturally to projects that represent those mixed emotions as a way of helping adolescents see that suicide isn't done in isolation. For example, if students are given the opportunity to create a collage, this could help students find ways to represent their feelings through art. Sharing the collages could help students begin to reach out to each other.

Finally, exploring some of the other recommended novels and web sites help continue the conversations in the classroom. Reading one novel is not likely to be enough support if you have students who are struggling with depression. Students might choose to read other novels and works of nonfiction in literature circles. Those texts can then lead them to journal articles and other resources.

CONCLUSION

There are many works of young adult literature that can help students explore the issue of suicide and depression and help them think about their own issues. If we want to help our students to become reflective, honest, and open in our classrooms, then we must provide them with literature that is meaningful, relevant, and appropriate to their lives. Although the topic of suicide is not comfortable to discuss, it is a reality in the lives of teenagers. Providing a vehicle for discussion through books that deal with the suicide of a peer, a friend, or a family member might help save a life.

RECOMMENDED READINGS

Fiction

Baer, Judy. (1991). *No turning back*. Minneapolis: Bethany House. ISBN: 1–55661–216–8 (6–8). PB, 142 pp.

This is a story of teenage romance. As Peggy pulls her life together, Chad falls apart. He is a loner and suffers from depression. When Peggy breaks up with him, the despair becomes overwhelming and Chad commits suicide.

Bunting, Eve. (1985). *Face at the edge of the world*. New York: Clarion Books. ISBN: 0–89919–800–7 (9–12). PB, 158 pp.

Jed's best friend Charlie commits suicide in their senior year. They had planned on going to college together, and Jed thought they had no secrets from each other. This is a story as much about friendship as it is about grief.

Cannon, A. E. (1991). *Amazing Gracie*. New York: Bantam Doubleday Dell. ISBN: 0–440–21570–6 (9–12). PB, 214 pp.

Gracie has to keep her new family together when her mother's depression leads to a suicide attempt. In addition to the obvious difficulty, she is dealing with a new stepfather, a needy six-year-old stepbrother, moving to a new city, and her first boyfriend. Readers will identify with fifteen-year-old Gracie's anxieties and fears.

Crutcher, Chris. (1989). *Chinese handcuffs*. New York: Bantam Doubleday. ISBN: 0–440–20837–8 (9–12). PB, 220 pp.

This is a story of two athletes who become friends; both share sorrow and secrets. Dillon's brother committed suicide in front of him, and Jennifer has been sexually abused. Together they try to survive and overcome the tragedies in their lives.

Dean, Pamela. (1991). *Tam Lin*. New York: Tom Doherty. ISBN: 0–812–54450–1 (12+). PB, 468 pp.

The traditional tale of Tam Lin is retold in a modern version that takes place in a Midwestern college town. Janet, her teachers, and friends are involved in unraveling the truth behind campus suicides.

Garland, Sherry. (1994). *I never knew your name*. New York: Ticknor & Fields. ISBN: 0–395–69686–0 (6–12). HC, 27 pp.

This is a picture book for young adults about neighbors who don't know each other. One of the boys commits suicide and the other wishes he had made the effort to know him—he didn't even know his name. The idea of reaching out to others is strongly present.

Gilbert, Barbara Snow. (1996). *Stone water*. New York: Bantam Doubleday Dell. ISBN: 0–440–22755–0 (6–8). PB, 168 pp.

Fourteen-year-old Grant has an envelope with a fable in it, written by his grandfather. He was instructed to open it if his grandfather was ever put in the terminal wing of his nursing home. The fable contains a request for Grant to help him commit suicide, and he must decide whether to honor his grandfather's request.

Hahn, Mary Downing. (1993). *The wind blows backward*. New York: Avon Flare. ISBN: 0–380–77530–1 (9–12). PB, 266 pp.

Shy, quiet Lauren falls in love with Spencer, the popular guy at school. She quickly realizes that Spencer is deeply unhappy and depressed. His despair is scary and causes him to contemplate suicide; Lauren tries to save him.

LeMieux, A. C. (1993). *The TV guidance counselor*. New York: Avon Books. ISBN: 0–380–72050–7 (6–8). PB, 184 pp.

Michael's father gives him a camera as he walks out of Michael's life. Looking at life through the camera lens helps Michael keep his family and friends at a distance. The turning point comes when he "accidently" jumps into the river and has to try to figure out for himself whether he meant to or not.

McDaniel, Lurlene. (1992). *When happily ever after ends*. New York: Bantam Doubleday Dell. ISBN: 0–553–29056–8 (6–8). PB, 168 pp.

Shannon tries to live with the suicide of her father. She knew he had been troubled since returning from Vietnam, but she thought her love for him would be enough to make him want to live. This book recounts her relationship with her father, as well as her relationship with her mother as they try to move on with their lives.

Mori, Kyoko. (1993). *Shizuko's daughter*. New York: Fawcett Juniper. ISBN: 0–449–70433–5 (6–8). PB, 213 pp.

When Yuki is twelve, her mother commits suicide and her father quickly re-marries a woman whose behavior is entirely motivated by appearances. Yuki excels in school, sports, and art. None of this is of consequence to her father or stepmother. When she leaves home for art school, she has a chance to re-connect with her mother's family and tries to make sense of her mother's tragic death.

Nixon, Joan Lowery. (1988). *Secret, silent screams*. New York: Bantam Doubleday Dell. ISBN: 0–440–20539–5 (9–12). PB, 180 pp.

After a string of suicides at Marti's high school, her friend Barry is found dead. Everyone assumes it is another suicide, but Marti doesn't believe that Barry would kill himself. She sets out to discover the truth.

Nunes, Lygia Bojunga. (1991). *My friend the painter*. New York: Har-court, Brace. ISBN: 0–15–200872–1 (4–8). PB, 85 pp.

Claudio, age eleven, remembers his artist friend who lived upstairs and the lessons learned in his friend's apartment. Prior to his suicide, the artist taught him about life through analogies to color. This book is written in the voice of Claudio over several days of poetic reflection about his friend. It may be difficult for some readers to follow the present, past, and dream sequences of this book, but it is well worth reading.

Pierce, Richard. (1994). *Frankenstein's children, book one: The creation*. New York: Berkley. ISBN: 0–425–14361–9 (8–12). PB, 200 pp.

Sara believes her love with Josh will last forever, until he commits suicide. Her grief is overwhelming until her grandfather Frank shows her the medical journal of Dr. Frankenstein. She is a scientist and thinks she can prove her everlasting love by bringing Josh back to life. This book is a modern recreation of the Frankenstein myth and incorporates the use of computers.

Schulte, Elaine. (1995). *Joanna*. Minneapolis: Bethany House. ISBN: 1–55661–624–4 (9–12). PB, 174 pp.

Joanna has troubles at home and doesn't fit in at school until she starts dating Matt. Then Matt's friend Melanie kills herself, and Joanna finds herself strug-gling to overcome the tragedy. This book has many religious references.

Shusterman, Neal. (1991). *What daddy did*. New York: Harper Keypoint. ISBN: 06–447094–6 (9–12). PB, 231 pp.

Preston's father murders his mother and tries to commit suicide. Preston and his brother are then raised by their grandparents while his father is in prison for the murder. When his father is released from prison, he wants his sons back, but Preston has not come to terms with his feelings about him. How can he forgive his father for murdering his mother?

Staub, Wendy Corsi. (1995). *Real life: Help me.* New York: Pocket Books. ISBN: 0–671–87274–5 (9–12). PB, 162 pp.

This book is written as a daily account of a teenager who is frantically trying to fight depression. Karen tries to hide her depression from her parents but is failing her classes and struggles to get out of bed. She thinks her mother wouldn't want a daughter who is crazy. Then Karen's mother commits suicide, and Karen is finally able to ask for help before it is too late for her.

Thompson, Julian F. (1994). *The fling.* New York: Penguin Books. ISBN: 0–14–037503–1 (9–12). PB, 201 pp.

This book is written in an interesting style that interweaves a story Felicia writes for a high school English class with her own life. It seems that what she writes about happens in her life after she writes it in her story. Her life changes after moving into a house that is a sanctuary for teens and meeting David, a troubled teen who eventually commits suicide. She writes "Experience is finding out that sometimes bad things happen, and all that we can do is cry and slowly make our peace with them."

Wartski, Maureen. (1996). *What are they saying about me?* New York: Fawcett Juniper. ISBN: 0–449–70451–3 (9–12). PB, 210 pp.

Meg has a hard time making friends at her new high school. Rea, her shy lab partner, becomes her friend but then commits suicide. Meg hears lots of rumors about Rea's reputation, and then finds her own reputation being talked about. This does not deter her from finding out the truth about Rea's life.

Zindel, Paul. (1993). *David and Della.* New York: Bantam Books. ISBN: 0–553–56727–6 (9–12). PB, 167 pp.

David is an aspiring playwright who develops writer's block after his girlfriend attempts suicide. He hires Della, an actress, to be his muse. He will write a play about teenage love and she will be the star. In the process, they both receive revelations about their pasts.

Short Stories and Poetry

Brooks, Martha. (1994). "Moonlight sonata." In *Traveling on into the light and other stories.* New York: Penguin Books. ISBN: 0–14–037867–7 (6–8). PB, 146 pp.

This is a collection of short stories about teenagers who meet one person who changes their lives and helps them step forward into their future. In one story, Jamie must deal with the suicide of his father and with his own drinking problem.

Janeczko, Paul. (1993). *Looking for your name: A collection of contemporary poems.* New York: Orchard Books. ISBN: 0–531–05475–6 (9–12). HC, 128 pp.

This is a collection of contemporary poems about conflict and the joys of life. Topics include suicide, war, violence, AIDS, peace, and loving relationships.

Shusterman, Neal. (1997). "Blue diamond." In M. J. Weiss and H. T. Weiss, eds., *From one experience to another: Award winning authors sharing real-life experiences through fiction.* New York: Tom Doherty. ISBN: 0–812–56173–2 (188–202). PB.

This short story is about two friends who take a road trip. One friend has decided to commit suicide and wants the other to go on one last fling with him. In the end, he really wanted his friend to save him.

Testa, M. (1995). "Dancing pink flamingos." In *Dancing pink flamingos and other stories.* New York: Avon Books. ISBN: 0–613–07582–X (9–16). HC.

Silvia feels guilty after her boyfriend Dominic commits suicide one month after breaking up with him. His friends are cruel to her and blame her. The person she receives comfort and encouragement from is the least likely—Sal, Dominic's karate teacher, the kind of guy who would have pink flamingos on his lawn.

INTERNET RESOURCES

American Academy of Child and Adolescent Psychiatry
http://www.aacap.org/publications/factsfam/suicide.htm
The AACAP represents over 7,000 child and adolescent psychiatrists who are physicians with at least five years of additional training beyond medical school. One interesting list on this site describes what a teenager who is planning to commit suicide may do.

American Psychological Association
http://www.psych.org/public_info/TEENAG~1.HTM
This site provides some research on causes of depression, facts on teen suicide, and an excellent bibliography of readings. There is also a listing of related mental health organizations.

American Academy of Pediatrics
http://www.aap.org/advocacy/childhealthmonth/ prevteensuicide.htm
http://www.aap.org/family/suicide.htm
Some things you should know about preventing teen suicide are discussed on this site. In addition, guidelines for parents are delineated.

Education Week
http://www.edweek.org/sreports/suicide.htm
This site is a complete transcript of a series published in *Education Week* on teen suicide. Several teens were interviewed for the article. There is also a section on the role of the school district in the prevention of teen suicide. Suicide rates by state and age group are also available.

National Mental Health Association
http://www.nmha.org/infoctr/factsheets/82.cfm
A fact sheet of teen suicide is provided with information on helping suicidal teens, recognizing the warning signs, and where to get more information.

Suicide Awareness/Voices of Education
http://www.save.org/cdcstat1.html
This site contains a question-answer section with the questions on suicide most frequently asked by students. There is also an area for students to go if they have a friend who is depressed, or if they are feeling depressed or have thoughts of suicide.

Yellow Ribbon
http://www.yellowribbon.org
This is a suicide-prevention site that provides an excellent list of warning signs and risk factors. It also provides teens with advice if they are in a crisis.

RESOURCES FOR STUDENT RESEARCH

American Psychiatric Association. (1997). *Teen suicide*. Washington, DC: The Association. Brochure.

Edwards, T. K. (1988). "Providing reasons for wanting to live." *Phi Delta Kappan* 70: 296–298.

Feinour, P. (1989). "These students are spreading a dramatic suicide message about teen suicide." *American School Board Journal* 11:29.

Frymier, J. (1988). "Understanding and preventing teen suicide: An interview with Barry Garfunkel." *Phi Delta Kappan* 70: 290–293.

Kaywell, J. F. (1993). "Stress and suicide." In *Adolescents at risk: A guide to nonfiction for young adults, parents, and professionals.* Westport, CT: Greenwood Press.

National Mental Health Association. (1997). *Recognizing adolescent depression.* Alexandria, VA: The Association. Factsheet.

Rasinski, T. V., & C. S. Gillespie. (1992). "Dealing with death and dying." In *Sensitive issues: An annotated guide to children's literature K–6.* Phoenix: Oryx Press.

Reese, F. L., & M. W. Roosa. (1991). "Early adolescents' self-reports of major life stressors and mental health risk status." *Journal of Early Adolescence* 11: 363–378.

Seibel, M., & J. N. Murray. (1988). "Early prevention of adolescent suicide." *Educational Leadership* 45: 48–51.

Stupple, D. M. (1987). "Rx for the suicide epidemic." *English Journal* 76: 64–68.

Wolf, J. (1988). "Adolescent suicide: An open letter to counselors." *Phi Delta Kappan* 70: 294–295.

Young, T. J. (1985). "Adolescent suicide: The clinical manifestation of alienation." *High School Journal* 69: 55–60.

REFERENCES

American Psychiatric Association. (1997). *Teen suicide.* Washington, DC: The Association. Brochure.
Garland, Sherry. (1994). *I never knew your name.* New York: Ticknor & Fields.
Opitz, Michael F., & Timothy V. Rasinski. (1998). *Good-bye round robin reading: 25 effective oral reading strategies.* Portsmouth, NH: Heinemann.
Peck, Richard. (1985). *Remembering the good times.* New York: Bantam Doubleday Dell.

Portner, Jessica. (2000). "Complex Set of Ills Spurs Teen Suicide Rate." *Education Week on the Web* (http://www.edweek.org/ew/ewstory.cfm?slug=31problems.h19).

Readence, John E., Thomas W. Bean, & R. Scott Baldwin. (1998). *Content area literacy: An integrated approach*, 6th ed. Dubuque, IA: Kendall Hunt.

"Finals"
Sara Holbrook

The accident.
The news.
Sped like a lighted fuse
to dynamite
our homeroom.
Facts were scattered
And confused.

Who was driving?
At what speed?
What road?
What curve?
What time?
How bad?
Oh, God.
Which tree?
Respirator. Coma.
Lifeflight. CPR.
Today's vocabulary words,
new adjectives
for "car."

The explosion left us staring,
unresponsive
with fixed eyes,
at
that blasted empty desk.
No retakes.
No goodbyes.

Index

About the Contributors

JANET ALLEN is an international consultant recognized for her literacy work with at-risk students. She is the author of *It's Never Too Late: Leading Adolescents to Lifelong Literacy* and *Words, Words, Words: Teaching Vocabulary in Grades 4–12* and coauthor of *There's Room for Me Here: Literacy Workshop in the Middle School.* Her newest book is *Yellow Brick Roads: Shared and Guided Paths to Independent Reading.* She has also written several articles and chapters on young adult literature and teaching. She taught high school reading and English in northern Maine until 1992, when she relocated to Florida to teach English and reading-education courses at the University of Central Florida. During her tenure at UCF, she directed the Central Florida Writing Project and assisted in the creation of the Orange County Literacy Project. Dr. Allen has received numerous teaching awards, including the Milken Foundation's National Educator Award. She has recently resigned her position at the university and is currently spending her time researching, writing, speaking, and conducting literacy institutes across the country.

CHARLIE AUBUCHON is an eighth-grade language arts teacher at McFadden Intermediate School in Santa Ana, California. She earned her master's degree at California State University, Long Beach, and has been published in NCTE's *Voices from the Middle.* She has participated in the California Reading and Literature Project and is a fellow of the Writing Project at the University of California at Irvine.

CARIN M. BEASLEY is a psychotherapist in private practice in Colorado Springs, Colorado. She is a doctoral student at Colorado School of Professional Psychology. Carin is a certified addictions counselor (CA-CII) and holds a primary certificate from the Albert Ellis Institute of New York in Rational Emotive Behavioral Therapy. In her practice she emphasizes a systems approach in helping individuals, couples, and families as they work through life's transitions.

DENISE P. BEASLEY is an English education instructor at the University of Central Florida, where she has worked for the past five years, and specializes in adolescent literature and literacy strategies in the content areas. For the past three years, she has written reviews of adolescent and professional literature for *VOYA* and served as a contributor to Diane Person's and Bee Cullinan's *Encyclopedia of Children's Literature*. Dee taught English and creative writing at a private high school and worked as the codirector of the Student Literacy Corps at UCF, a federal grant that provided literacy instruction to homeless children and adults. She is currently working on a Ph.D. in general education, with a focus on literacy and online learning, from Capella University.

JAN CHERIPKO has been assistant to the publisher of Boyds Mills Press, a children's book publishing company owned by *Highlights for Children* magazine. He also teaches writing and literature at the Family Foundation School, a private school located in rural New York State for at-risk teens. Mr. Cheripko is the author of *Imitate the Tiger*, a young adult novel about a high school football player who has a drinking problem. *Imitate the Tiger* won the Joan Fassler Memorial Book Award given by the Association for the Care of Children's Health. It was also an International Reading Association Young Adult Choice, a Parent's Media Guide selection, New York Public Library Best Book for Young Adults, and an American Booksellers Pick of the List. Mr. Cheripko also wrote *Voices of the River: Adventures on the Delaware*, a photo essay about a 10-day, 215-mile canoe journey that he took with a fourteen-year-old boy. His latest book, *Get Ready to Play Tee Ball*, is a photo essay about the basics of how to play tee ball.

CYNTHIA G. CLARK earned a B.A. in organizational communications from the University of Central Florida and later returned to complete the certification process as a language arts teacher for grades five through nine. She also has earned a master's degree in pastoral ministry from Loyola University, New Orleans. After spending seven years as a classroom teacher, she joined the student assistance program and has worked as a Student Assistance and Family Empowerment (SAFE) coordinator on school sites, and on the district level, for eight years. She has written and developed curriculum for students from kindergarten to twelfth grade on topics such as drug awareness, prevention, and conflict management. Presently, she is SAFE coordinator at Howard Middle School in Orlando, Florida.

ANNE E. COBB has taught language arts in secondary settings and is currently teaching English education courses at the University of Central Florida, where she received her M.Ed. in English language arts education. While at UCF, she coordinated the Central Florida Writing Project, organized and directed a reading program for local at-risk students, and was a member of the Literacy Initiative serving homeless adults in Orange County, Florida. Currently, she is the coordinator of Dr. Janet Allen's *It's Never Too Late* literacy institutes offering professional development to teachers around the country.

ROBERT CORMIER (1925–2000) was a distinguished author of many highly acclaimed books, including *After the First Death; Eight Plus One* (a short-story collection); *Now and at the Hour; I Am the Cheese*, an ALA Notable Book for Children, an ALA Best Book for Young Adults, and a School Library Journal Best Book of the Year; *Take Me Where the Good Times Are, Fade, The Bumblebee Flies Anyway*, an ALA Notable Book for children and an ALA Best Book for Young Adults; *We All Fall Down; Other Bells for Us to Ring*; and *The Chocolate War*, an ALA Best Book for Young Adults, a New York Times Outstanding Book of the Year, and a School Library Journal Best Book of the Year. He was the recipient of numerous teaching awards, including the Young Adult Services Division/School Library Journal Author Award, which recognizes authors "whose books have provided young adults with a window through which they can view their world and which will help them to grow and to understand themselves and their role in society."

SHARON DRAPER, the 1997 National Teacher of the Year, is a professional educator, as well as an accomplished writer. She is the recipient of numerous other educator awards, including the 1997 Milken Family Foundation National Educator Award. She was one of the first teachers in the nation to achieve National Board Certification in English/language arts. Her twenty-five years in the classroom, together with a love of reading and writing, have resulted in three young adult novels, *Tears of a Tiger, Forged by Fire*, and *Romiette and Julio*. She has also published numerous poems and short stories. *Tears of a Tiger* has received numerous awards, including the 1995 American Library Association/Coretta Scott King Genesis Award for an outstanding new book and an ALA Best Book for Young Adults Award for 1995. *Forged by Fire*, the sequel to *Tears of a Tiger*, is the 1997 Coretta Scott King Award winner, as well as the winner of the ALA Best Book Award and the Parent's Choice Award. Her books in the *Ziggy and the Black Dinosaurs* series are favorites for middle readers around the country.

MARIBETH EKEY specializes in grief work in her writing, speaking, and therapy. She has a private practice in Fullerton, California, where she sees individuals, couples, and groups seeking help with relational struggles, parenting issues, and unresolved losses. She directed marital seminars for New Life Clinics, doing extensive teaching and group work with couples in distress. She has also done extensive training in psychology, teaching psychology at the graduate level, supervising psychology interns and teaching for lay counseling programs at local colleges and churches. In 1998 she wrote an article, "What Honoring Our Fathers Really Means," published in the *Orange County Register*. From 1995 to 1999, she was a regular guest host on the New Life Live national program, a radio talk show dealing with marital, parenting, and relational issues. She received her doctorate of psychology from Rosemead Graduate School in La Mirada, California. Her book, *Shattered Hopes, Renewed Hearts*, deals with facing and working through the losses and disappointed wishes that go with marriage, parenting, and being a child of imperfect parents.

PATRICIA H. FEDOR is the children's specialist with Wuesthoff Brevard Hospice and Palliative Care in Rockledge, Florida. She holds a master of arts degree in counseling and a bachelor's degree in business administration from Rollins College. Pat has been involved with hospice grief work for over ten years following work with Big Brother/Big Sisters and the Girl Scouts in an executive staff capacity. She works closely with the Brevard County School System in conducting grief groups in the schools as well as serving the individual needs of grieving children in the hospice families.

RALPH FLETCHER has written books for young readers and writing teachers. As author and consultant, he has worked at schools around the United States and abroad helping teachers create a supportive environment for young writers. His pedagogical texts include *Walking Trees: Portraits of Teachers and Children in the Culture of Schools; What a Writer Needs; Breathing in, Breathing out: Keeping a Writer's Note-*

book; and *Craft Lessons: Teaching Writing K–8*. His fictional works include *Spider Boy; Twilight Comes Twice*; and *Fig Pudding*, an American Library Association's Notable Book. Poetry collections include *Ordinary Things: Poems from a Walk in Early Spring; Buried Alive: The Elements of Love*; and *I Am Wings: Poems about Love*, an American Library Association's Recommended Book for Reluctant Young Adult Readers. He has degrees from Dartmouth and Columbia and is a former member of the Teachers College Writing Project in New York City.

KYLE E. GONZALEZ currently teaches ninth grade at Boone High School in Orlando, Florida, where she works with struggling readers. She is the coauthor of *There's Room for Me Here* (1998) with Janet Allen and has served as a facilitator in Janet's *It's Never Too Late* literacy institutes. Kyle earned her M.Ed. in English education at the University of Central Florida. She was named the 1996 Teacher of the Year at Lakeview Middle School, where she worked with at-risk readers before to moving to the high school level.

SARA HOLBROOK began writing poetry for her daughters to record the joys and trials of growing up. Since 1990 she has worked as a poet in schools, at conferences, and in other venues, sharing her poems with children and educators. She writes adult poetry, as well, and as a member of the Cleveland Slam Team, Sara has competed at the Slam Nationals, a national competition for performance poets. She is the author of *Nothing's the End of the World; Am I Naturally This Crazy; I Never Said I Wasn't Difficult; The Dog Ate My Homework; Which Way to the Dragon;* and *Chicks Up Front*.

PAUL B. JANECZKO didn't start out to be a writer. He started out as a kid in New Jersey who had two major goals in life: (1) survive one more year of delivering newspapers without being attacked by thugs from the public high school and Ike, the one-eyed, crazed cur that lurked in the forsythia bushes at the top of the hill; and (2) become more than a weak-hitting, third-string catcher on his sorry Little League team. He claims failure at both. But it was the *Hardy Boys* (and his mother) who got him started as a reader and, eventually, a writer. His book, *Brickyard Summer*, was a 1989 ALA Best Book for Young adults. The poet's anthologies of modern poetry are recognized as the finest in the field: among them are *Looking for Your Name; Preposterous: Poems of Youth; The Music of What Happens: Poems That Tell Stories; Strings: A Gathering of Family Poems; Poetspeak: In Their Work; About Their Work*; and *The Place My Words Are Looking For*. He's also the author of

Bridges to Cross (fiction) and *Loads of Codes and Secret Ciphers* (non-fiction).

JULIE JOYNT is a middle school resource teacher in Brevard County, Florida, who is currently working under a three-year federal grant for drug prevention and school safety. She has been a classroom teacher for twelve years with the last five spent teaching high school drama. She holds a master's degree in English language arts education from the University of Central Florida and has spent the last four summers working for Dr. Janet Allen in her *It's Never Too Late* literacy institutes. In her new position, she works with middle schools to identify risk and protective factors within the school and surrounding community that relate to the use of alcohol, tobacco, other drugs, and violence issues. Upon identification of the schools' needs, she will help them design prevention programs that can be integrated into the existing curriculum in order to reduce the number of students that might get involved in drugs or violence.

MYRNA LEWIN serves as a therapist focusing on the psychological and emotional conditions of individuals, couples, and families. She also provides substance and addiction counseling and serves as a guardian ad litem for children of divorce. She specializes her focus on women who have been sexually abused as children. Ms. Lewin received her B.S. in behavioral science from the University of Maine, Presque Isle, and a master's degree in social work from Boston University.

MAUREEN McGARTY is on the faculty of Emory University's Psychoanalytic Psychotherapy Training Program and maintains a private practice in Athens, Georgia. She received her Ph.D. in clinical psychology from Fordham University and completed psychoanalytic training at the William Alanson White Psychoanalytic Institute, New York. For over twenty years, she has specialized in the treatment of depression, trauma character disorders, and women's issues. She cowrote, with Ira Moses, Ph.D., "Beyond Neutrality: Analytic Disclosure in the Interpersonal Field" in *The Handbook of Interpersonal Psychoanalysis*. Her articles have appeared in the *Journal of Contemporary Psychoanalysis* and the *Hillside Journal of Clinical Psychiatry*. She participated in the American Psychological Association program Warning Signs: A Youth Anti-Violence Initiative.

ANGELA SHELF MEDEARIS'S desire to write books for children was the result of working with second-graders who had difficulty reading. She went on to become the founder of Book Boosters, Inc., a nonprofit organization dedicated to tutoring elementary school children who need a boost in their self-esteem and help with their reading. Mrs. Medearis has written more than 67 award-winning books for children. Her books have sold more than 2 million copies worldwide and are featured on a line of *Storytime Videotapes* which are narrated by Mrs. Medearis. Her works are found in schools, libraries, and bookstores around the United States and have been translated into Spanish, French, Dutch, and Japanese. Her book, *The Princess of the Press: The Story of Ida B. Wells-Barnett* is a 1998 Carter G. Woodson Honor Book award winner. Some of her other titles are *Rum-A-Tum-Tum, Picking Peas for a Penny, Our People, Annie's Gifts, Treemonisha, The Freedom Riddle*, and *Skin Deep and Other Teenage Reflections*, a poetry collection. During the last school year, Mrs. Medearis spoke to more than 50,000 children and adults around the United States about storytelling, reading, and the art and craft of writing.

STEVE PUCKETT is the senior minister for the Melbourne Church of Christ in Melbourne, Florida, where he has served for sixteen years. The heart of his ministry has always included an active involvement in the community. He served for eight years as a chaplain for the Melbourne Police Department and for nine years as the school and football chaplain for Palm Bay High School. He has taught in high school and middle school. Steve has presented at the FBI's Critical Incidence Stress Debriefing seminar in Quantico, Virginia. He also served on Brevard County, Florida's Critical Incidence Stress Debriefing team.

JOANNE RATLIFF is an associate professor of reading at Texas A&M University–Corpus Christi. She teaches both graduate and undergraduate literacy and field experiences in reading. In addition, Dr. Ratliff is the current coeditor of *The State of Reading*, a journal for the Texas State Reading Association.

MELANIE WEBER is an intermediate-school English language development teacher. She earned her master's degree from Pepperdine University in counseling psychology and has been working as a marriage, family and child therapist intern for five years.